LANDFORMS LIGHT & LIFE

Toadstool Geologic Park in Photos and Poems

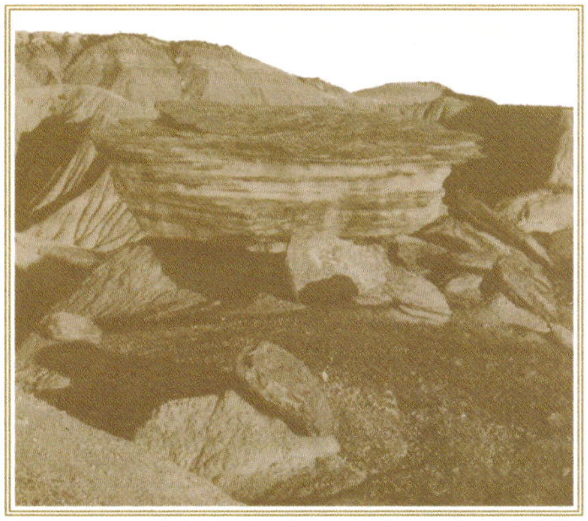

Photos

Dan Brooks

Poems

Jack Maze

Landsforms, Light & Life

ISBN-13: 9780984807321

Cover and Book design: Cristina Juarrero

Printed in the United States of America

"This volume is dedicated to those who have felt the magic and beauty of Toadstool and those to come."

Contents

Preface

This book has been a labor of love and a celebration of life. As always, we are supremely indebted to our designer, Cristina Juarrero de Varona. Cristy couples extraordinary creative energies and spirit with an excellent knowledge of natural history gained during her training as a UNESCO nature interpreter in her native Cuba. As with our previous projects, Cristy edited poems and photos, helped create a pleasing flow, and kept up the spirits of two aging authors. And she did this always with enormous grace and cheerfulness despite working at full-time job and being a wife and mother. Our appreciation is unbounded.

- Lincoln and Vancouver, August 2012

Introduction

Inevitable

Wind, water
Eternal, seeking
Earth's crust
Firm, malleable
Plants
Signposts of the seasons

They met
In the western prairies
The wind, the water
Sculpted the earth's crust
Plants added a veneer of life
To flats, slopes, gullies, ridges

It`s called Toadstool

Sit, look, think

Wait
For euphoria

Hills, carved by water;
Flats decorated with plants;
All embraced by light.

Photos & Poems

Dynamics of Dawn

Dawn's a good time of day
It's cool
The air is fresh
Bird songs are starting
Predators are seeking cool spots
To pass the heat of midday.
Antelope are starting to graze
Ever watchful for coyotes.

There's no morning sun
Remnants only of the night
In the horizon's shade.

The first sign of dawn is a lightening to the east
An intensity concentrating the day's sunshine
Carrying the promise of warmth.

Light

Dawn's light contacts first
Slopes facing east.

It's then reflected
Some back to its origin
Some forward connecting the slopes
To this layered rock.

The rock takes the light into its varves
Filters, purifies, sanctifies it
Imbues it with the soul of the rock
With the spirit of the earth.

The rock calves beget
Progeny that, each one
Bearing light now sanctified
By the earth's spirit.

Progeny now free to disperse
So the slope, the rock
Stand not in isolation.

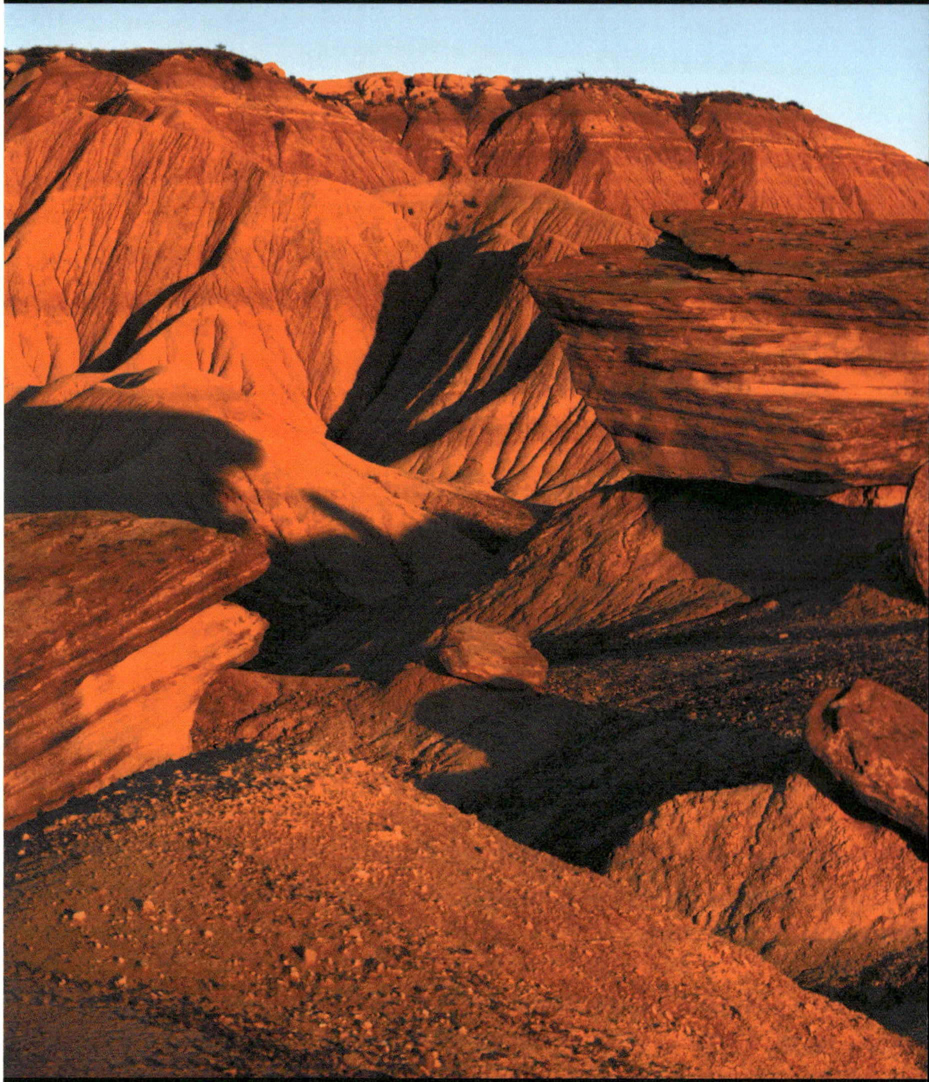

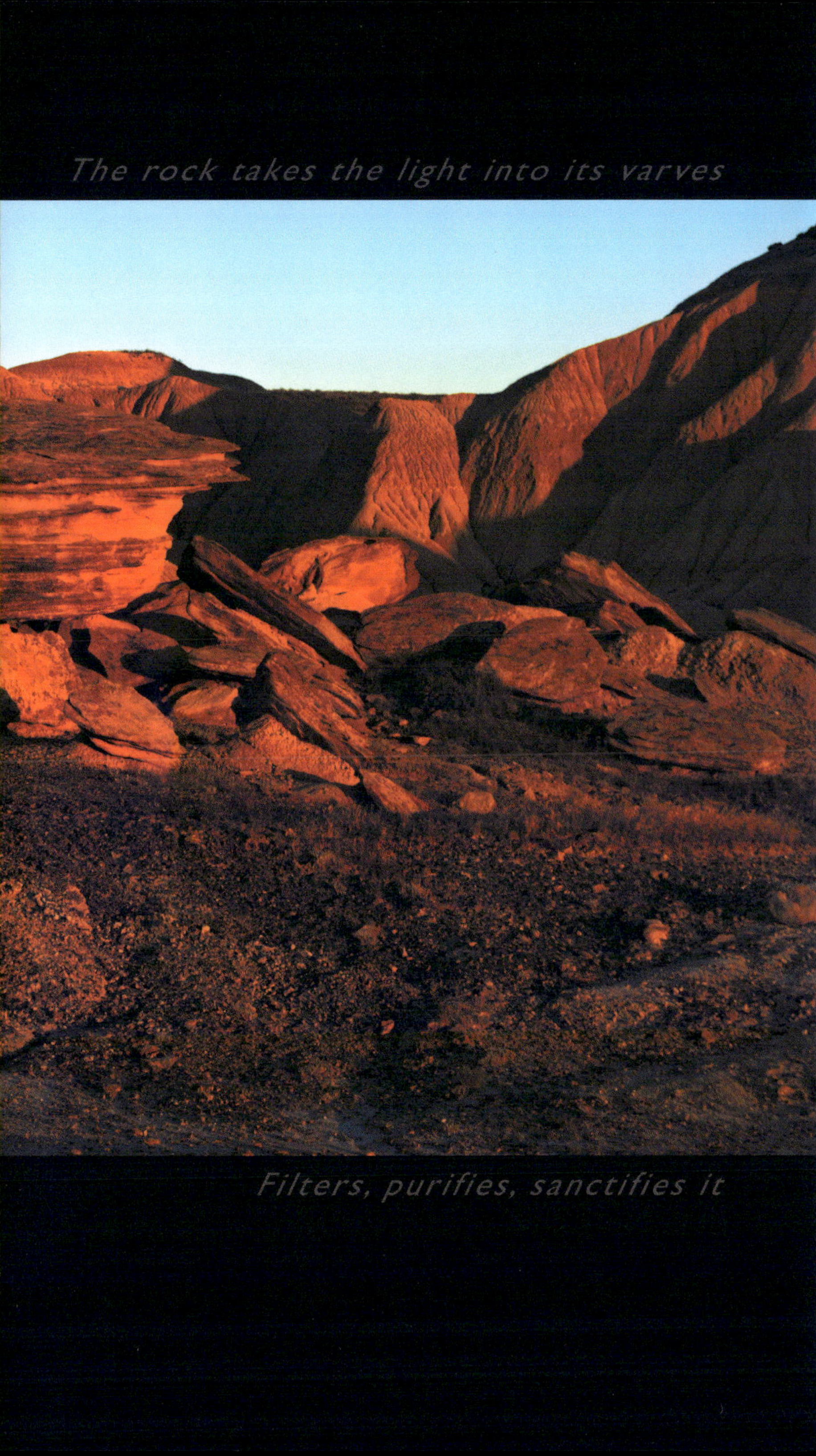

Morning's Symphony

It's carefully planned
The sun, the rocks, their shadow.
The stage is set for

Morning's symphony
Played on strata in red rock
By the rising sun.

And what's revealed are
Ancient history's archives
Light trapped years ago,

Now revealed by dawn's
Light reflecting to connect
Today to the past.

Don't try to escape
The past by hiding in nooks
Offered by the rocks.

History, like dawn
Cannot be denied and both
Will waken your day.

And then let you pass
So you can seek the knowledge
Promised by the hills.

Dawn

The sun peeks over
The eastern horizon.
The shadows stretch
Covering the morning steppe.

There's a promise here.
An aromatic wisdom of the day
Generated by the sun's warmth;
The odors of dry grass and sage.

Soon daylight will spread everywhere
Carrying away the experiences of the night,
The good, the bad, soon all part of the past.
And the steppe can prepare for the coming night.

In anticipation of another dawn.

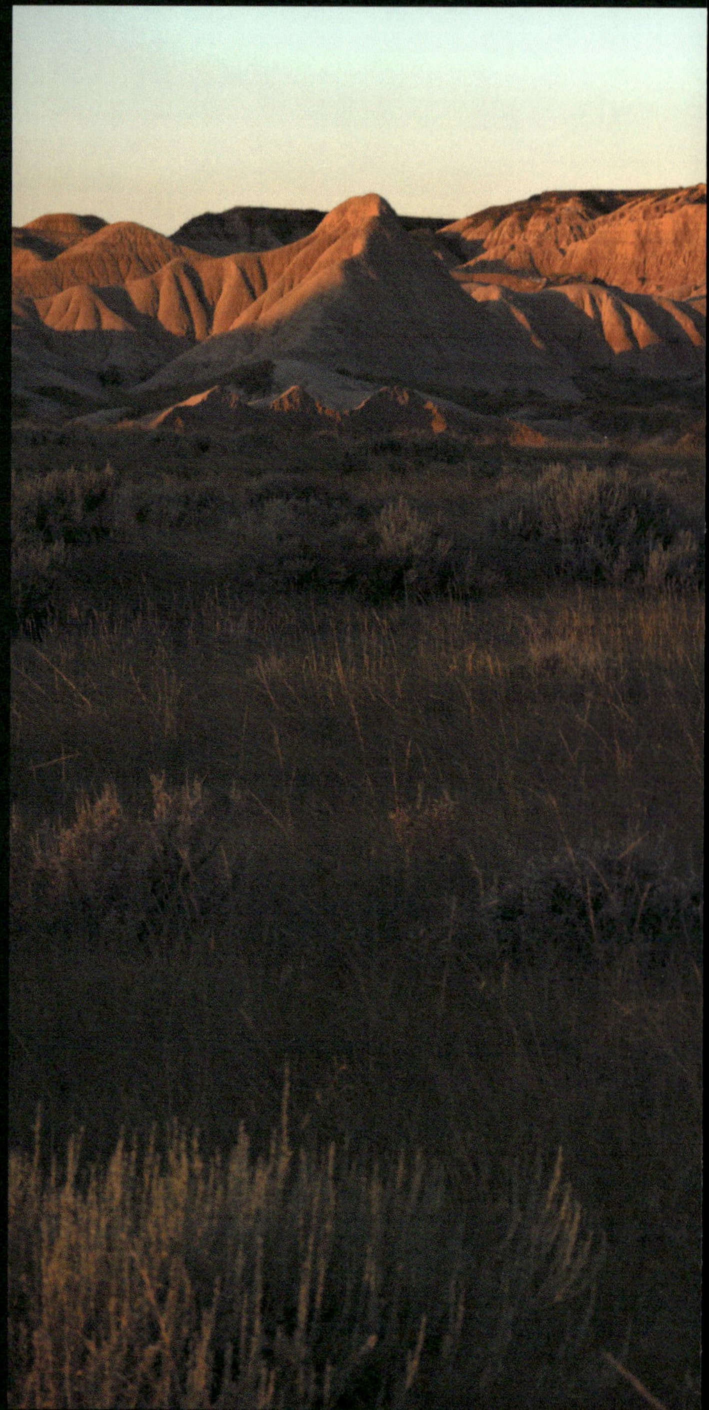

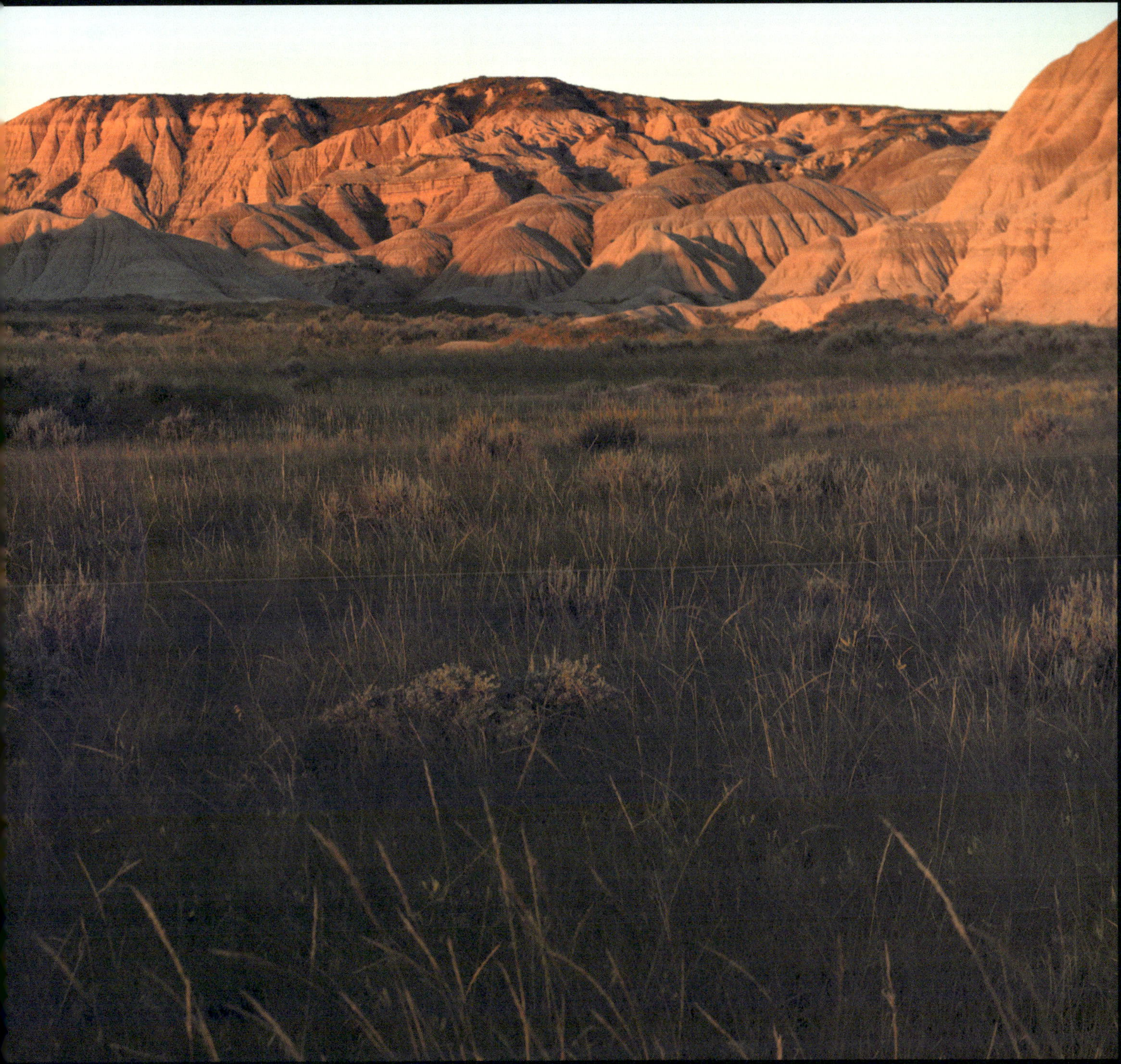

Early Morning

What more could one want?
The sun rising behind you
It's light reflected in a peak.

And that patch of grass
Sitting there below the peak
Partly shaded, mostly in the sun.

Is that grass after anything?
A bit of water draining down from the peak?
A place to hide from grazers?

Or maybe it's there by accident
Nothing profound
It just survived as a bit of prairie.

The sun rising behind you

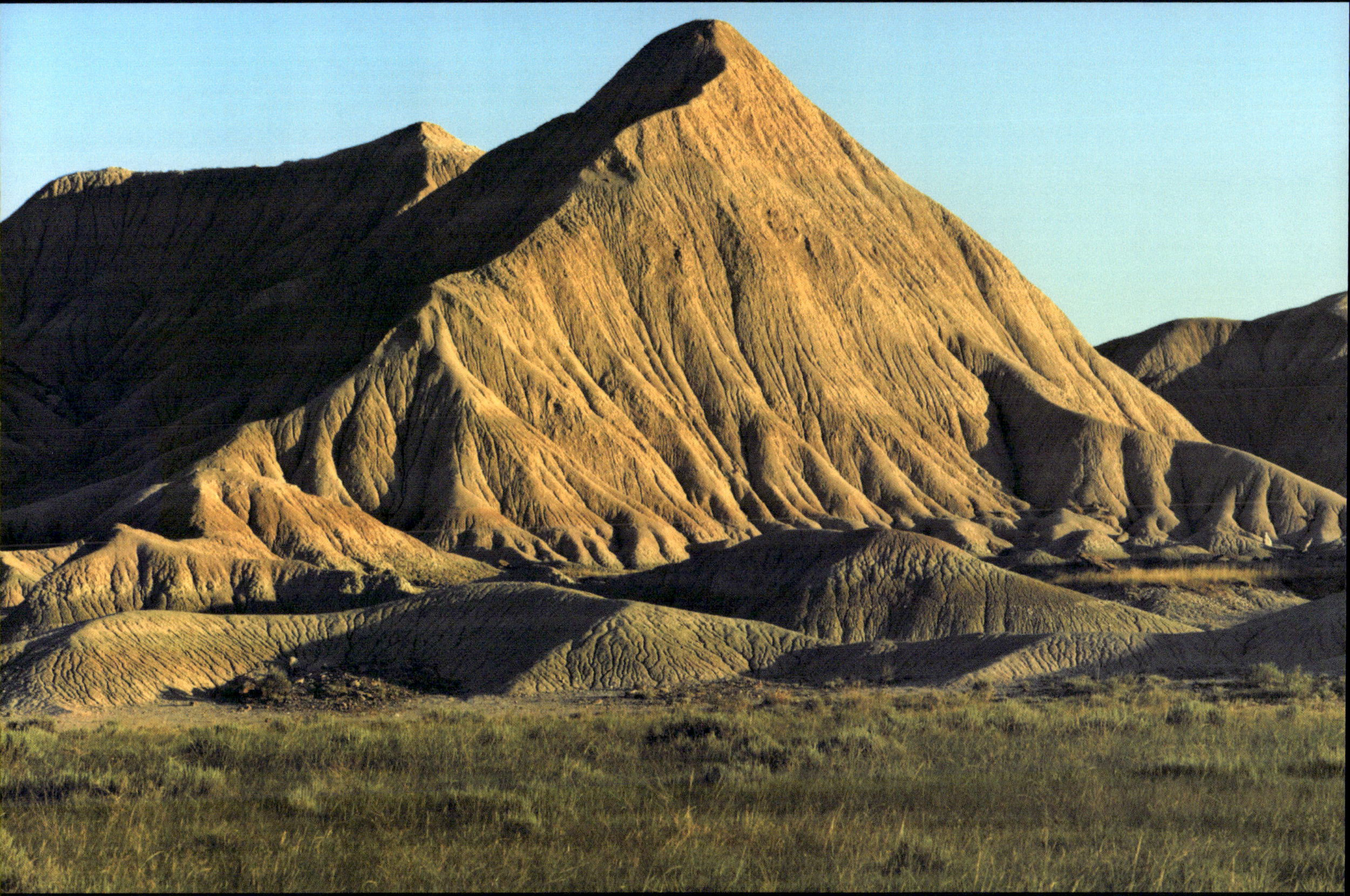

It's light reflected in a peak

Earth Awakening

Even the boulders
Genuflect to the rising
Sun, catching its warmth.

The earth gently wakens
As the sun
  Seeks out crevices
        And
  Reflects off edges
        And
  Flat surfaces.

It's the light, the warmth;
Impetus for the earth to
Prepare for the day

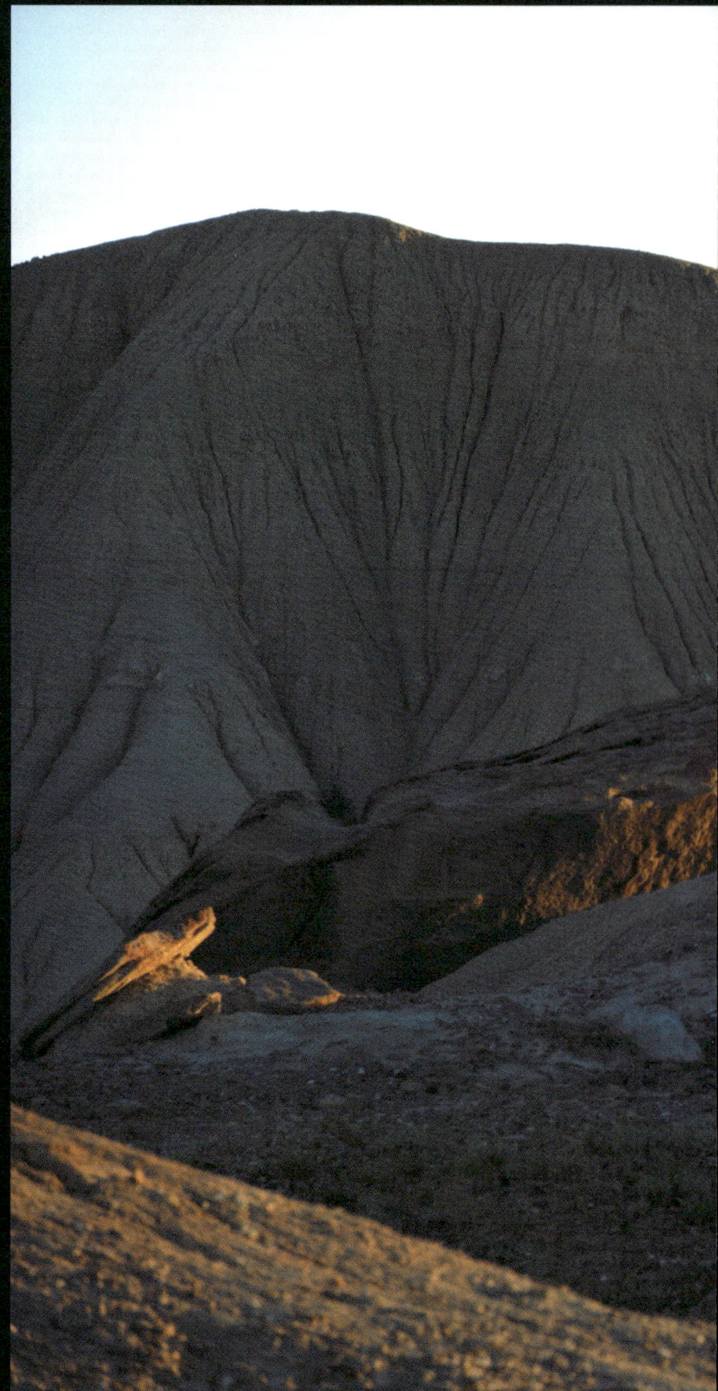

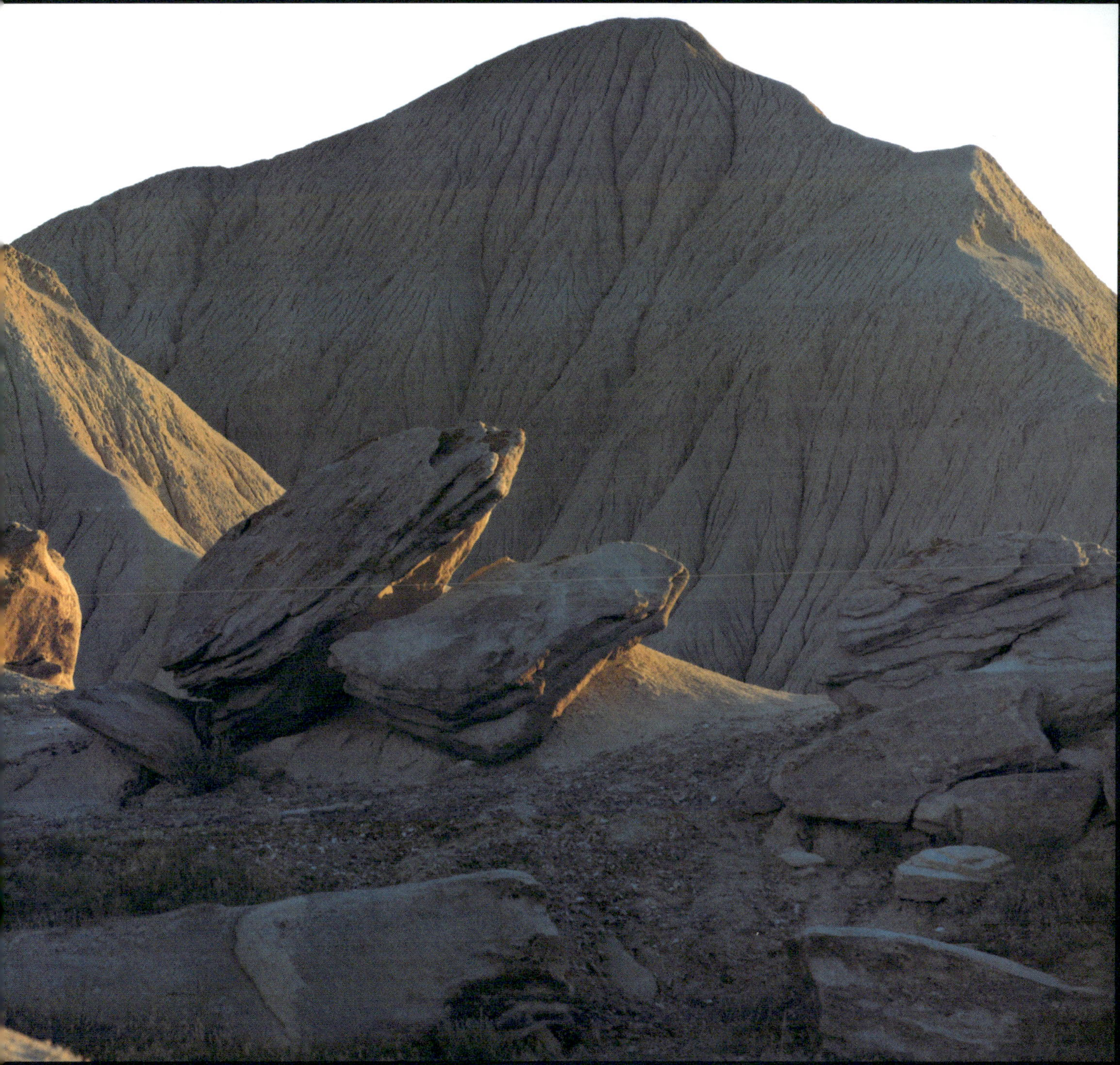

Tchaikovsky's First

It is now the time.
Our presentation today,
Tchaikovsky's First.
Soon the music will echo
Across water-cut ravines.

Led by opening horns,
Followed by piano chords
The kind rarely heard
Of beautiful complexity
Enhanced by the canyon walls.

You're carried along
Until the plants enter in
And mute the music
For peaceful contemplation,
A respite leading to the

Final crescendos

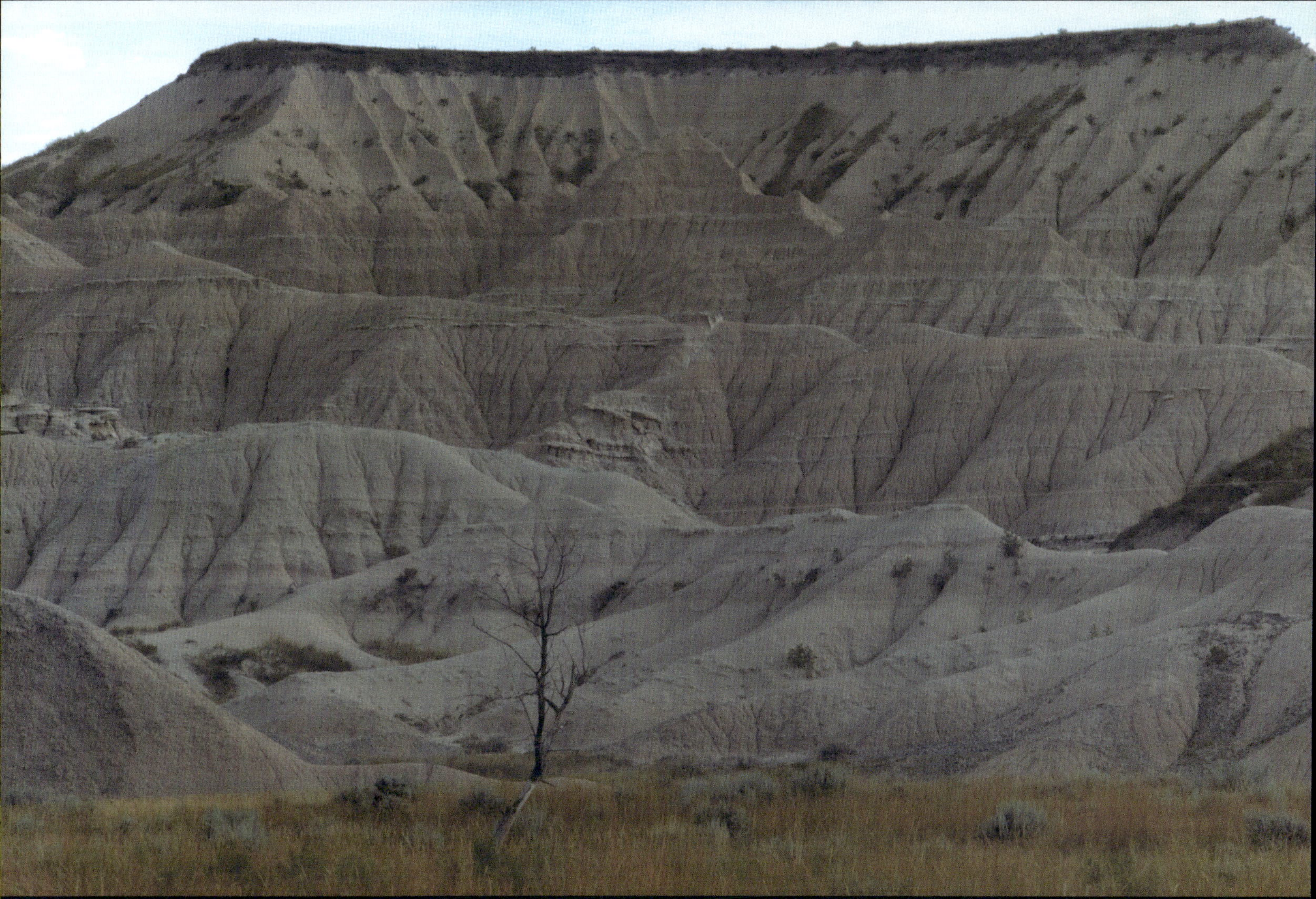

Revealed

It's what happened here.
A ridge seems to have dissolved
To reveal that knoll,
Sharp-pointed, erosion-scarred,
Dotted with scattered green plants.

It stands inviting.
To sit, to look and to dream
Of what's found beyond.
Some boulder strewn steppe, perhaps.
Or an open prairie view.

Unimpeded,
  Into the far distance,
  Into the far future.

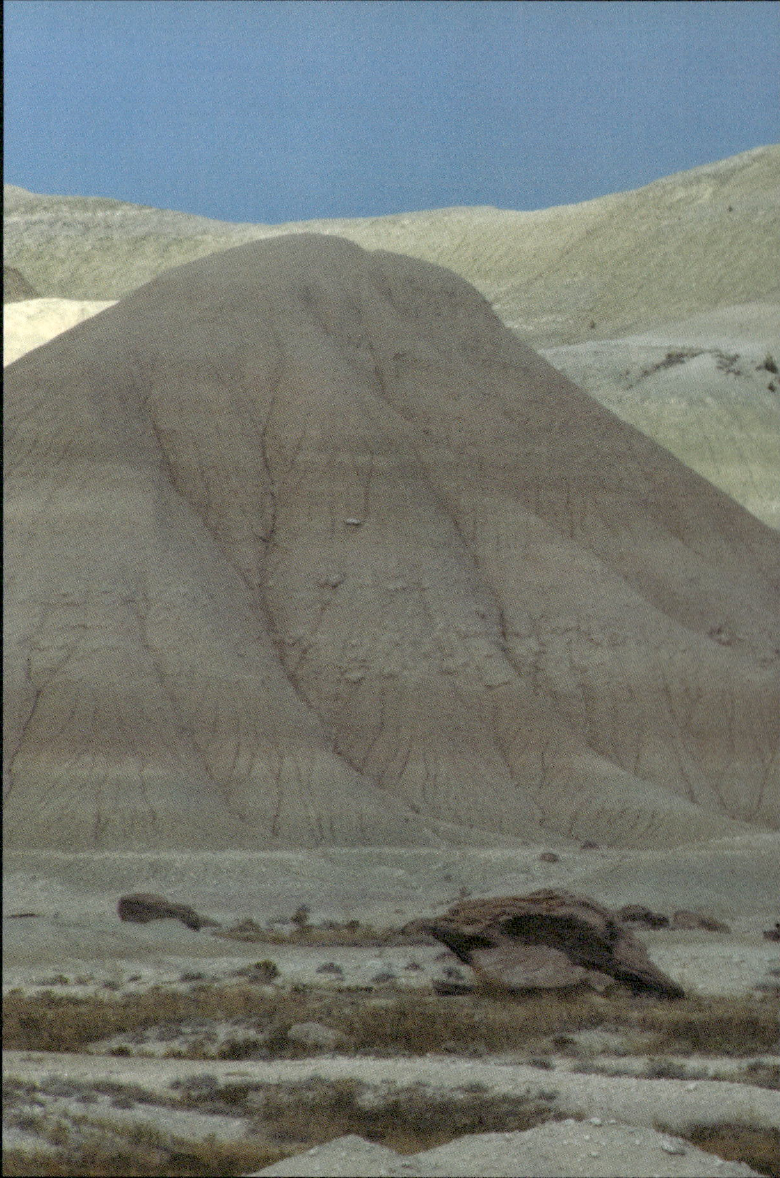

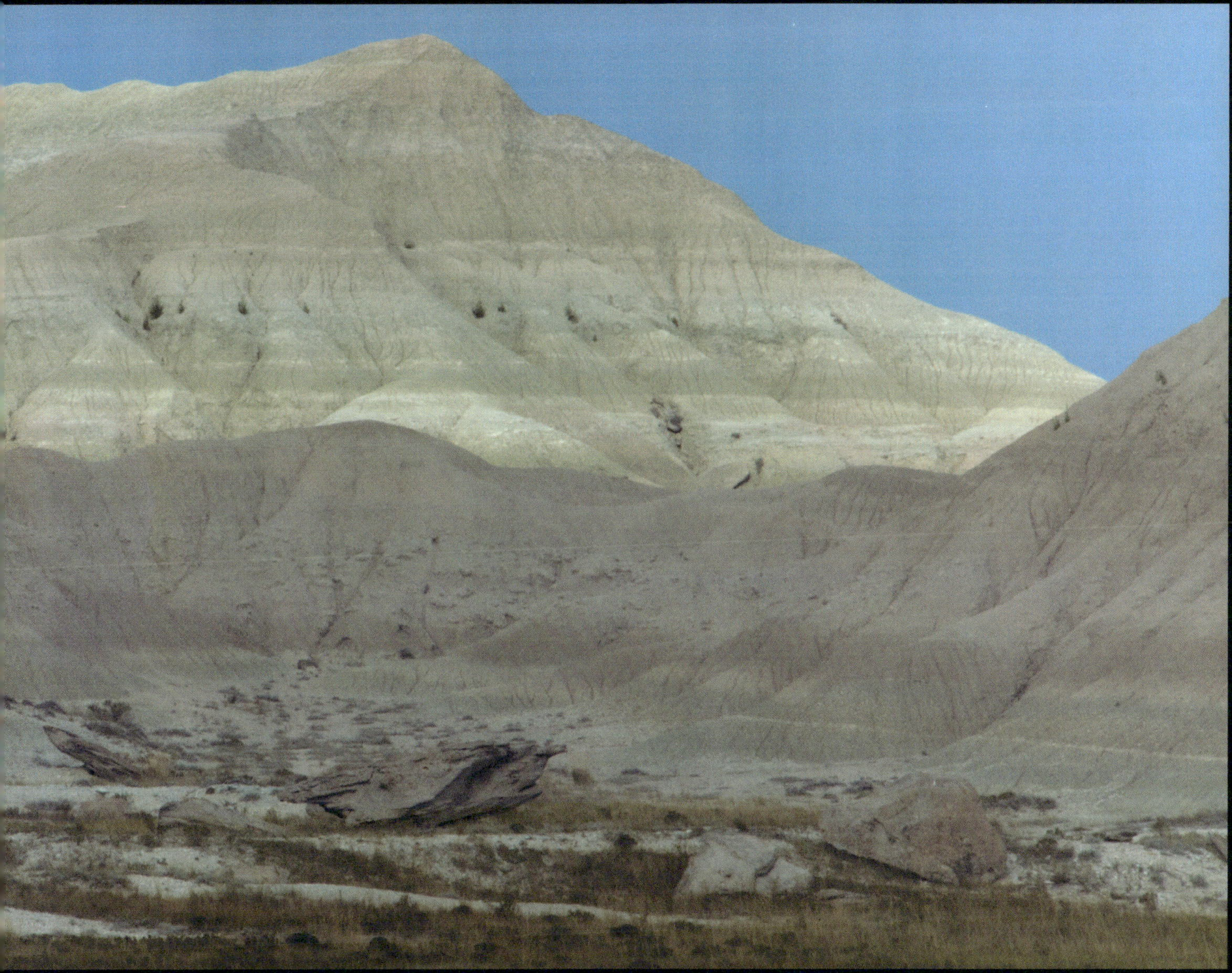

Meeting

The boulders gathered along the ridges
Looked down at the plants who've just arrived.
Tired and travel-damaged, those plants
Brownish, many devoid of leaves.
The boulders' emissaries roll down a little draw
To meet their living counterparts.

It's an annual event
Plants seeking the wisdom of the boulders,
Granted by the goddess to help the plants
Survive the oncoming winter.
The goddess was pleased.
She knew her creation would be renewed in spring.

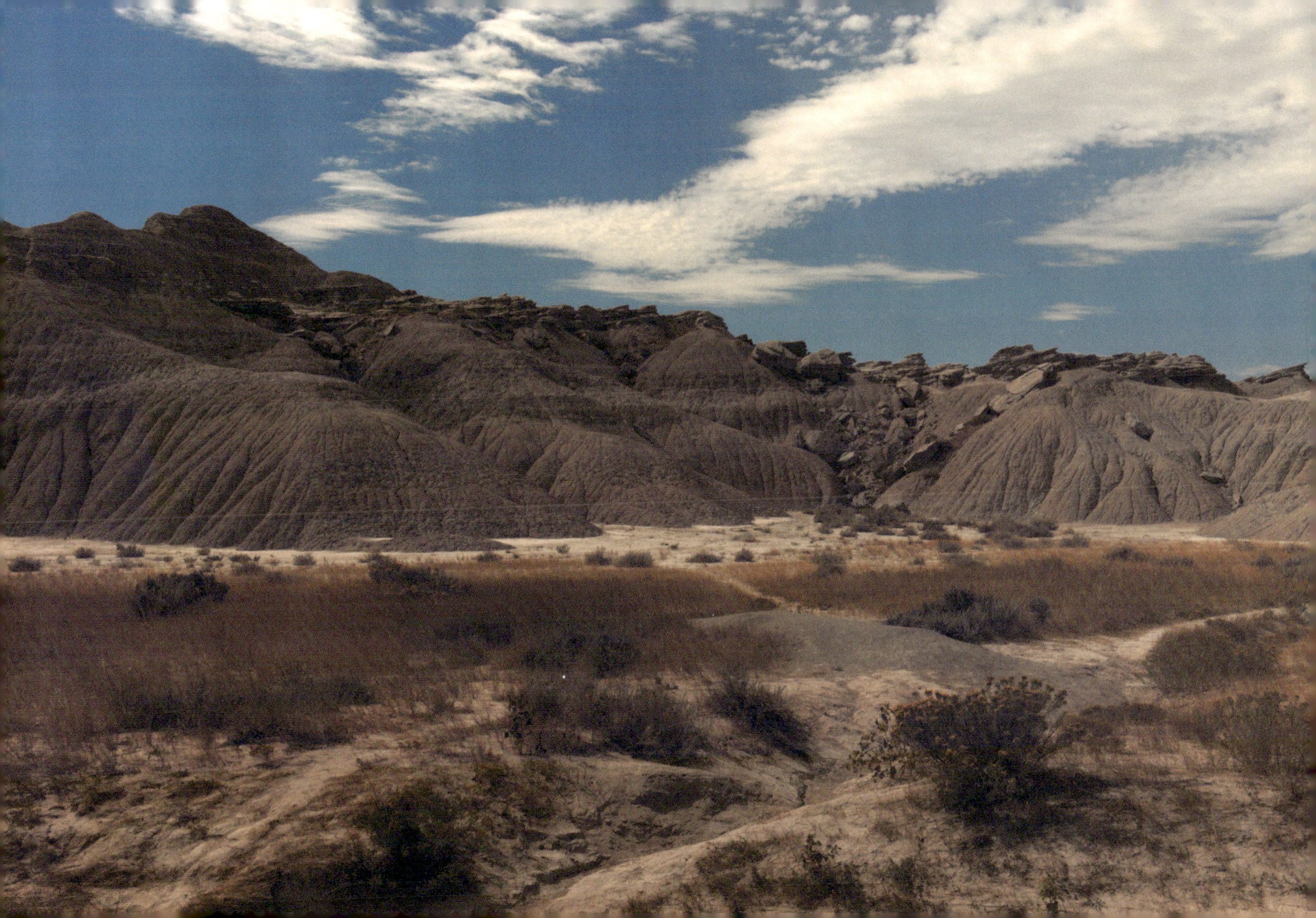

Just a tree

It was just a tree
A small one
Growing among grasses and shrubs
Along a flat
Below some hills.

It was just a tree
A small one
It died.
The skies turned gray in sorrow
To mark its passing.

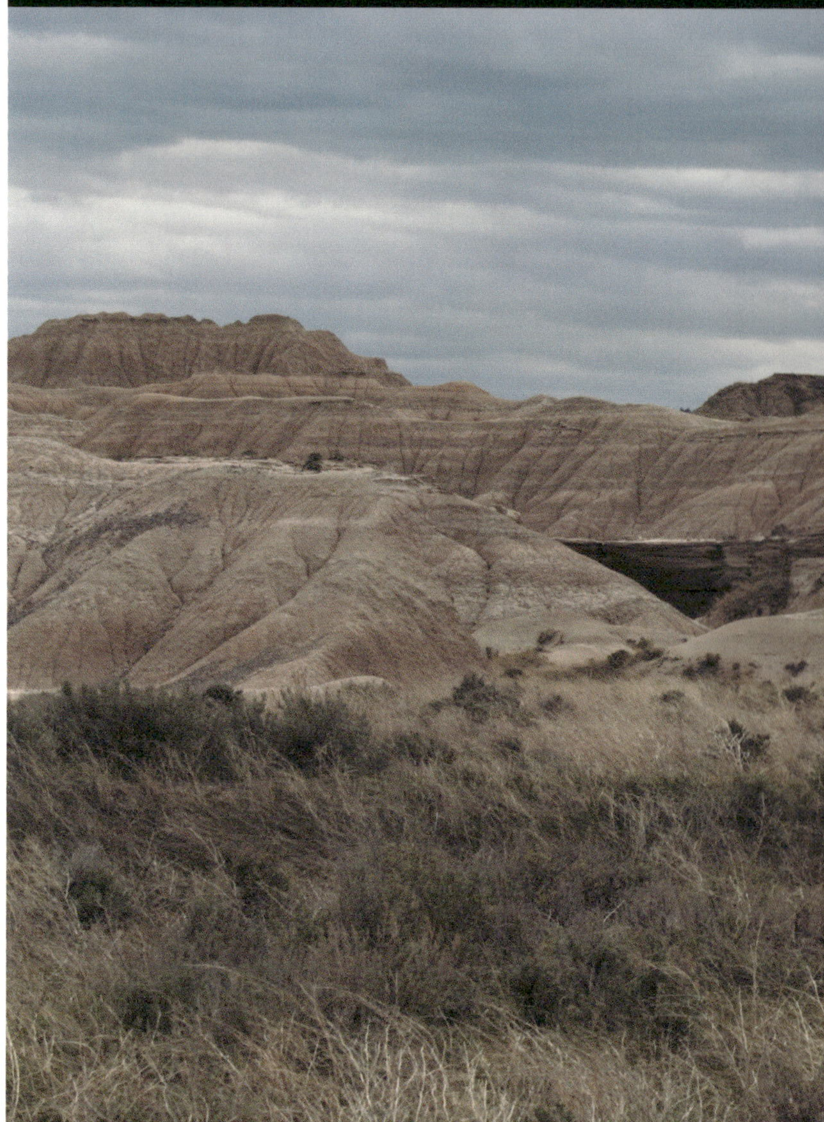

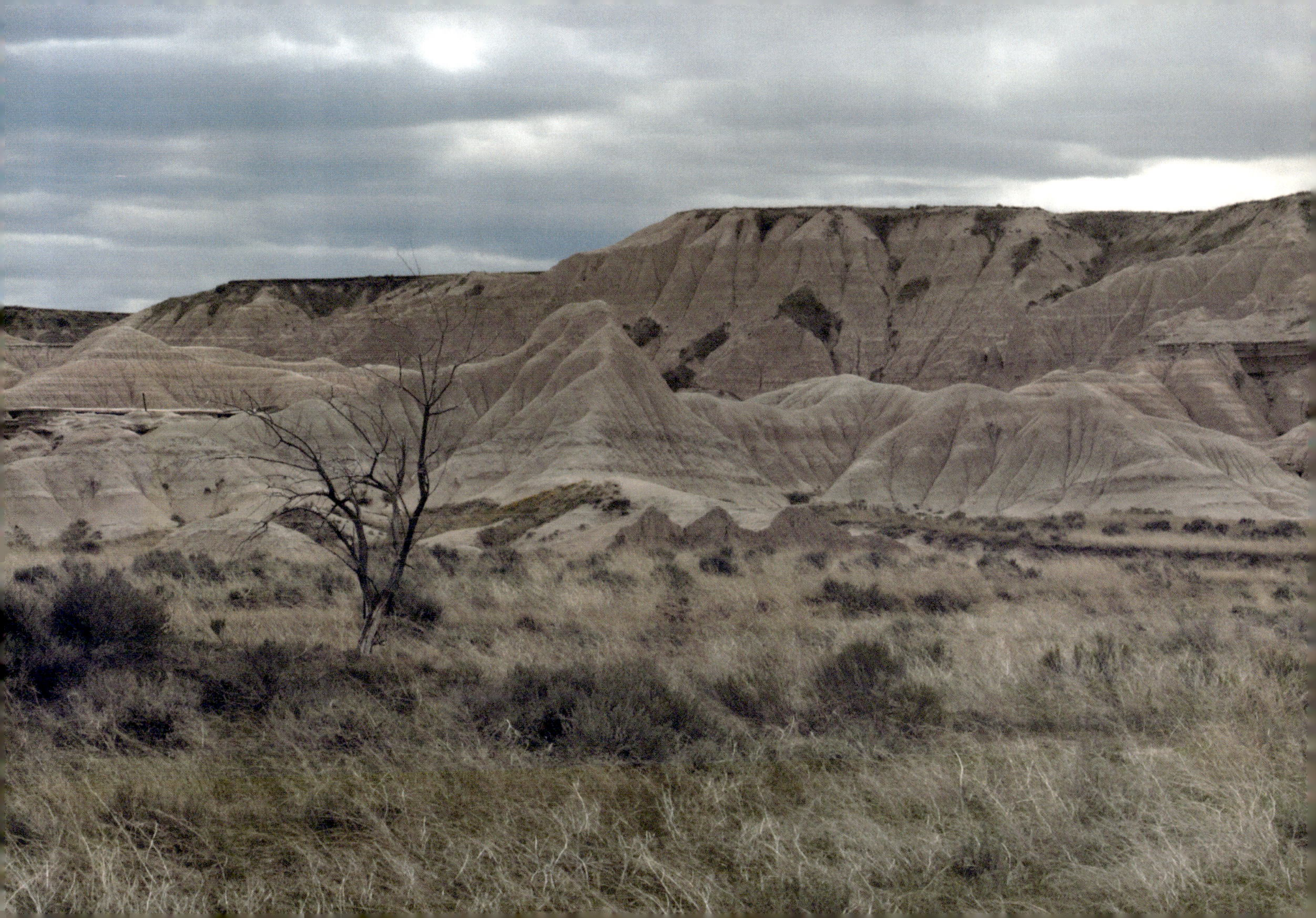

Spell

It's not very large,
  Not very high.

Sandwiched between
  Blue sky above, almost cloudless
  Vegetation dried tan beneath,

Its furrowed white surface attracts
  First the eye
  Then the mind
  Finally the imagination.

And look with your imagination,
  The furrows on the surface start to shimmer
  As in a dance of desire

    To

Draw you into their spell.

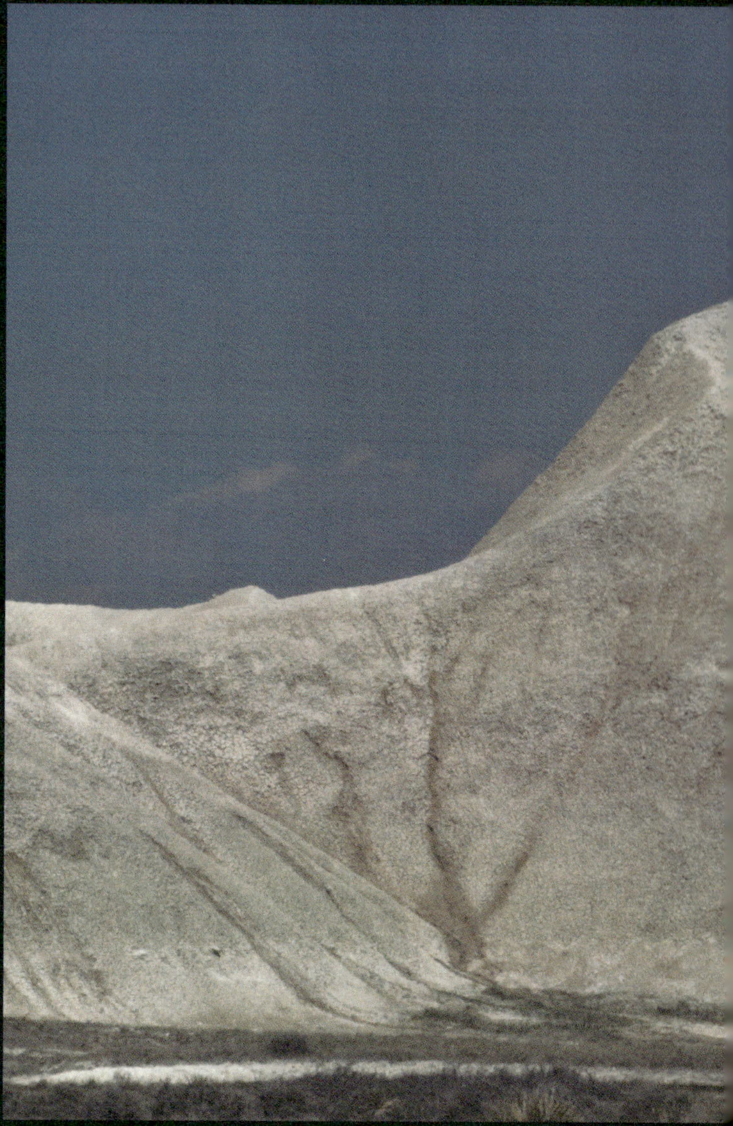

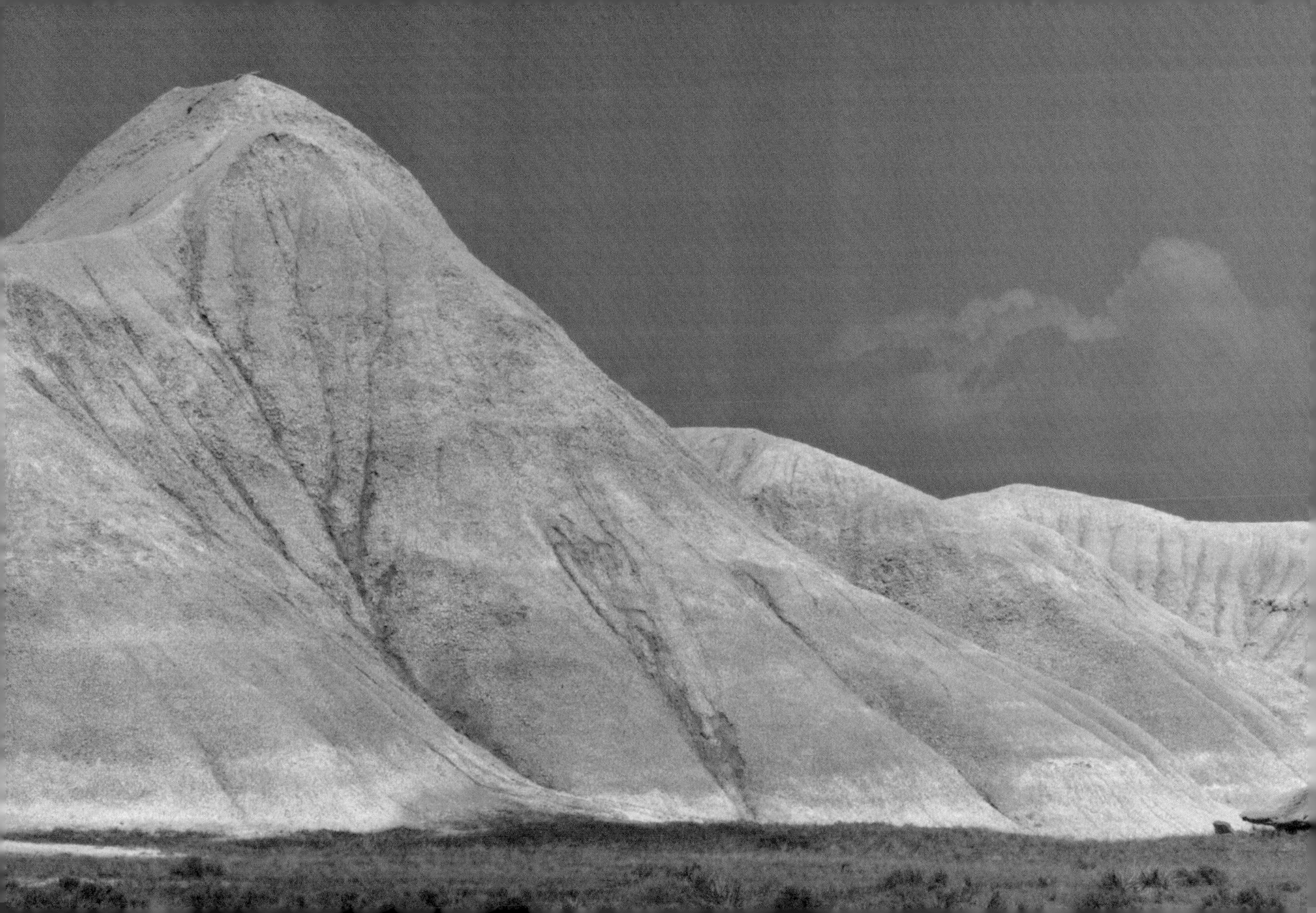

Conundrum

As the eye wanders, there's differences
Starts with a complex jumble of rock
  Festooned with a few bushes.
Then there's furrowed slopes, simpler
  And without plants.
Then the flat land, simplest
  But with more plants, obviously.

But nature's usually not like that
It starts out simple and becomes complex
   Bacteria to plants
   Egg to chicken
   Life, child's to adult.

Maybe the eye's not starting in the right place.
But no one ever read nature as descending
    From plant to bacteria
    From chicken to egg
    From adult to child.

So why the conundrum?

Maybe I've missed out time.
  Rocks to slope to flat land
    One time.

Bacteria to plants, egg to chicken, child to adult
   Different phases.

All carried along through time.

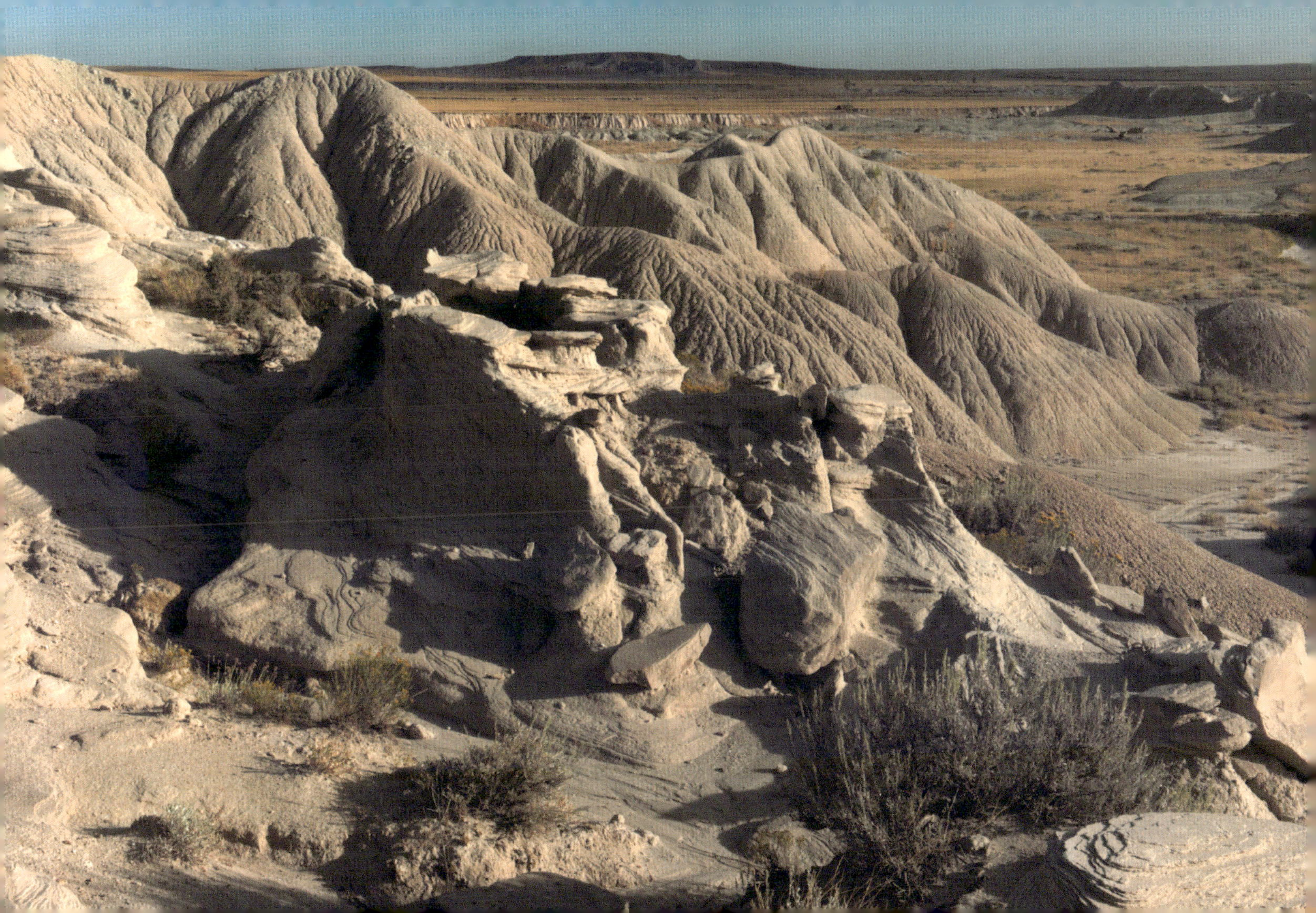

Altruism

The hill stands tall
  Sharp peaked
  Rugged, strong

Guardian against encroachment
  Stopping advancing steppe
  Frustrating its plans.

They seem to stand, opposed
  The hill rising
  The flat land below.

But this is illusion.

Look closely.

That tower of strength seems unaware
  Of the runnels carved in its side
  Left behind as running water
    Ate away at its strength
    Carrying it to the encroacher.

In truth there is no opposition
But there is sacrifice.
You can see the many wrinkles on the hill
  Wrinkles left behind when the hill gave of itself to the flat land.

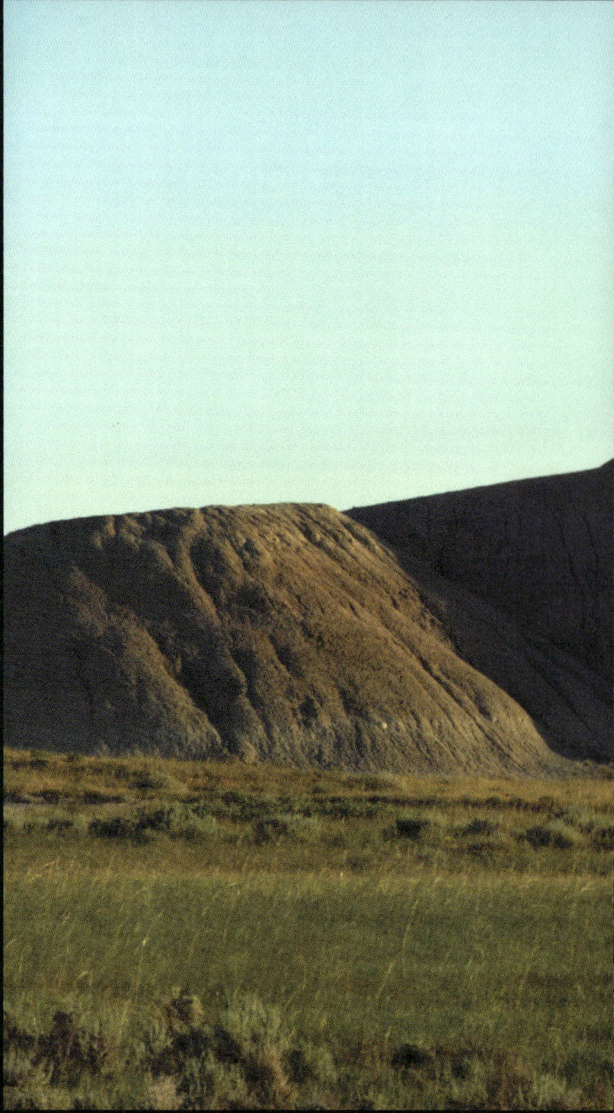

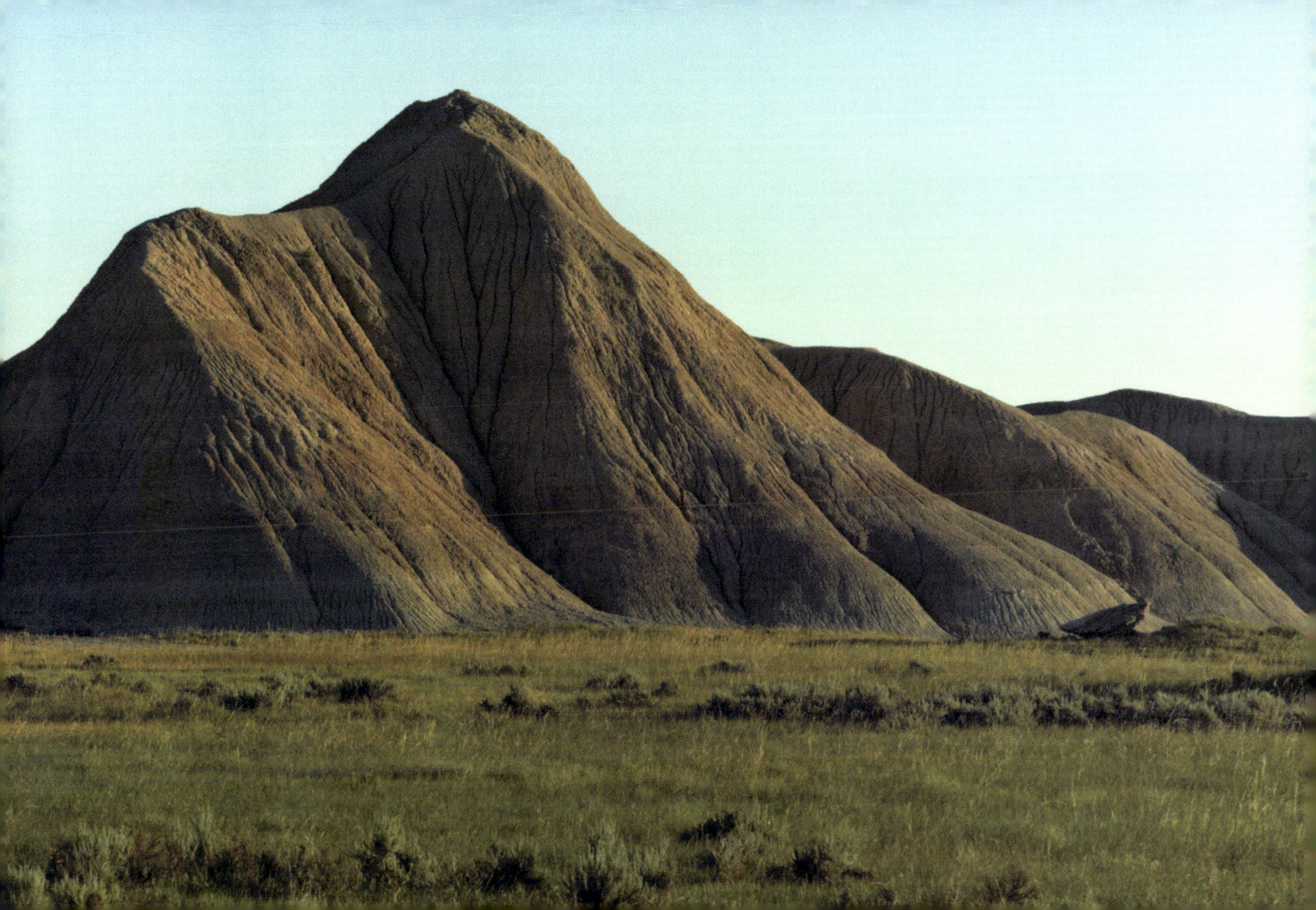

Benediction

You've come to me
   Seeking my blessing.
   Granted.
But I have more to give.

My water
   Given by my clouds
   Taken by my hills
   Delivered to you
See its passage in rivulets on slopes.

My body
   Represented by my earth
   Taken from my hills
   Delivered to you
See it grooved by my water.

Take all this and make it your own
   My spirit as your blessing
   My water and body as your body.
Then rest.

Winter's coming,
 And with its passing
 You should sleep
 You'll be refreshed body and spirit
Ready to carry the message of my spring.

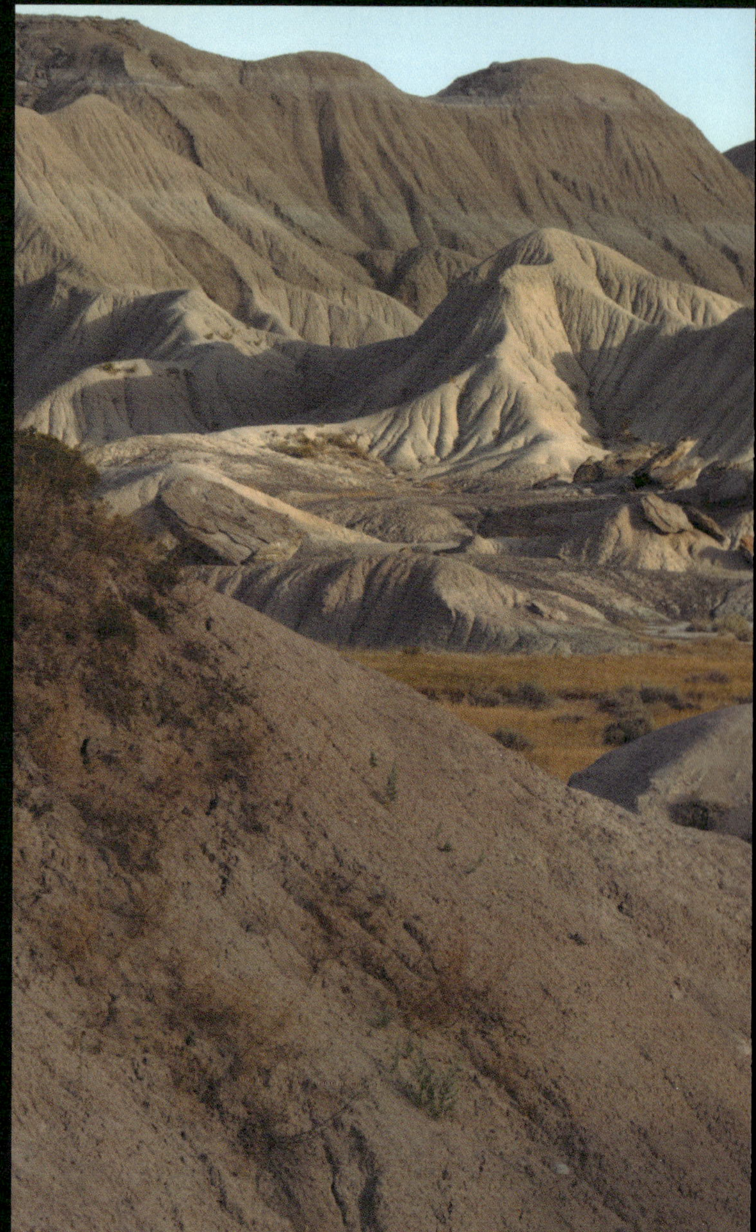

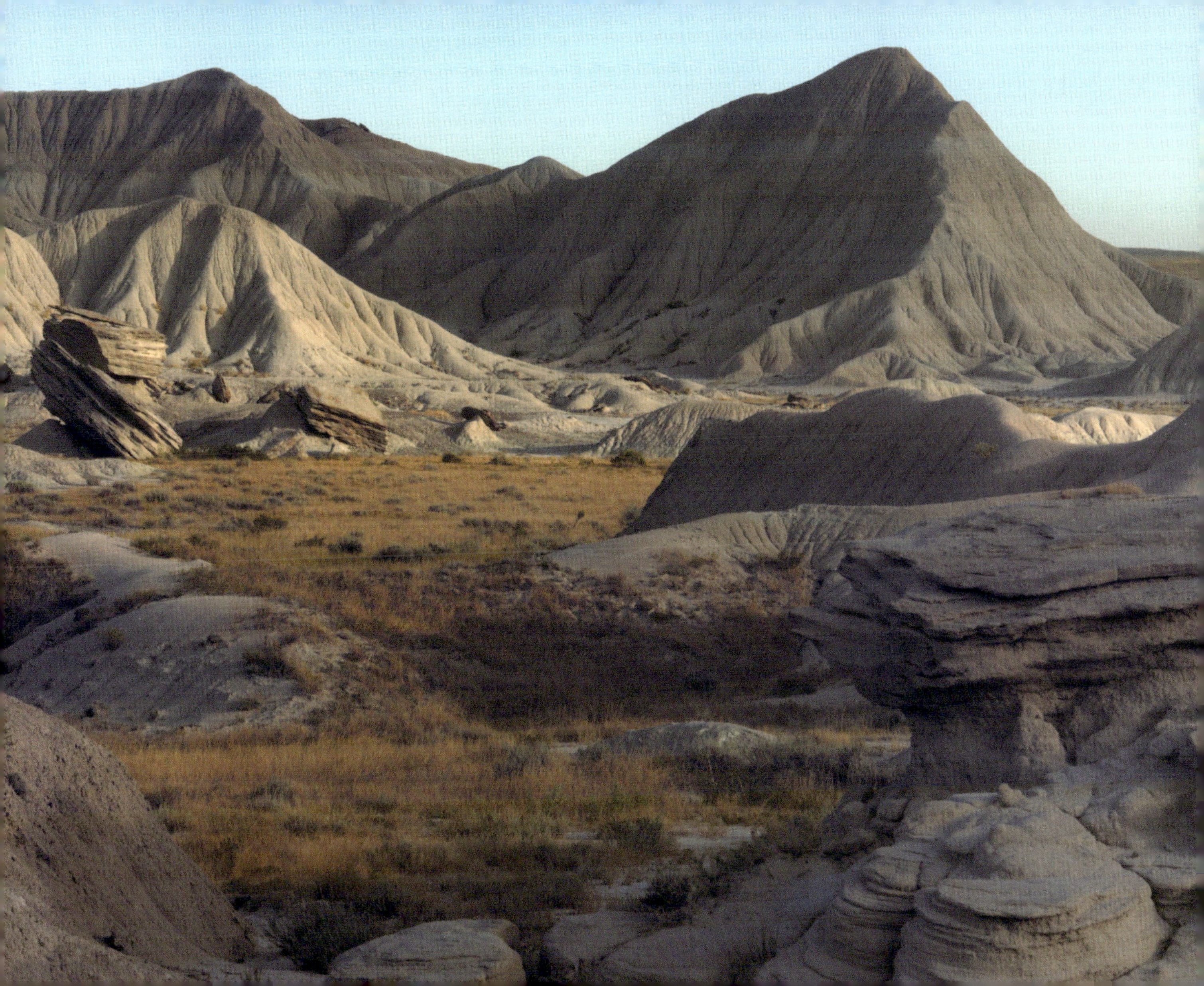

What's Going On

I just arrived to see rocks galore,
Some on the valley floor,
Some in that gully.

But what's happening?
Are the gully rocks trying
To escape their kin, or to join?

Maybe they're advance scouts
Reconnoitering in preparation
For a war of the rocks.

That must be it.
The clouds are arriving in anticipation,
Hoping to share in the spoils.

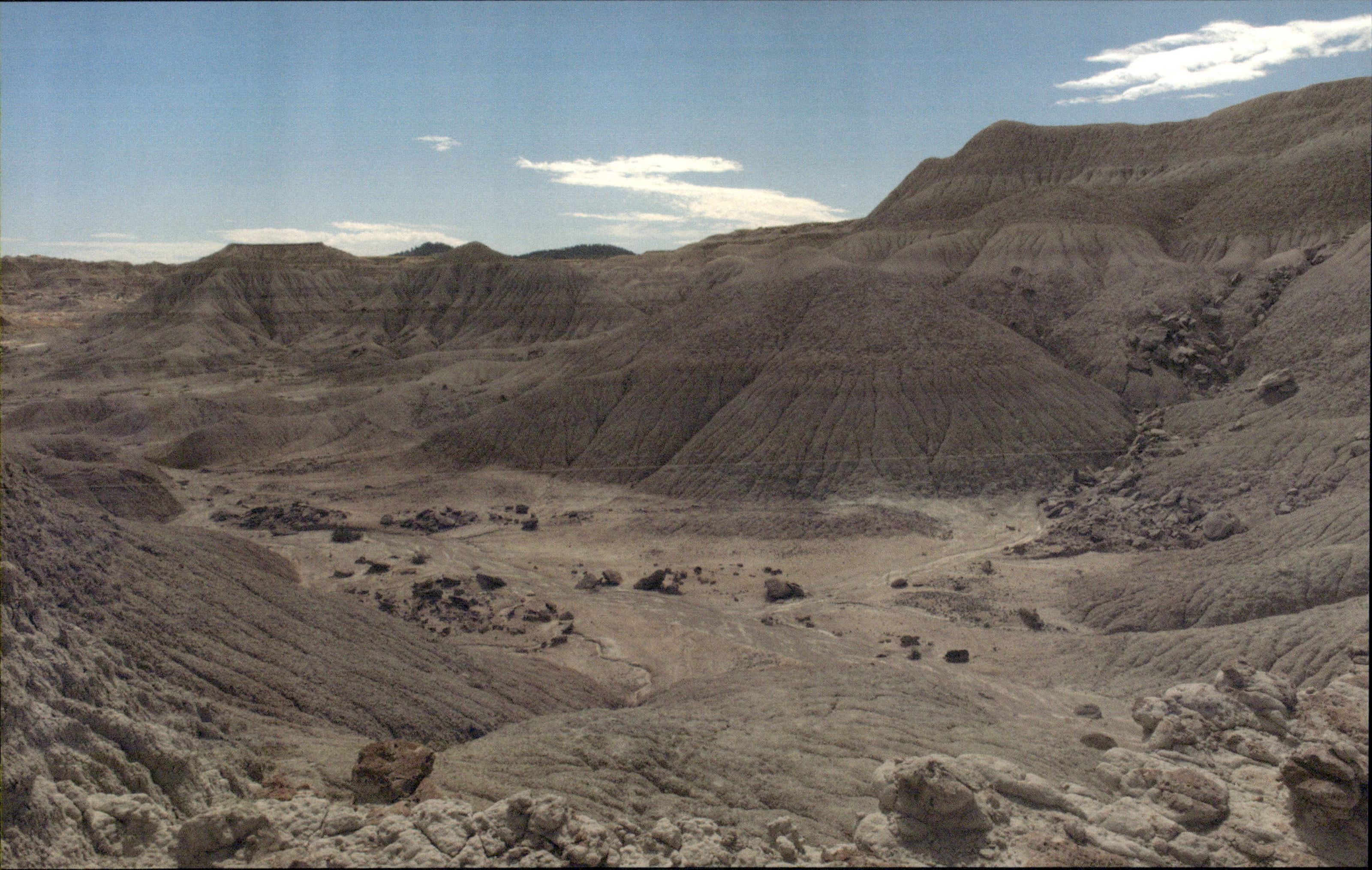

Peeking

Clouds must want to know.
Why else would they be peeking
Over the hillsides.

But what do they seek?
The origin of those rocks
Basking in the sun?

They know already
A bigger question looms
What's missing from here?

Where have the plants gone?
Doubtful the rocks scared them off
To hide in some nook.

No, the clouds are checking
To see if all is ready;
For the new spring.

Better find the plants
Favorites of the goddess
Her messengers.

Needed to carry her meaning east
To waken the Sand Hills so spring
Can arrive again

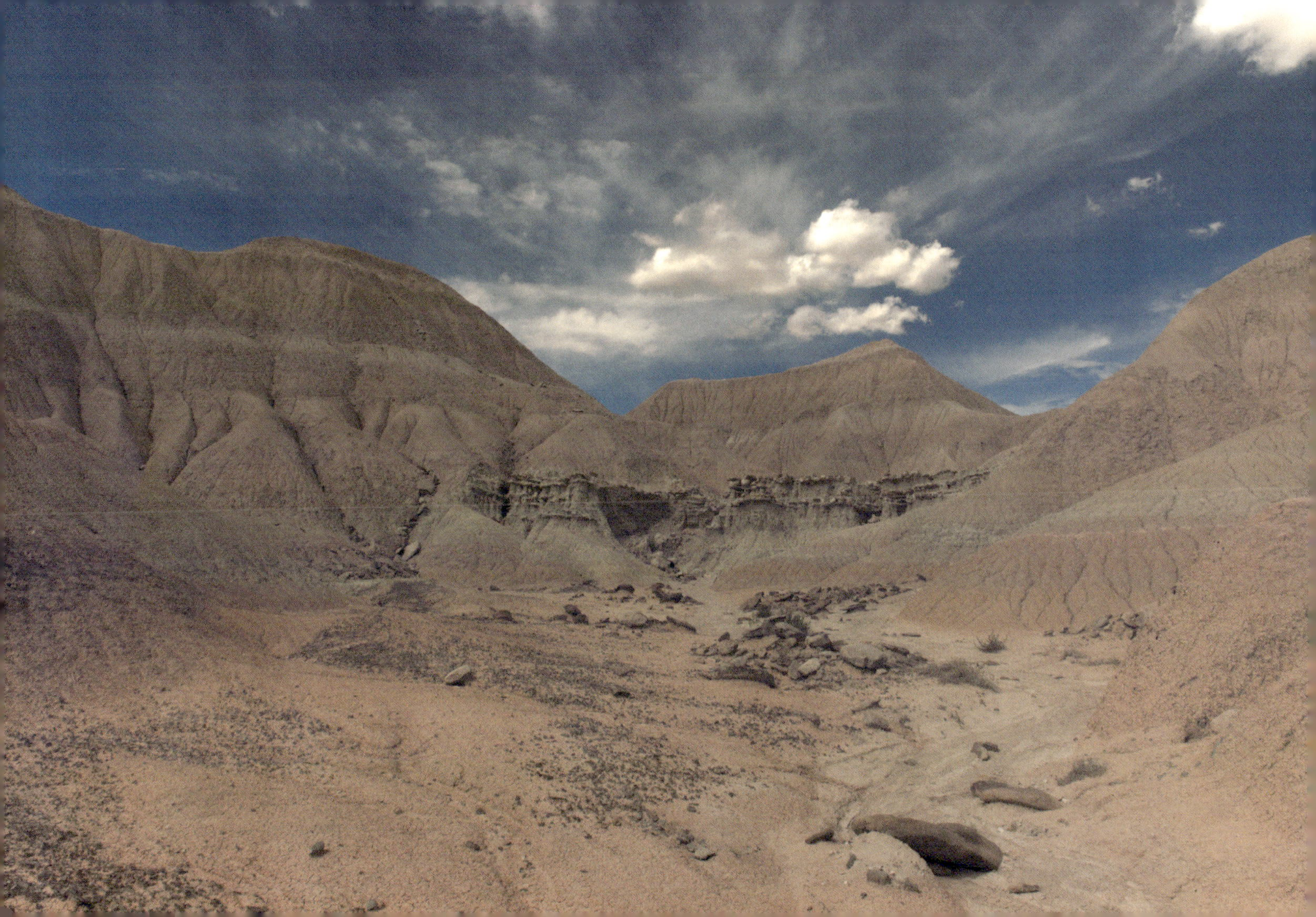

Reason

Reason

It dominates.

The force which brings order
  So grasses and shrubs form a steppe,
  So a course appears for water when it flows,
  So there`s a mesa offering plants a sanctuary,
  So there`re swales where snow can slowly melt
    To nourish small plants,
  So there`s a ridge defining the nave
    Where supplicants can wait
      For the order meant for them,
        For contentment.

Organizer

There was chaos
Gasses, shrubs, little trees tumbled over each other,
It was steppe, but a confused steppe.

Then a ridge appeared,
Stark white, furrowed by erosion;
It was preparing the land.

A dominating edifice arose.
The plants now had a focus;
They abandoned their confusion,

Found the flow around each other,
Allowing harmony to emerge,
Driving chaos from the steppe.

To move lightly in the wind.

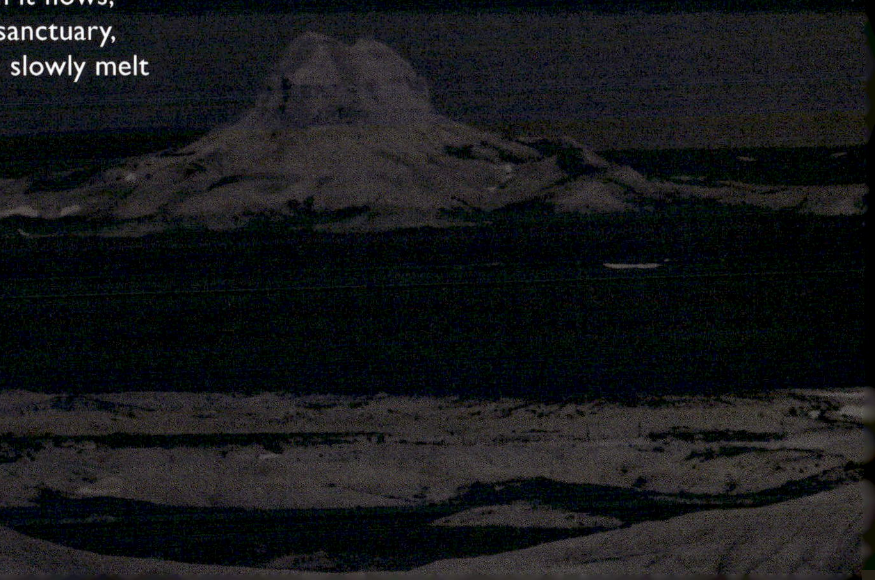

Focus-I

There's a lot out there, I think.
I seem to sense things,
  A ridge cut by erosion,
  A dry water course with small trees
  A steppe on flat land,
  A low mesa.

But I can't be sure.
There's an obelisk.
  It dominates the land,
  Leaving all else fog bound
  A fog not from the obelisk
  One brought by my eye.

A choice has been made,
Intense focus over calm musing.
  Is this choice to be rued?
  It is like life.
  Decisions, decisions, decisions,
  With none cast in stone,

    Even an obelisk.

Focus-II

The eye can't waver.
The obelisk won't let go.
But the choice was mine.
To abandon my freedom
For the safety of knowing.

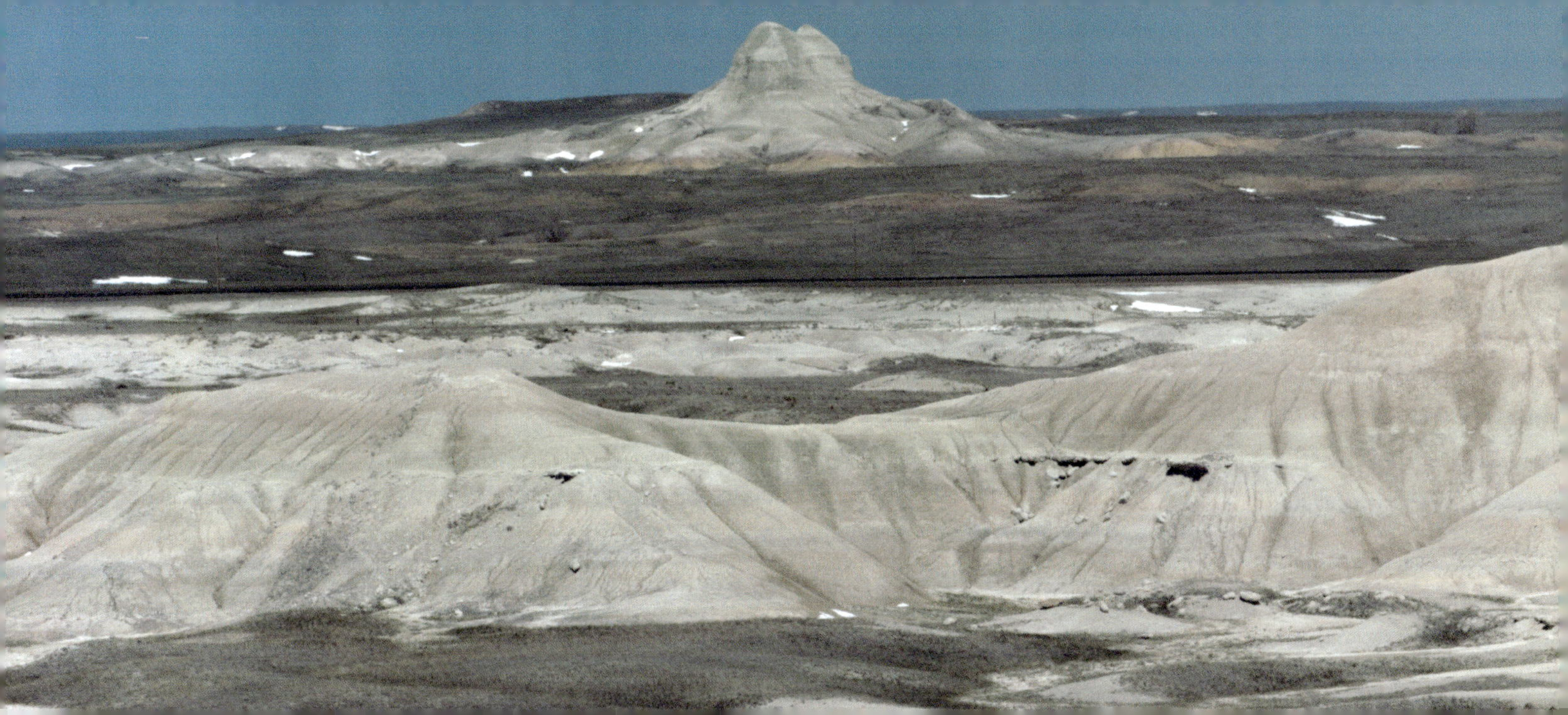

Shadow

That shadow there
Can it block the erosion
Eating at the hill?

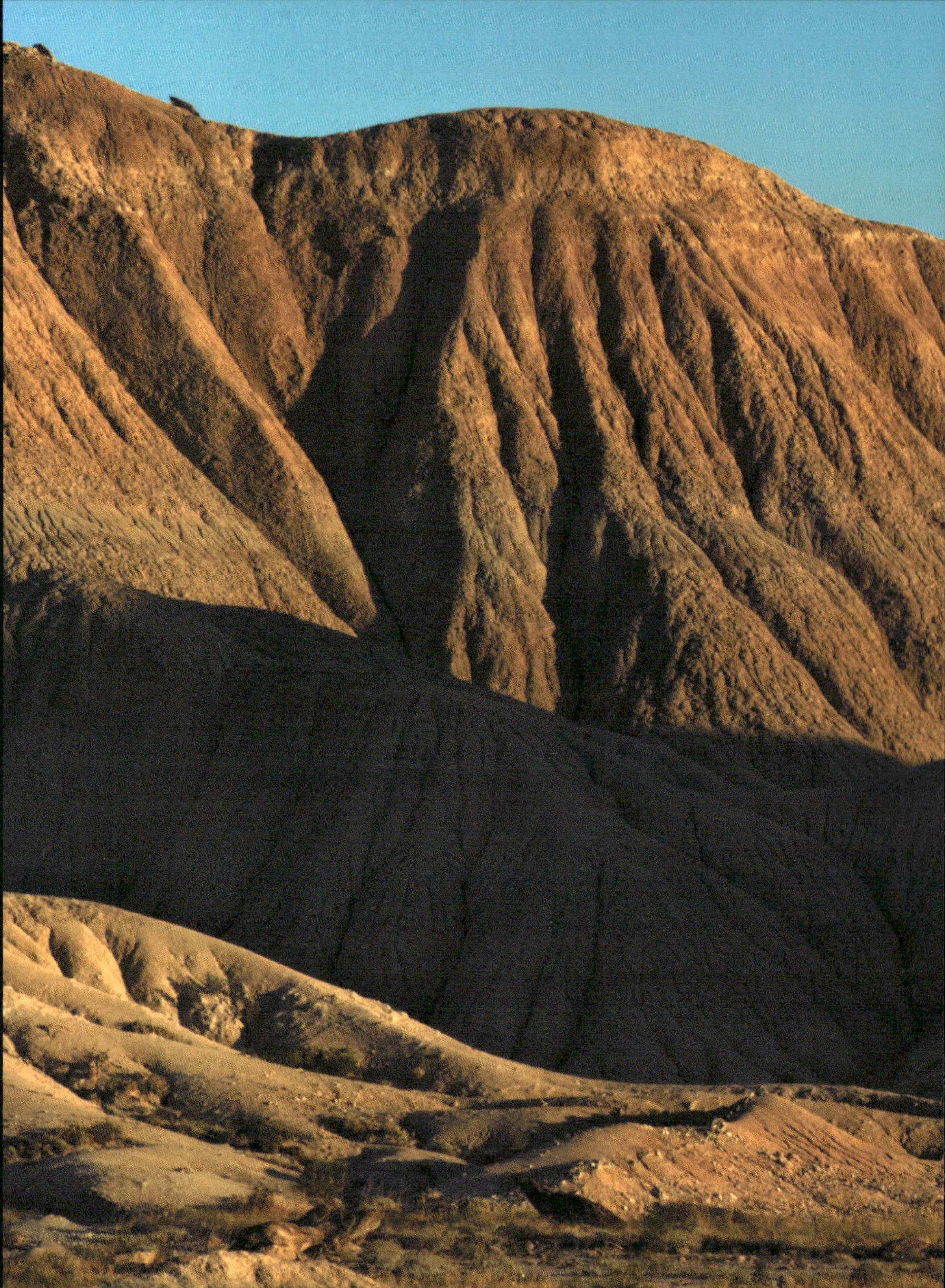

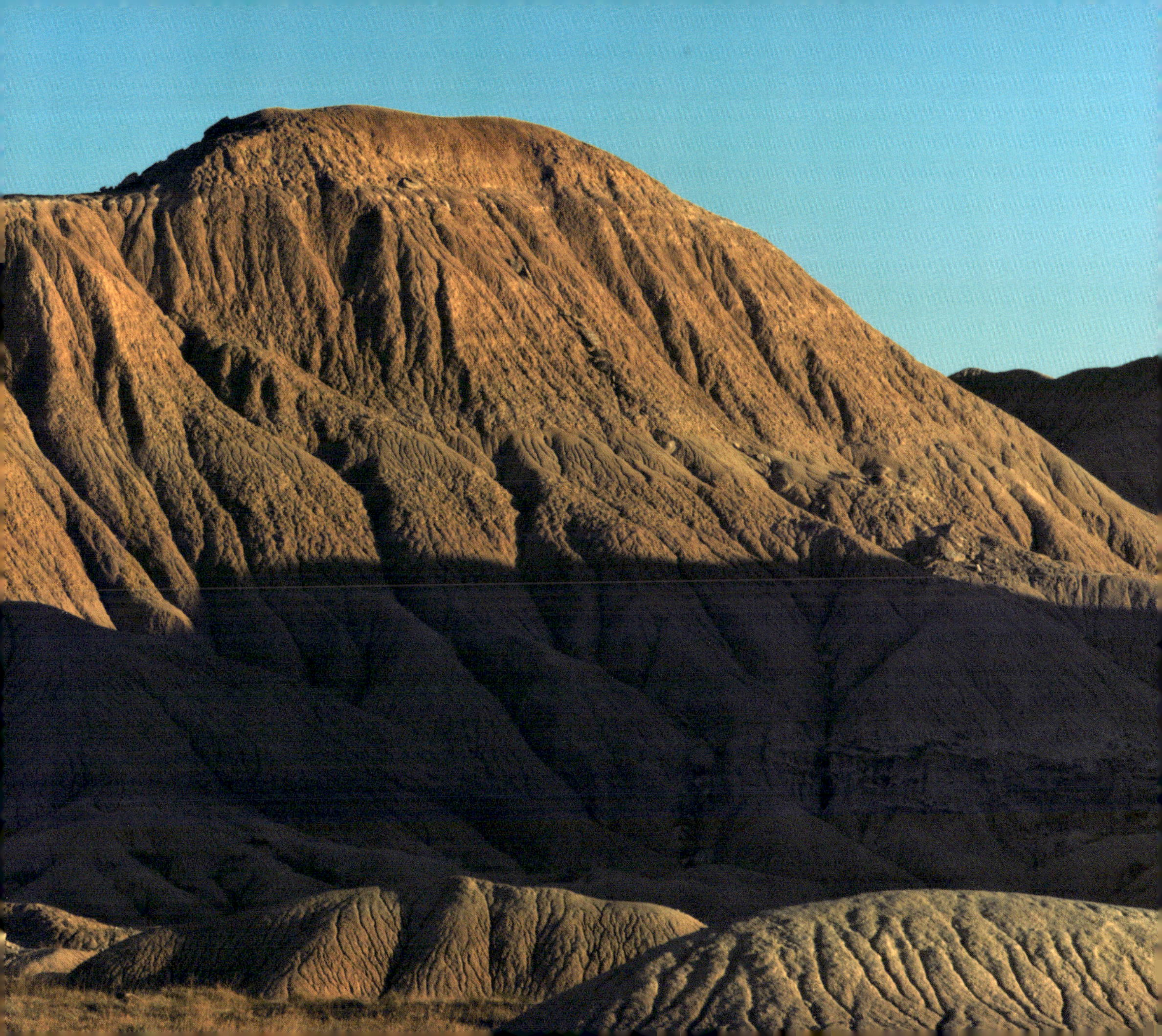

Prepared Temple

The clouds have come from the west
To inspect,
To be sure the Temple's ready
For the Goddess to return.

The altar's in place
The grasses, the shrubs,
Her steppe worshippers,
Await in their pews.

The hills have bared themselves
In supplication.
Open to receive her first light
Streaming from the east.

All is ready.

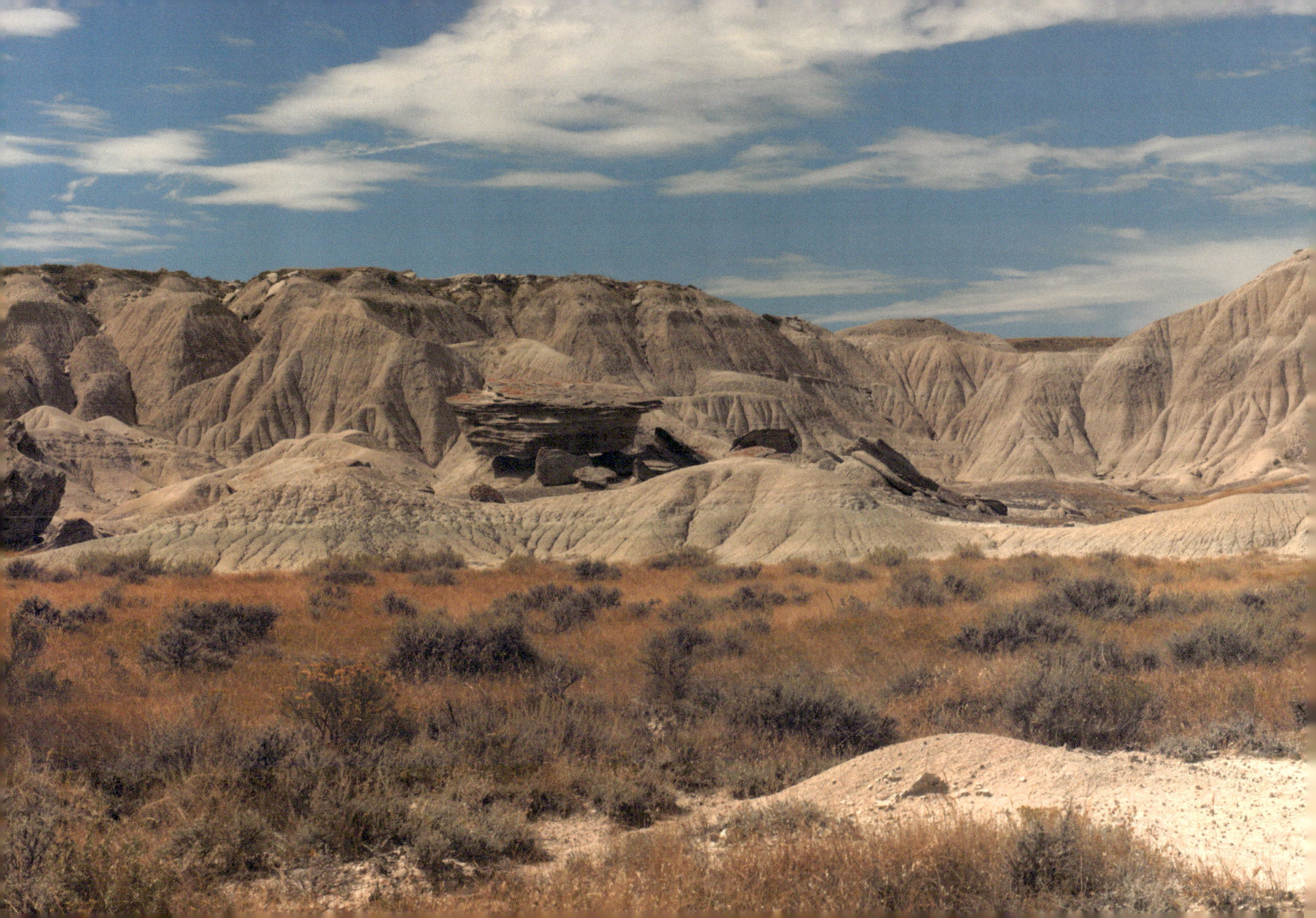

Changes

They're not large
Those hills.
But they dominate
They use the morning sun
Reflecting brightly
To elicit devotion
From those
Sitting scattered at its base.
The hills're slowly changing
The wrinkles on their slopes
The sign of age
Left behind as the rain
Collected and then followed gravity's urge
Carrying along bits of the hills.
Both are deposited at the base of the hills.

They're many and small
The plants
Supplicants
At the base of the hill.
They take the water
Delivered by the hill.
They take the body
Donated by the hill.
And incorporate them
The water and the body
As part of their own..
That ownership is brief
The body
The water
Both released when the plant dies.
To be taken up again
In the spring
As plant begats plant.

Slow and continual change in the hills
Rapid change in the plants.
Why does this happen?

It is the wish of the goddess of life
Of renewal
Of beauty.
The majesty of the hills is there
Season after season.
The plants mark the passing seasons,
The youth of spring
The maturity of summer
The aging of fall
The death of winter.

Why does the goddess wish this?

The slow change in the hills,
The background beat of the bass fiddle;
The rapid cycling of the plants,
Jazz, improvised on a beat,
Artie Shaw, Benny Goodman, Louis Arstrong
At their best.

The goddess loves music.

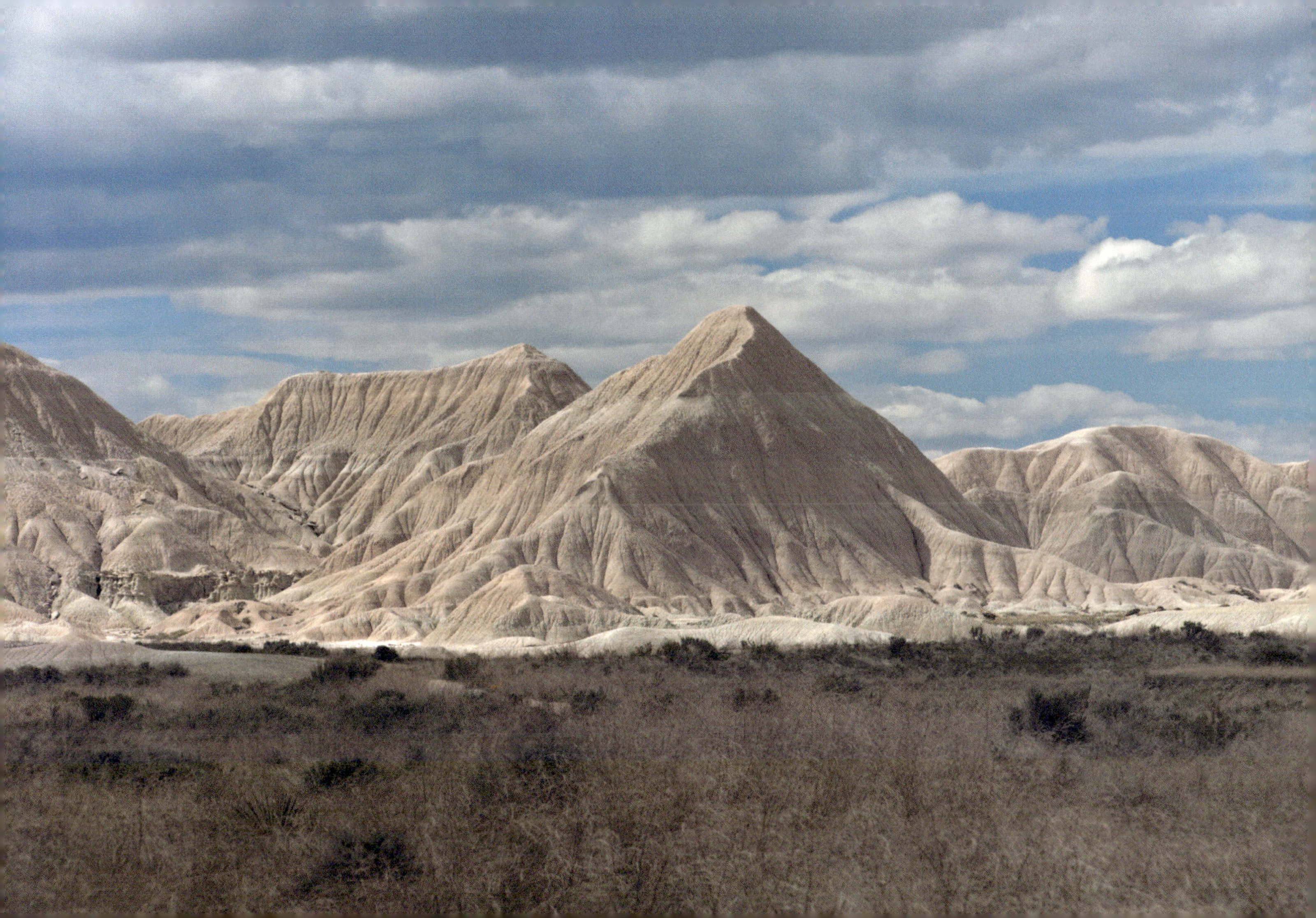

Who's this?

Plants stare at the rocks.
Impressive, imposing, but
Don't they ever move?

Are the plants jealous?
Nope! They're dynamic, changing
With passing seasons,

Not stuck in one pose
Preening, but for whom? Not
Mother Nature. She likes plants.

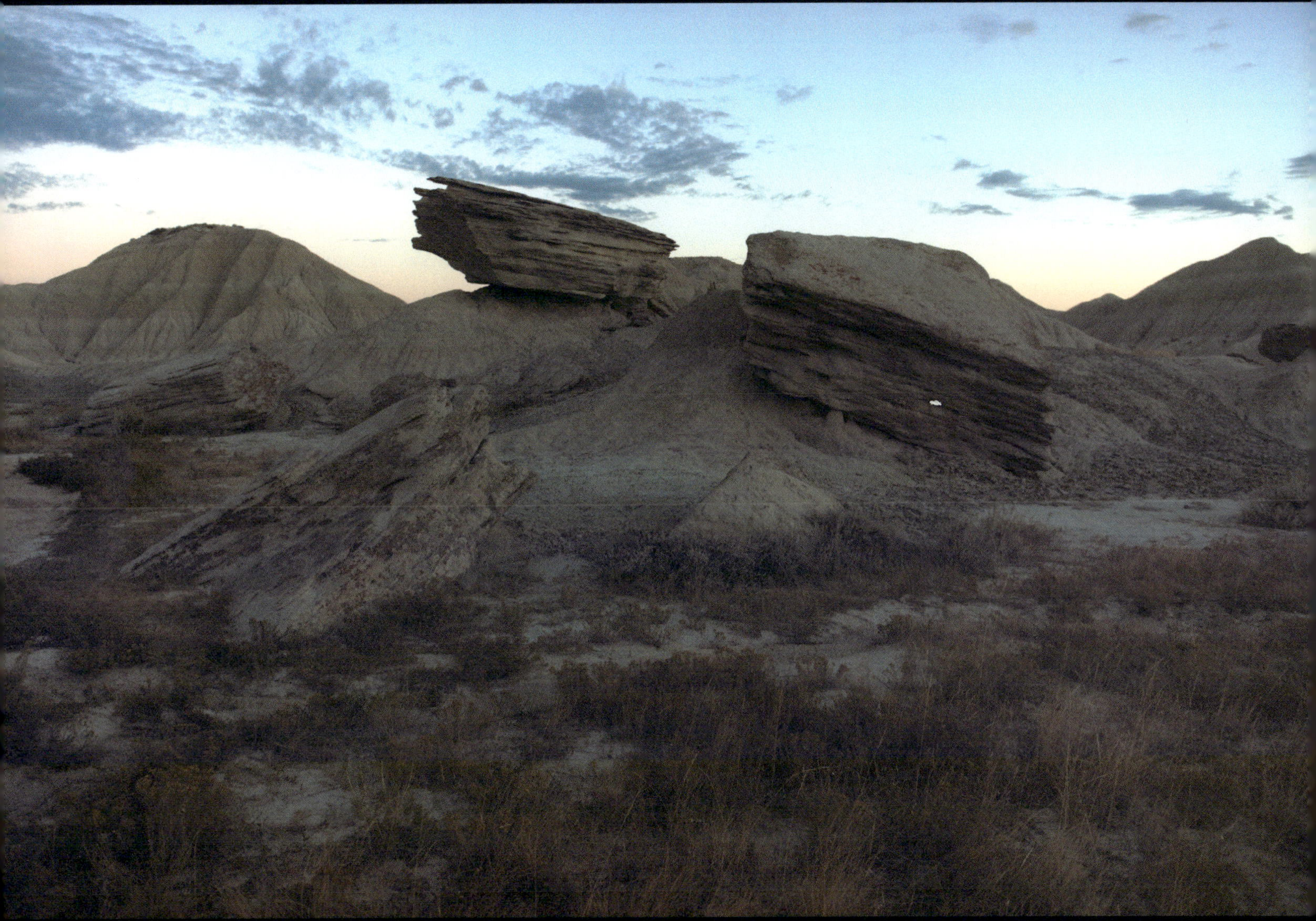

Master

I am the master

Do you doubt that?

Look at me! What do you see?
A lightening bolt
Hurled by the gods
Turned to stone by an earth
Grateful for the gift.

Would you doubt the will of the gods?

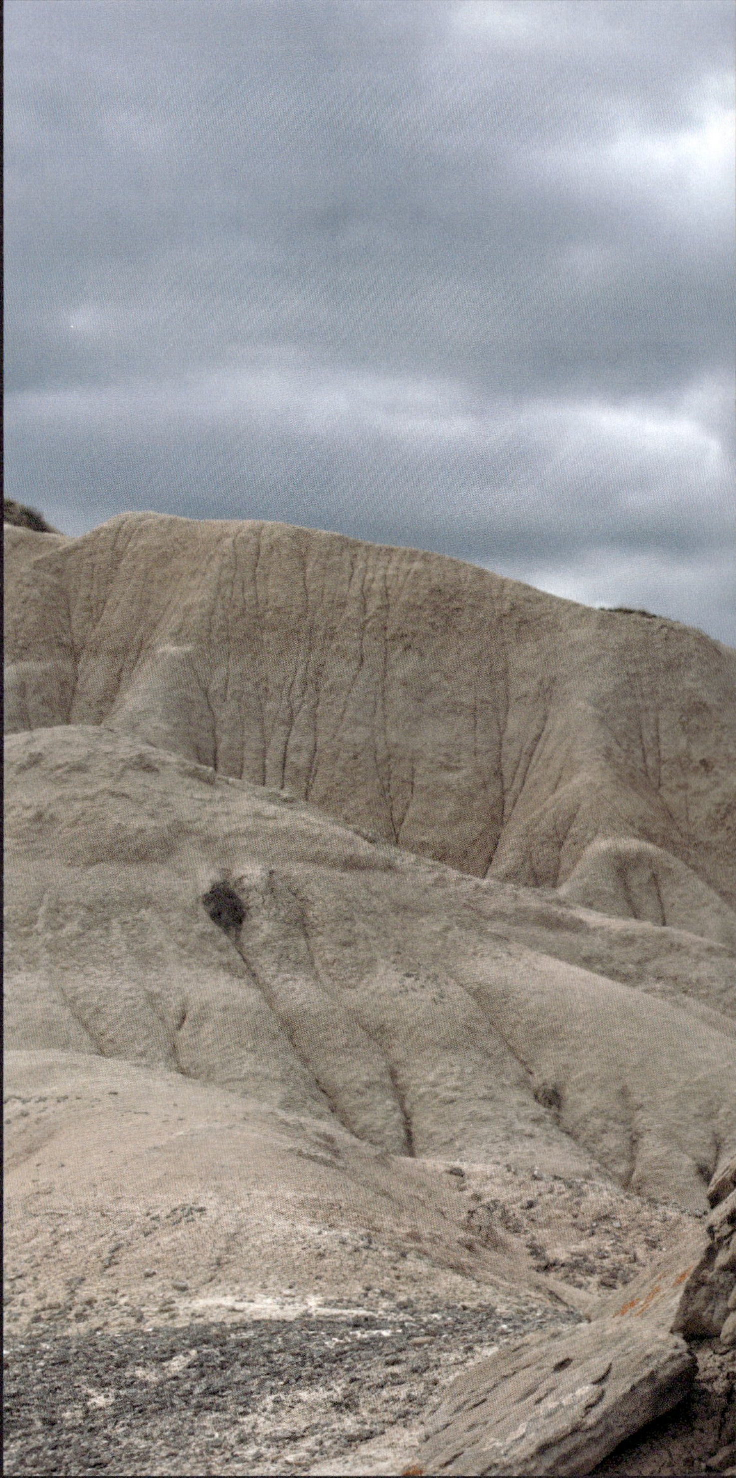

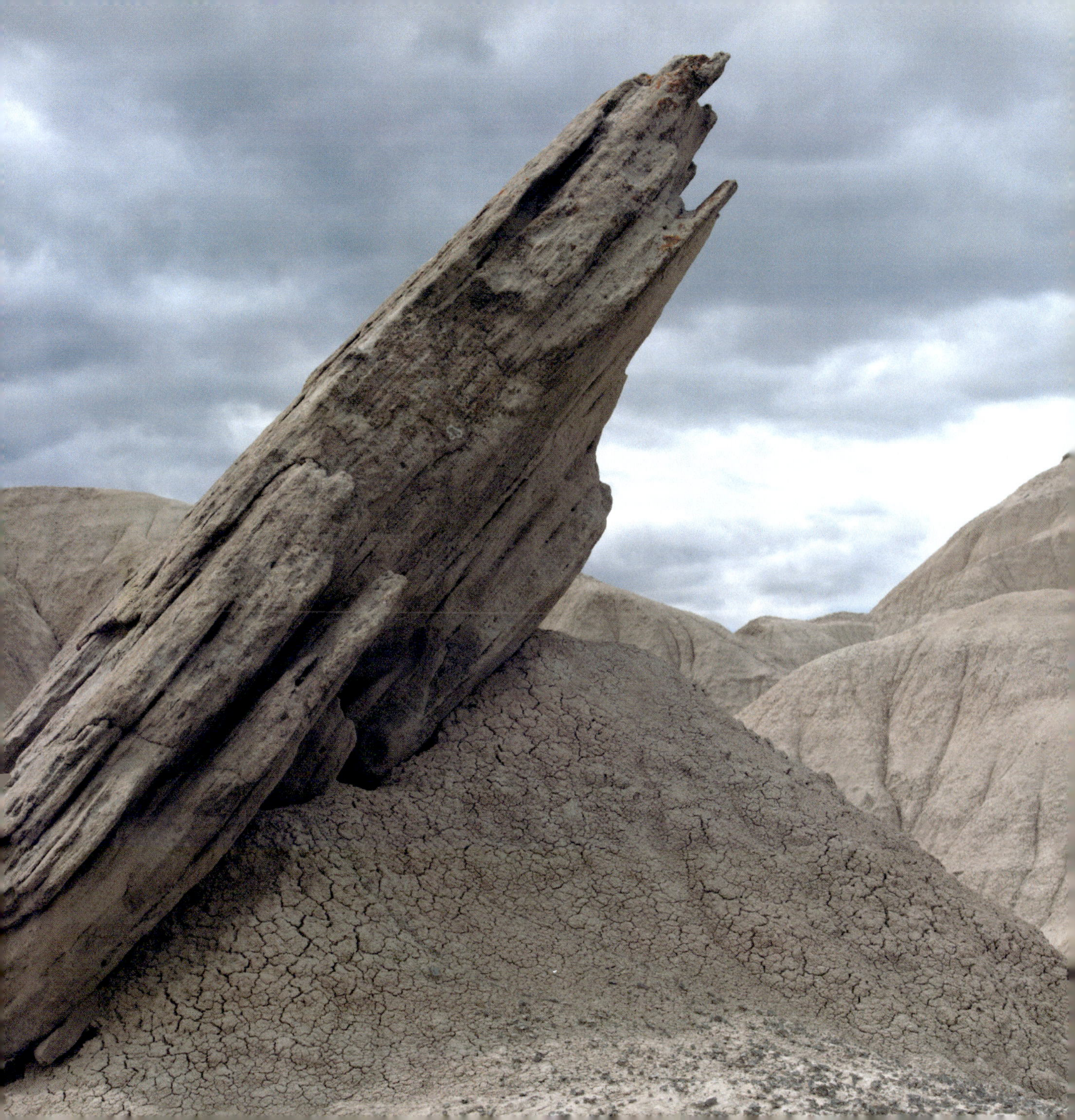

Hubris

It was drab, uniformly gray
Low hills and flat surfaces.
The rocks didn't like the drabness
They decided it was time for a change.
They used rain, wind, dust
Smoothed surfaces, created crannies, carved rocks.

The rocks saw and they were pleased, sort of.
More was needed.
They took ice and whittled blocks from stone.
They prepared to stack these blocks
Into towers, edifices to reflect their glory.

They rested and then glanced, disappointed
At the fine bits left over from their efforts.
They saw something beyond their ken
Things that appeared, as if by magic, yearly
Self-organizing, self-directing into things
Intricacies beyond rocks's grasp.

The rocks looked.
Their efforts faded into the trivial.
They left their blocks where they fell
Littering flat surfaces.
Monuments to hubris.

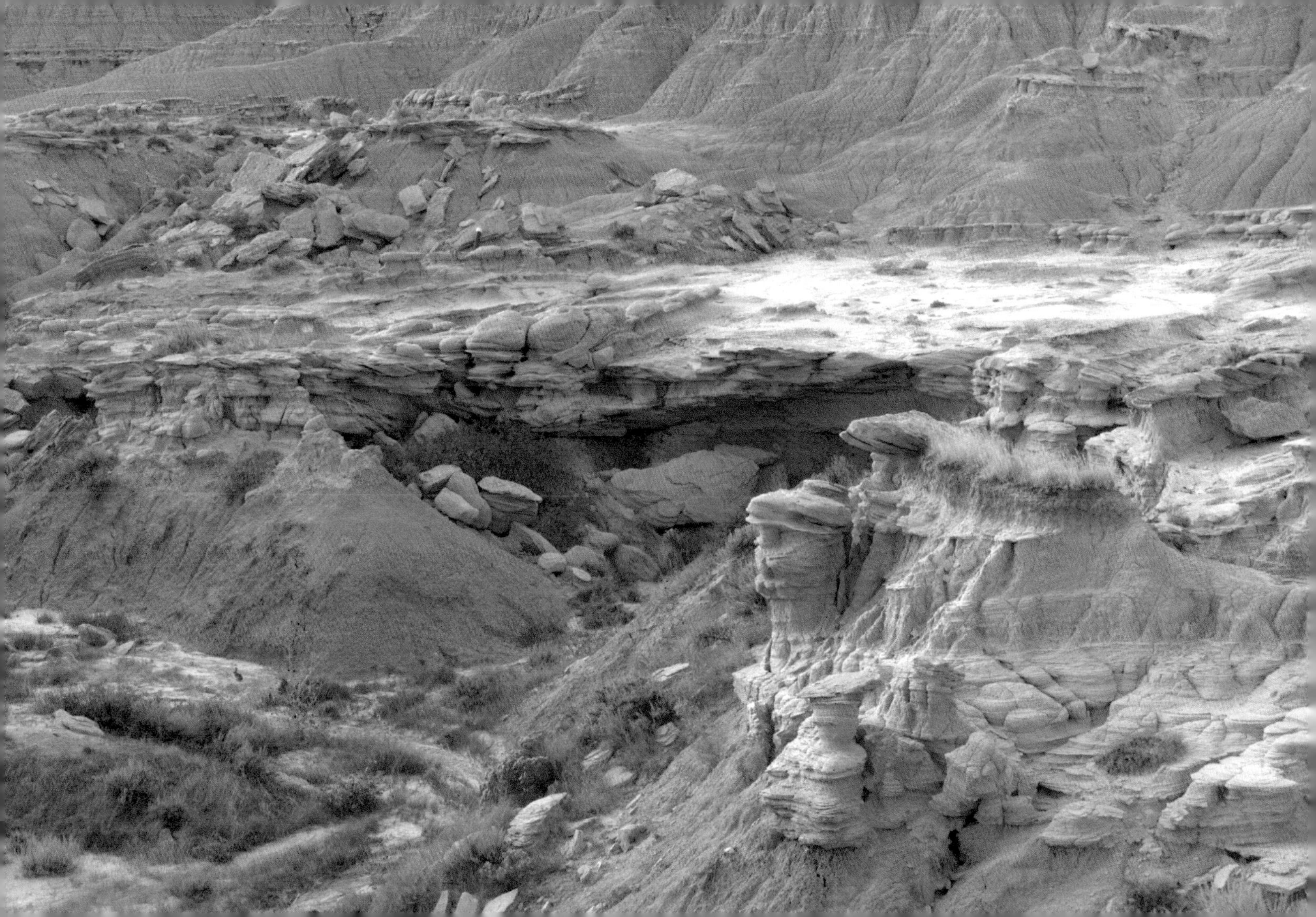

Jumble

Better be careful.
If you wander away
Into that jumble of rocks and bushes
You might be trapped
In chaotic intricacy.

That's not necessarily bad.
The play of sunlight through the day,
Creating moving shadows
And patterns of reflection
Is inviting.

Should you find yourself trapped,
Ricocheting nook to cranny to bush
Pay very close attention
Surely secrets are hidden there,
Maybe some of your own.

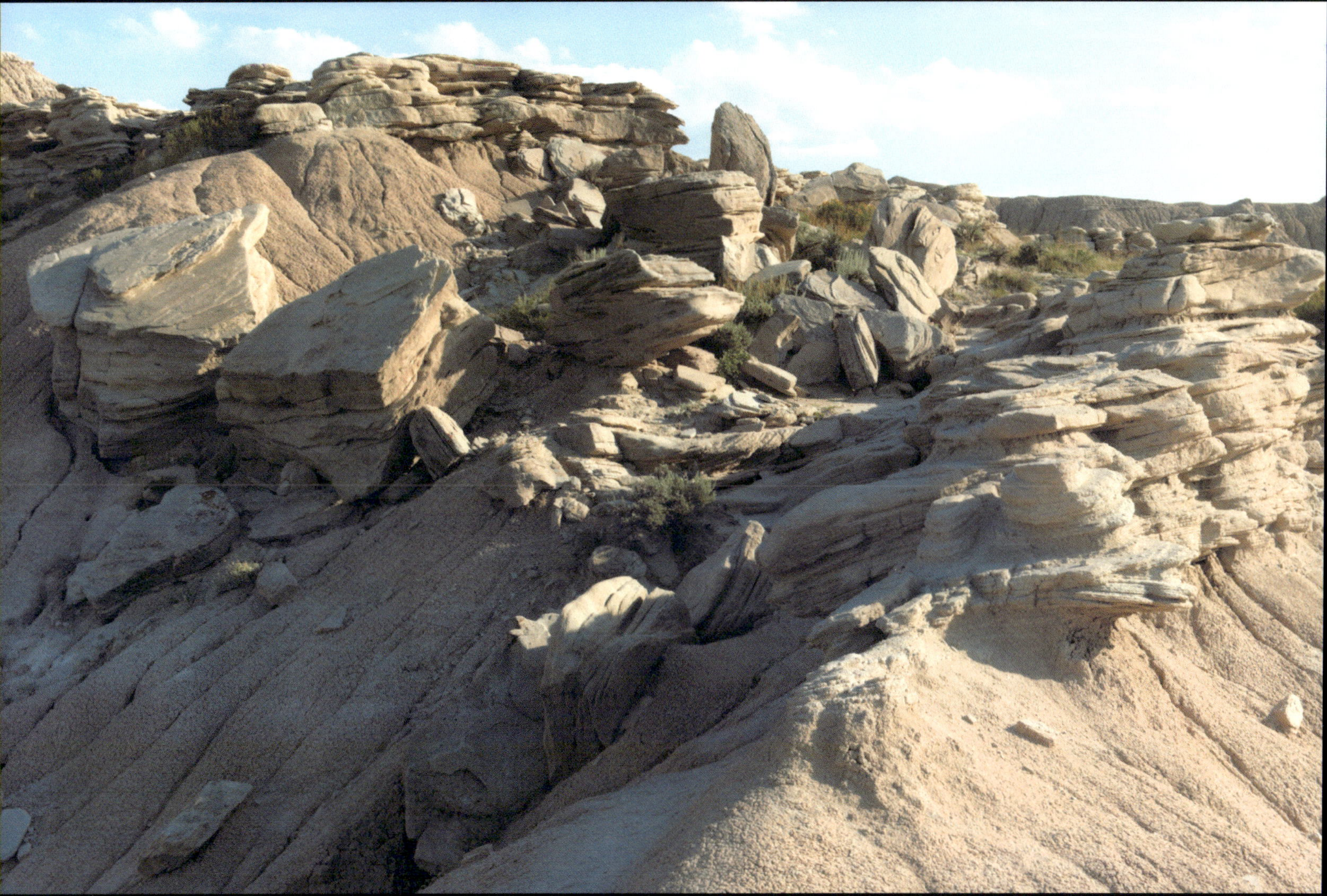

Lonely Waiting

I'll simply wait here
To see what comes from that vault.
I can't see in there
Maybe it will be a friend.
I'm by myself, and lonely.

Lonely Escape

The crypt was crowded,
Essences vying for room
In tightly cramped space.
Cowering before the light,
Fearful of the outside world.

Then one ventured out.
The light, the water, the air
Gave its soul substance.
And with that mortality.
Now it needs companionship.

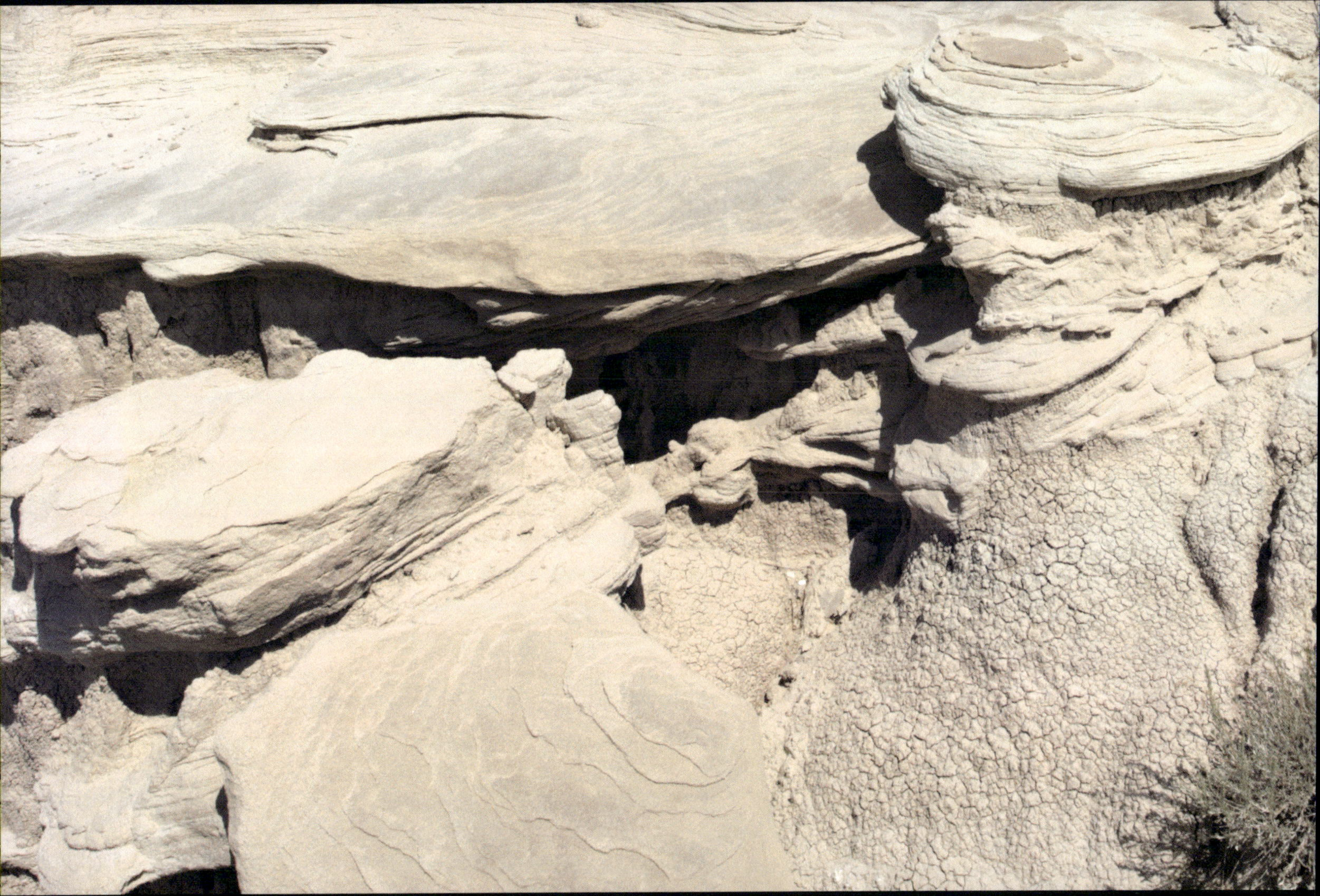

Shadows

Shadows wander across grey
  Different shades
  Different textures
  Different shapes.

With the promise that as the day passes
  Views change
  Views intoxicate
  Views transform

Rocks and soil
  Into a reason to spend a day in the sun

Shadows from a moving sun
To create new scenes.

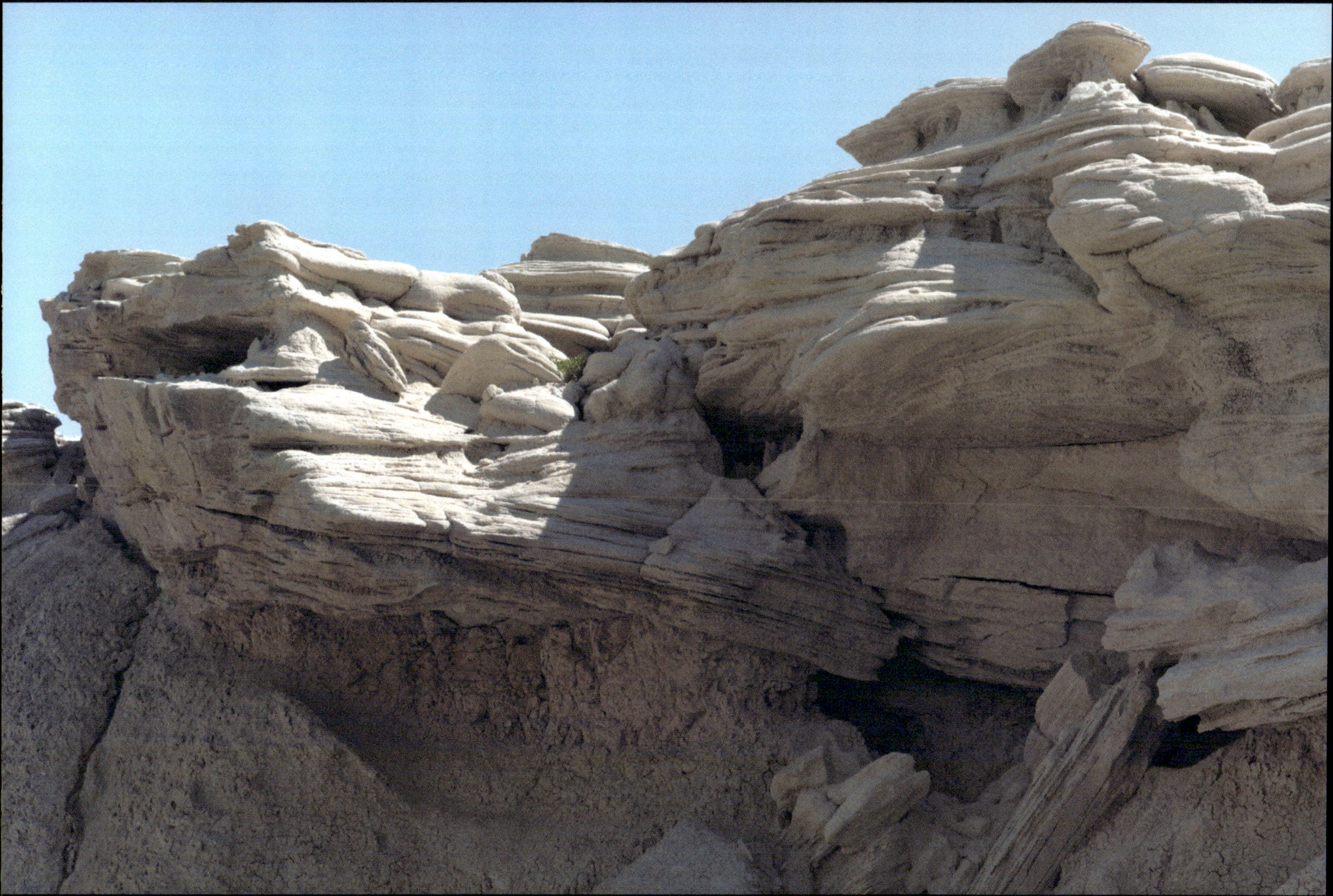

Permanent

There's a contrast here.
Boulders, indurate, layered
Oozing permanence.
But the base is friable.
Perhaps there's some delusion?

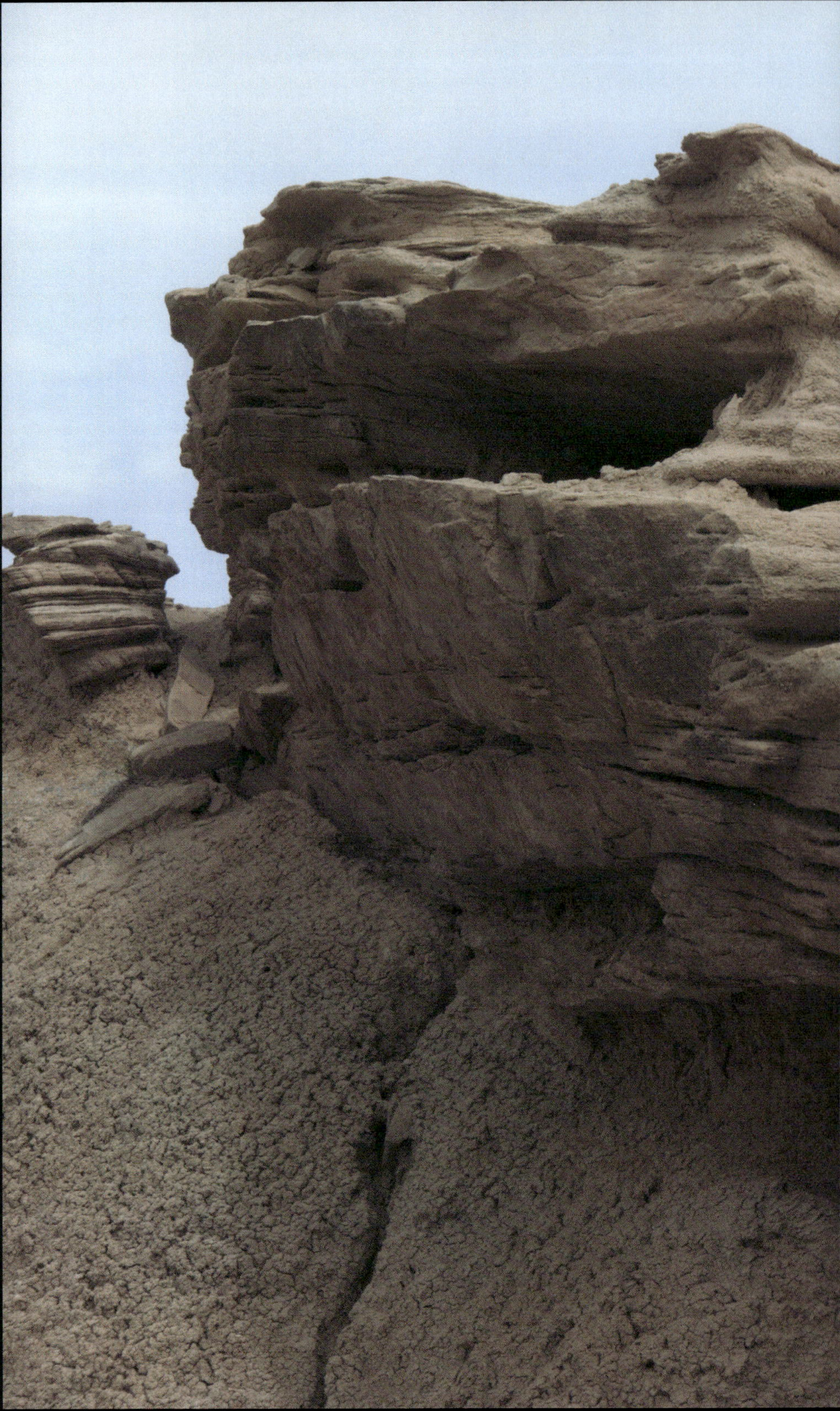

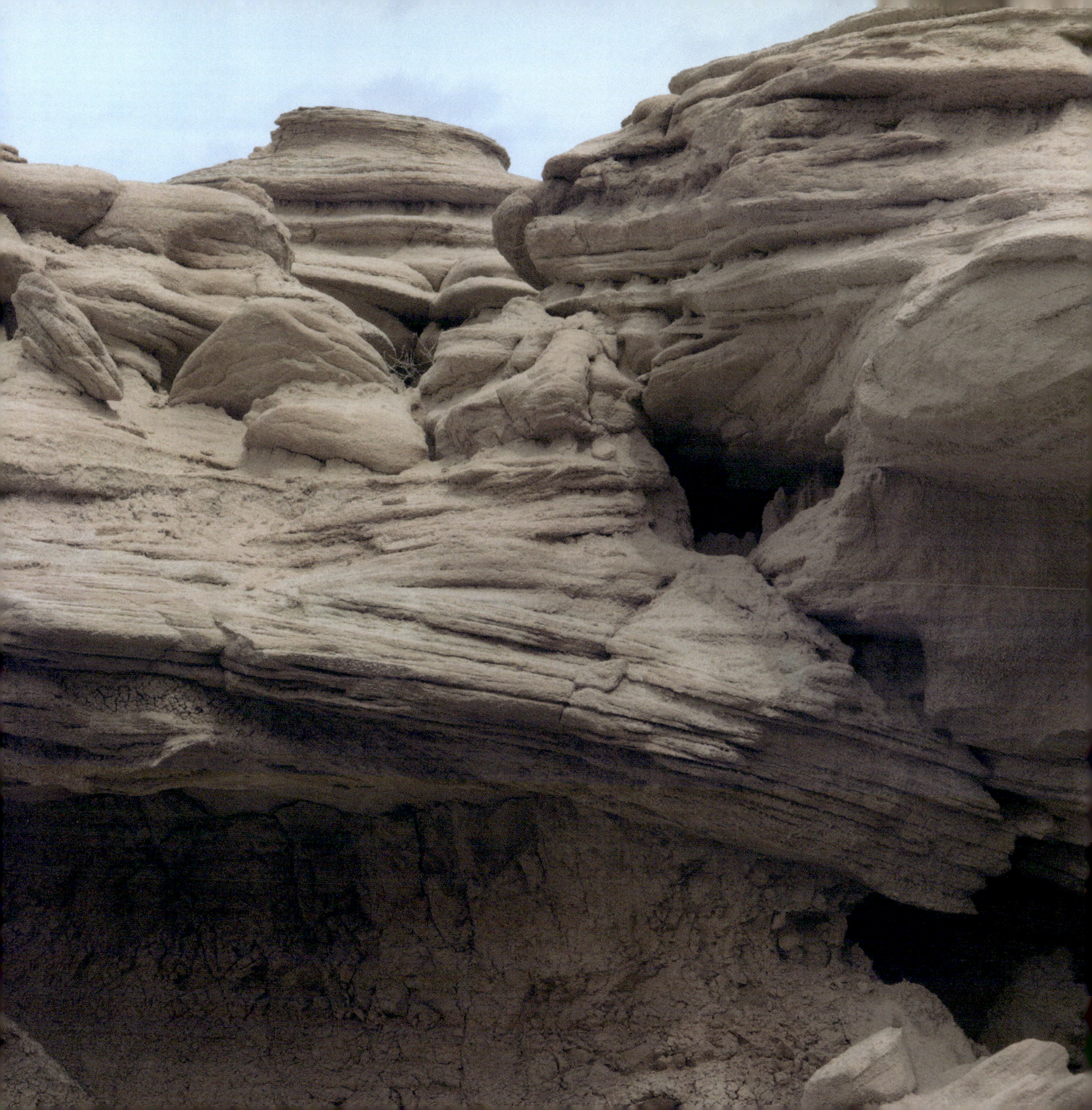

Secrets

Are they only rocks,
Wavy edged, rounded, smooth,
A dull gray color?
Look where the rocks are worn away.
Crests parallel the edges.

There's a history
Of tiers laid one on another
Each clearly outlined.
To savor Nature's plan
Just look below the surface.

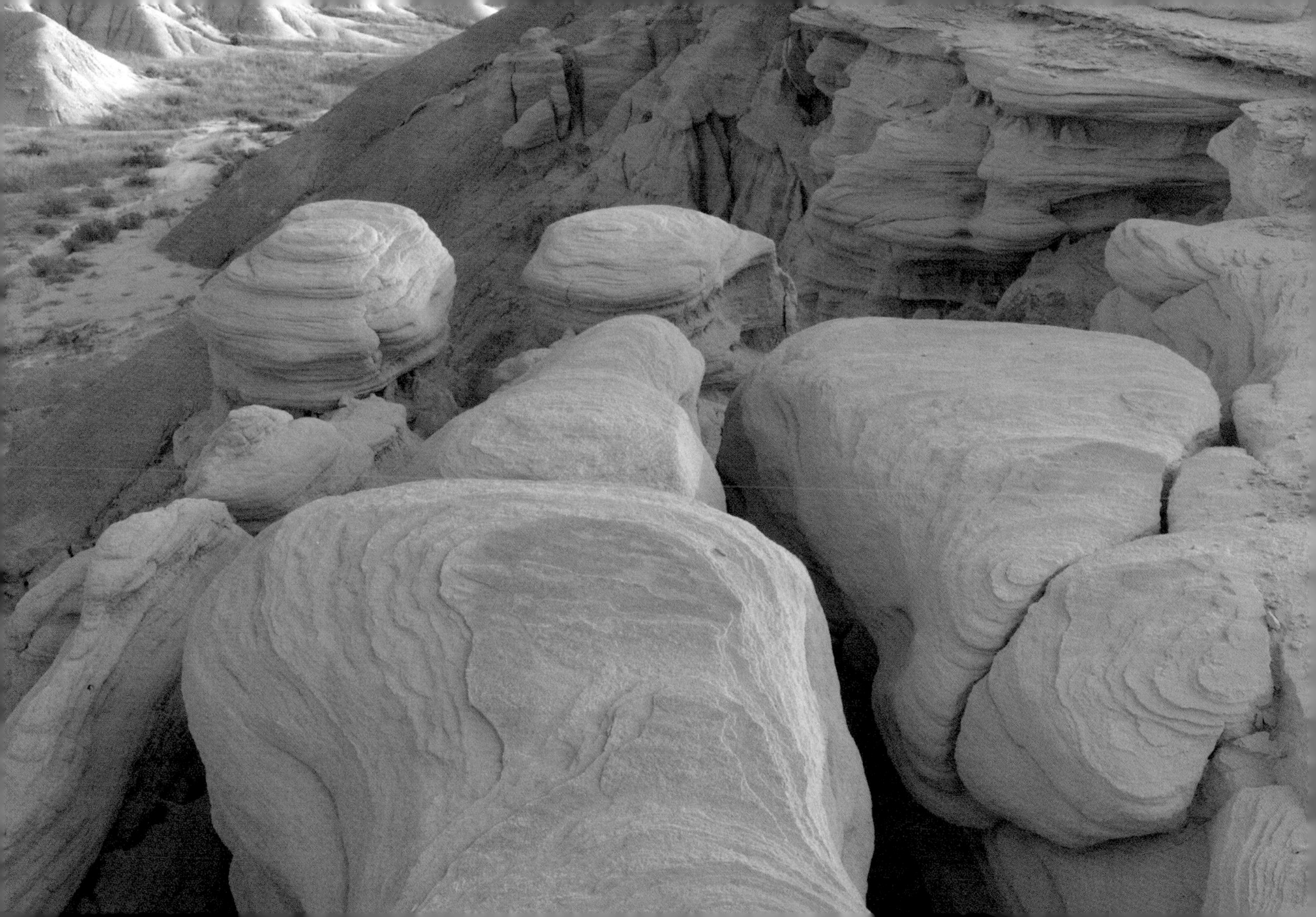

Subtlety

Light and Shadow

First there was the light
Intense, showing no mercy;
Everything revealed.
But there was not much to see
Surface, blinding white.

So rocks were added
Layered, diverse forms and shapes
They intercept light
The light is still intense, but
But now carved into shadows.

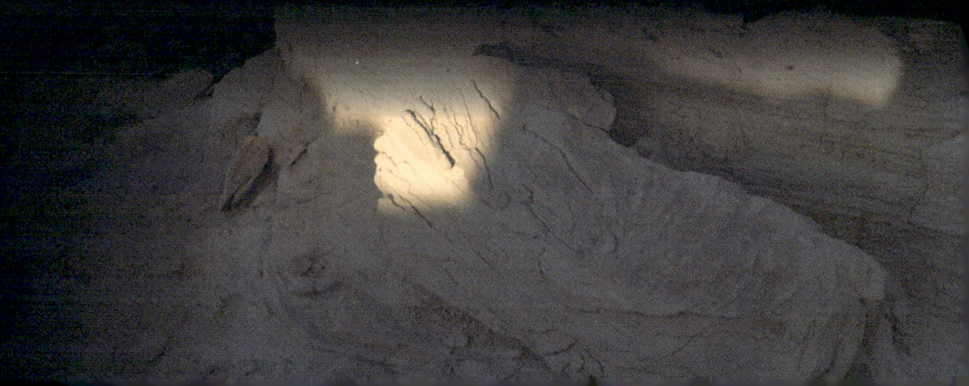

Subtlety

An intensity
Focuses the eye and mind
On reflected light.
But hiding in the shadows,
An absorbing subtlety.

Light and Balance

The light possesses
An intensity, balanced
By its own shadow.

Balance

That flat rock seems precarious.
Is it balanced by opposing forces
Intense light and shadows?

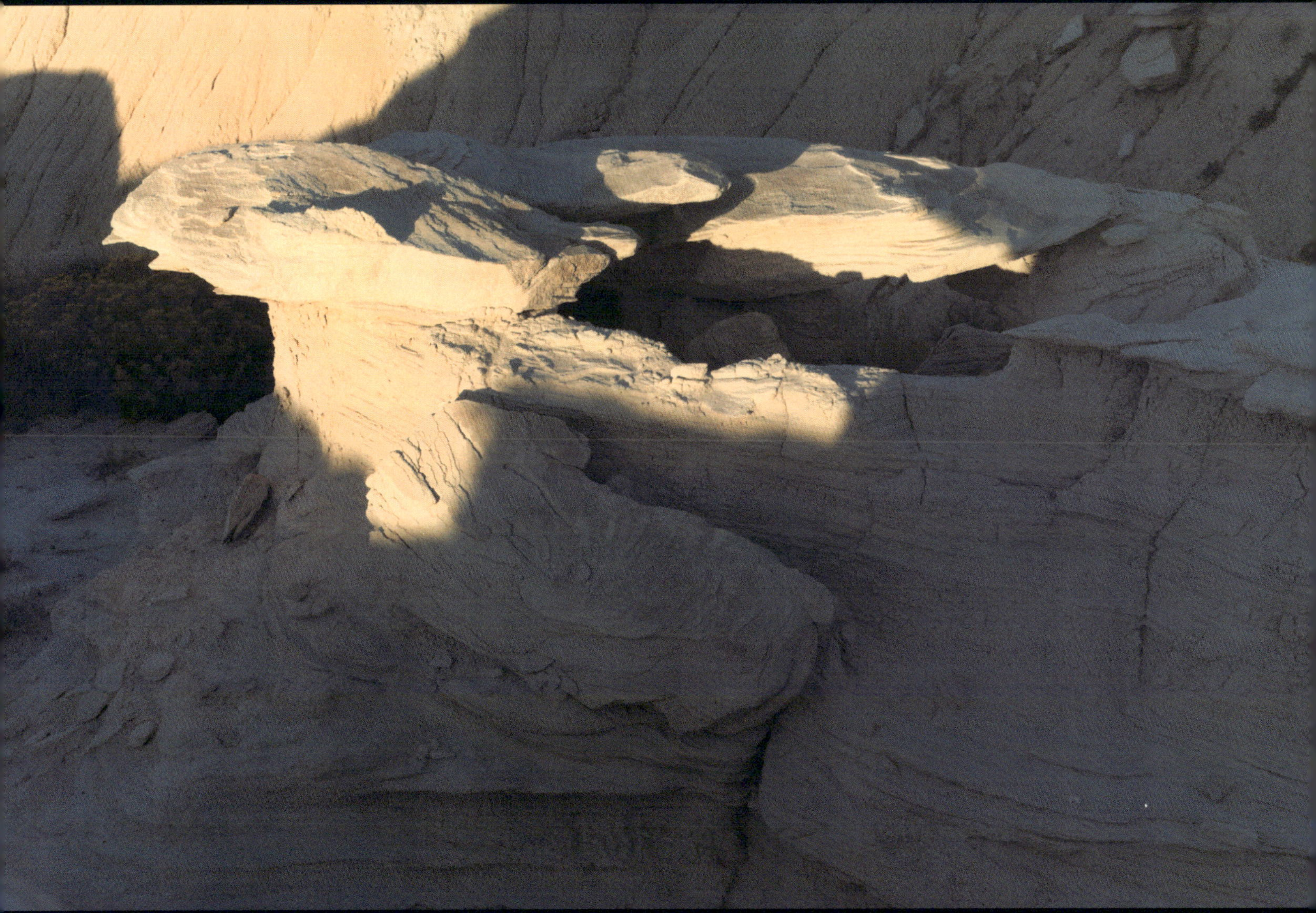

Swirls

Swirls, undulations
Eddies frozen in time, nooks
Crannies, everywhere.

Follow me inside
Maybe we will understand
These convolutions.

We turn left, then right
We clamour up on ridges
We rappel back down.

We lose ourselves in
Labyrinths lined with roughened walls
Following dim light.

We've taken samples
They've been pulverized then they've
Been analyzed then

Described in detail.
And what do we really know?

Swirls, undulations
Eddies frozen in time, nooks
Crannies, everywhere.

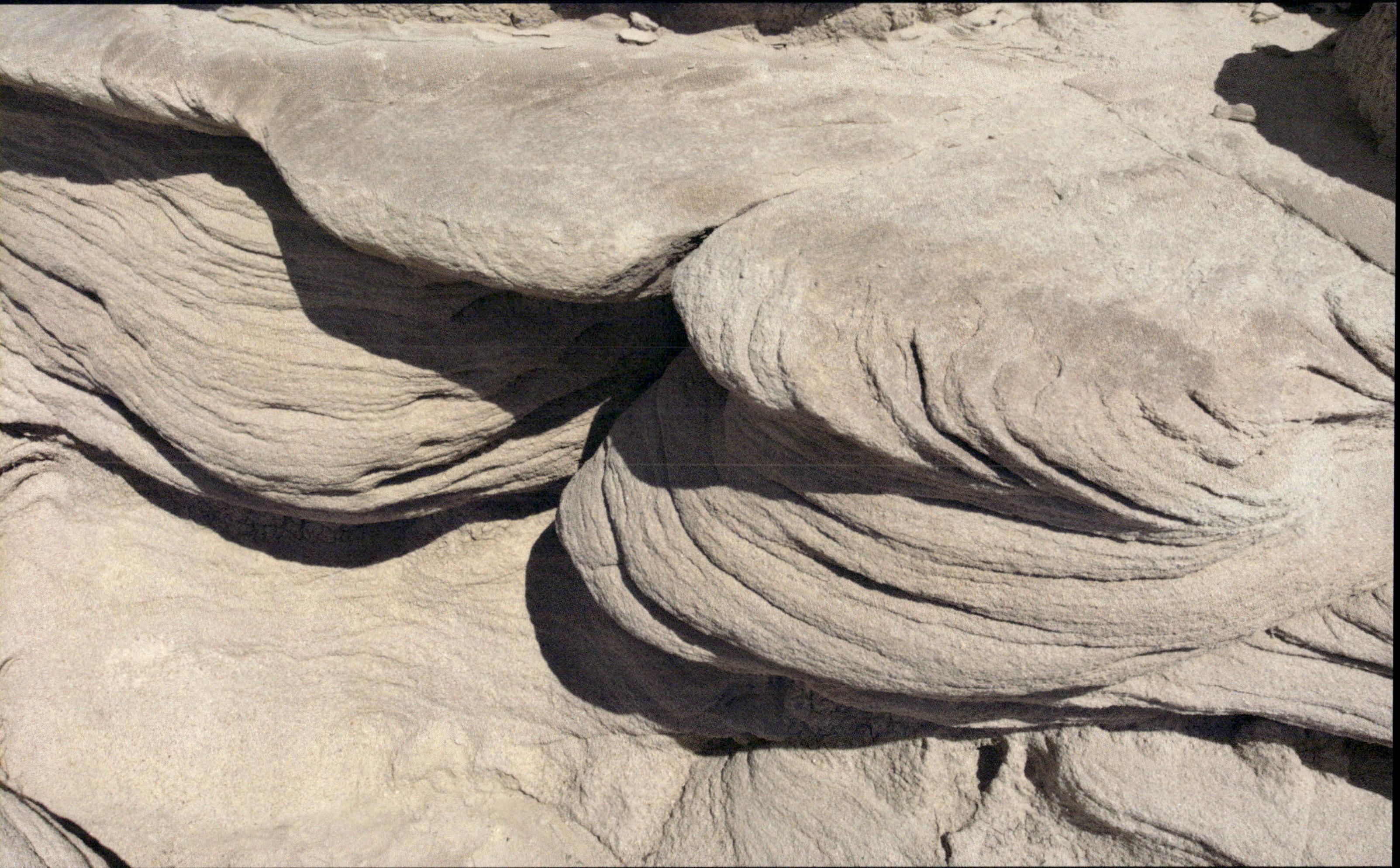

Winter Den

It's all organized,
Rain and rocks, interacting

Horizontal layers to the left
Vertical columns to the right

And in between
A shallow gully, a protective den.

This looks a good place,
Protection from winter's cold
And future's assured.

All this done
Using ancient rocks and recent rain,
So the shrubs will have a haven
Where they can overwinter and rest.

The goddess needs rested shrubs
When she wakens the spring.

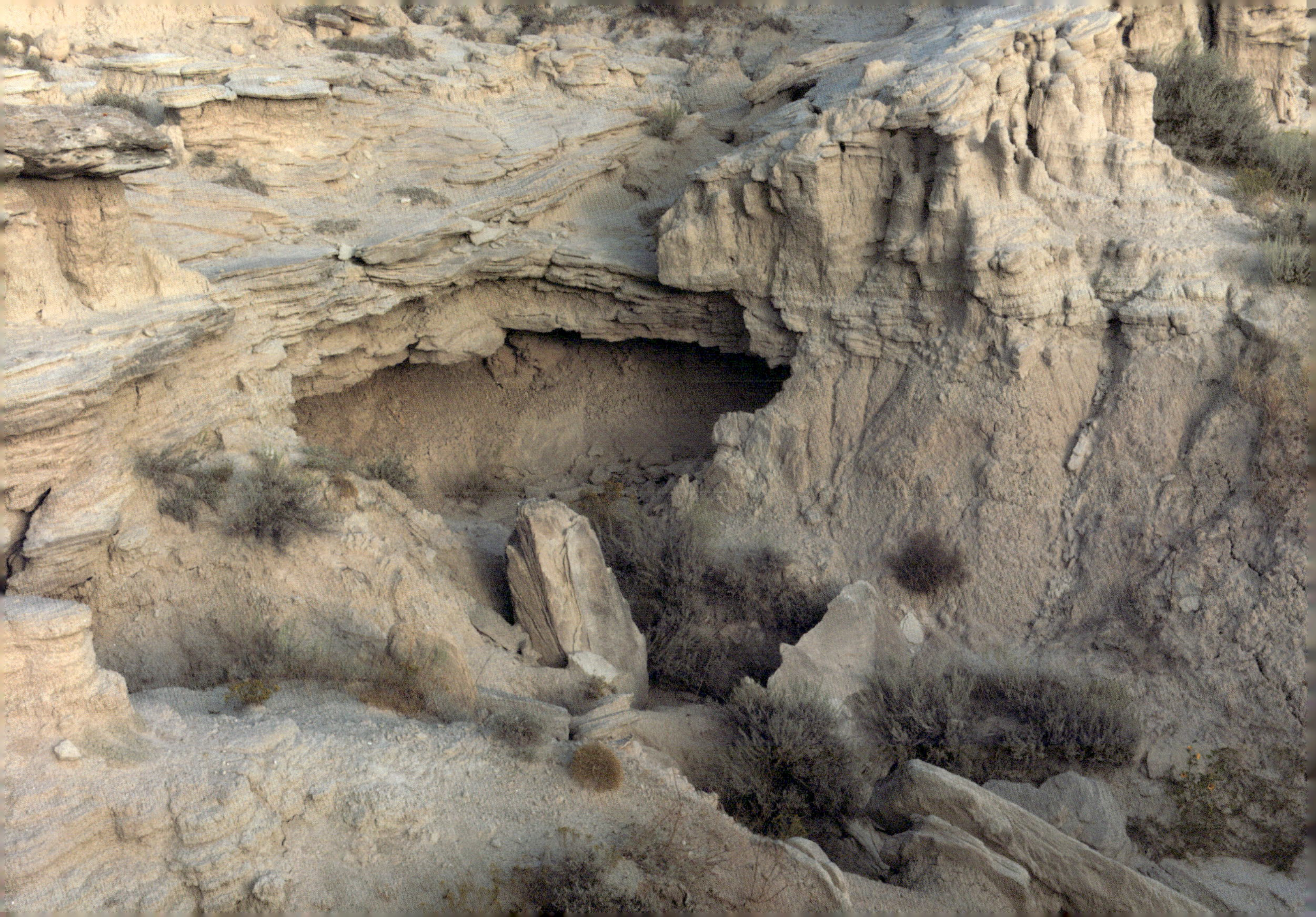

Toadstool Sphinx

Look at me!

I guard the dead.
I protect the path to the gods;
You must satisfy my curiosity
To go beyond the pale.

I see all.
I hear all.
I know all.

I am the Toadstool Sphinx.

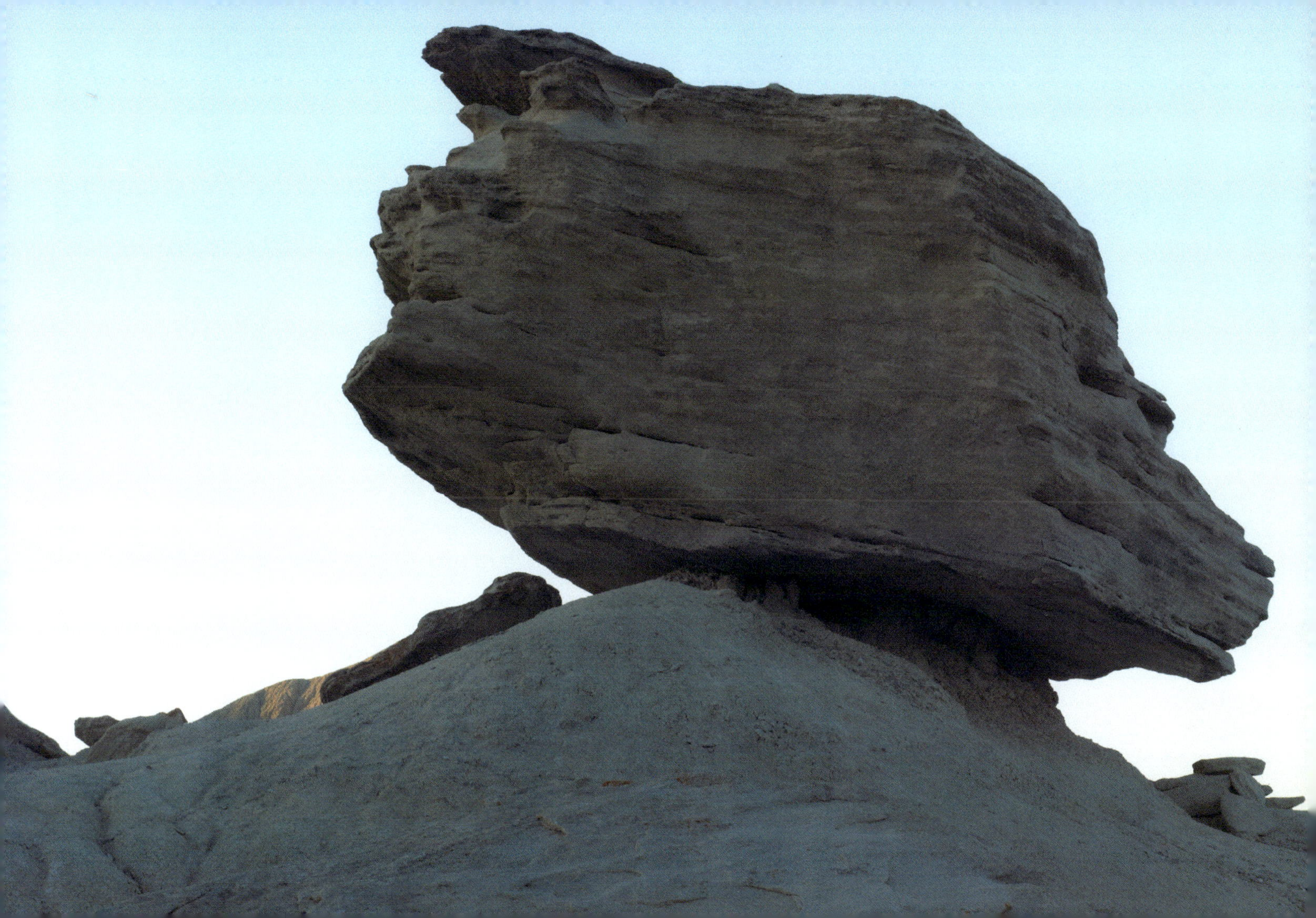

The Trade off

Dare you question me!
Dare you doubt my majesty!
I'm here at the top
And why do you think that's so?
I've been chosen by the gods.

But there was a price paid.
They demanded a trade off.
I'm the royal one
But mobility's been lost
Freedom's been sacrificed too.

I guess you can't have

Everything.

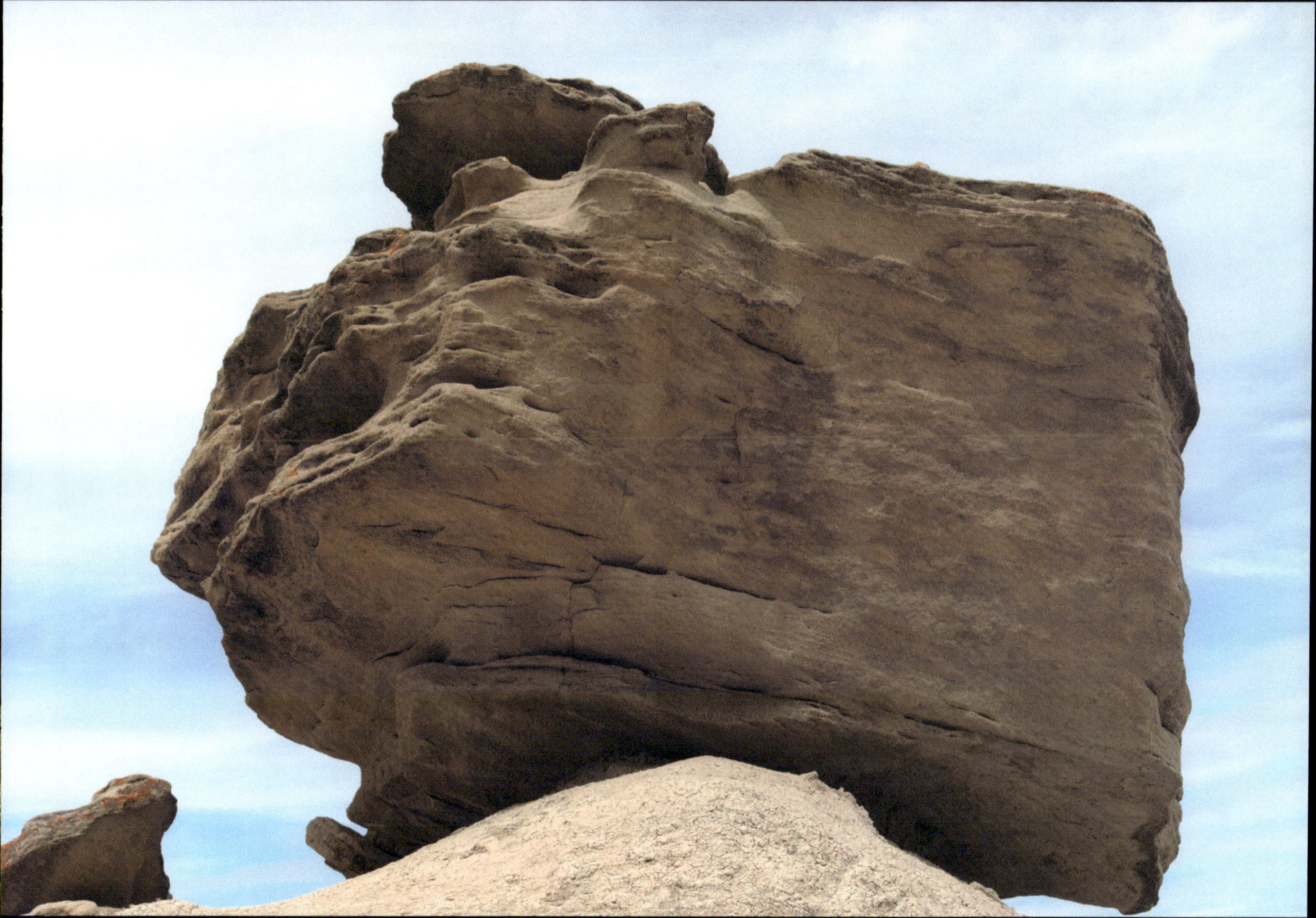

A Place

Thwarted Plans

The plans had been made.
The required bulk was there
As was the stern look.
But Mama Nature didn't approve
And transformed all to rock.

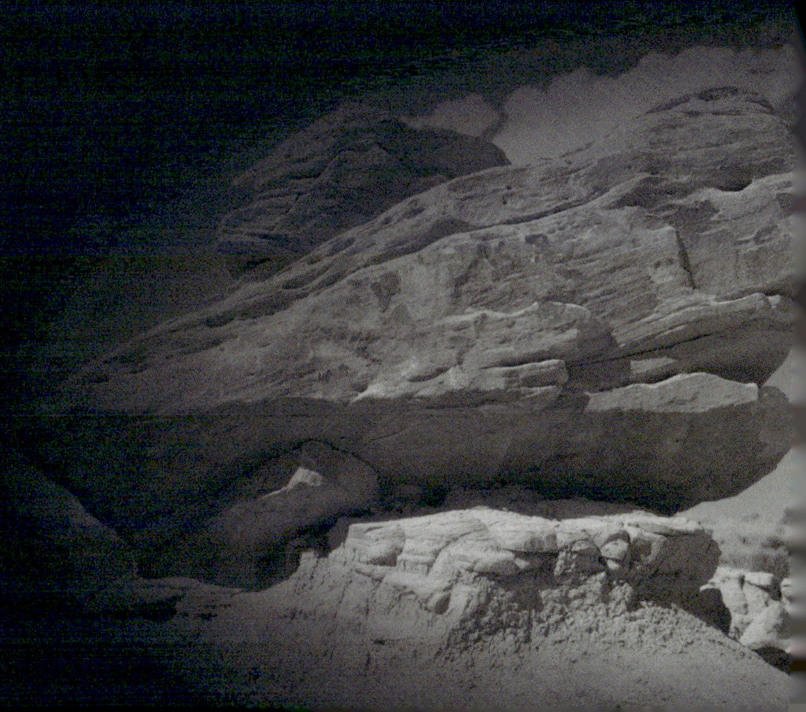

A Place

Just travelling through.
The trip had been tiring
The scenery dull.
But here shadows and sun play.
Here's a place to stay and watch.

Patience

Waiting, open-mouthed,
Anticipating, with joy
Her planned arrival.
She didn't come. Still he waited
With the patience of a stone.

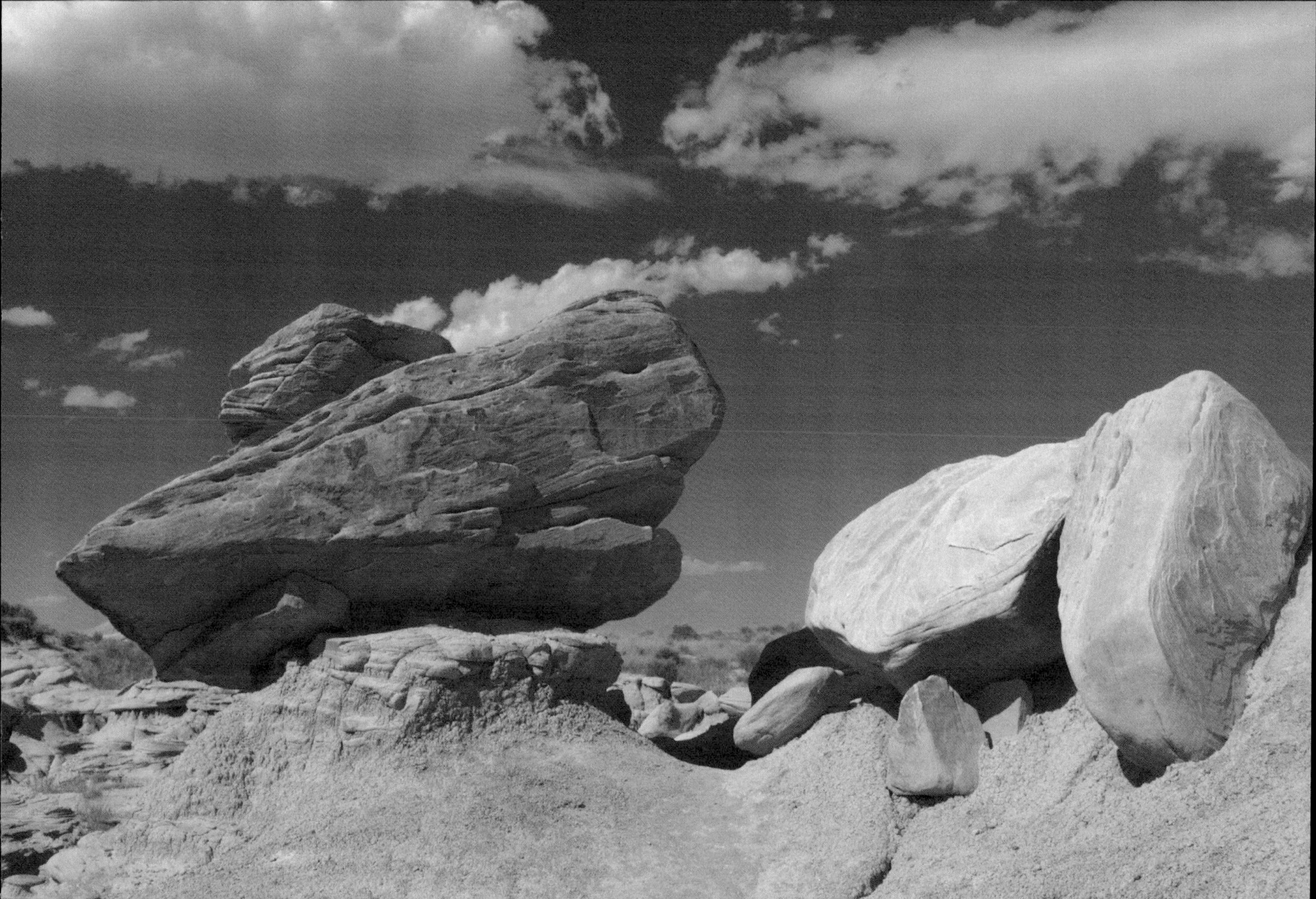

Plato Was Wrong

There is the allegory of the cave
One of Plato's big ideas
Who argued we live in a world of shadows;
We can never know the truth.

It's an appealing, interesting idea
But also an excuse;
To accept ideas without critical thought
A place to hide from reality, decisions, the future.

But look here!

Can you stand in these shadows,
this cave?
And feel any desire to stay there?
Could you miss the promise of a dawn?

Could you miss the promise of a dawn?

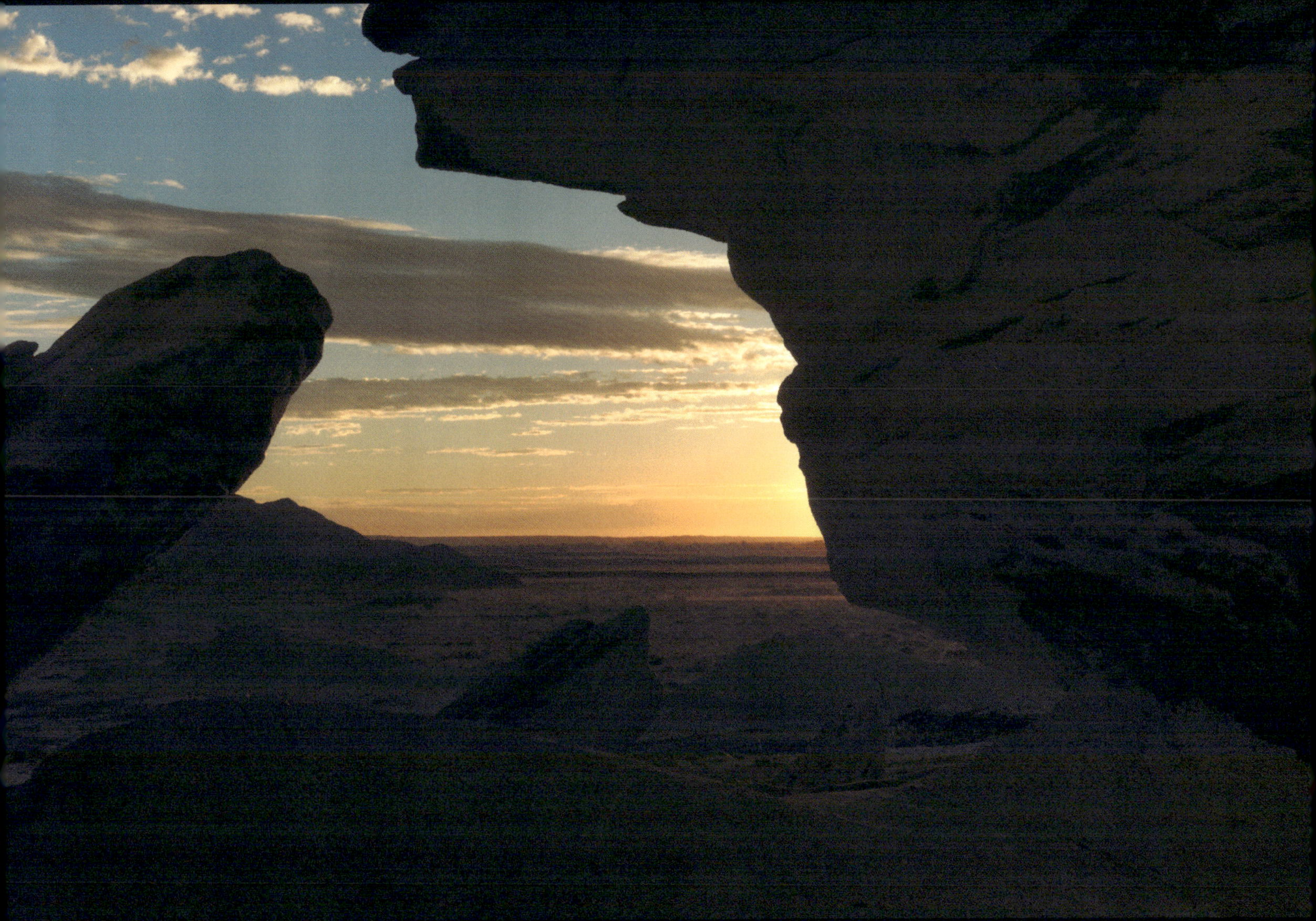

Transformation

Rocks go tumbling down
To the flat where they're transformed
Into scattered shrubs.

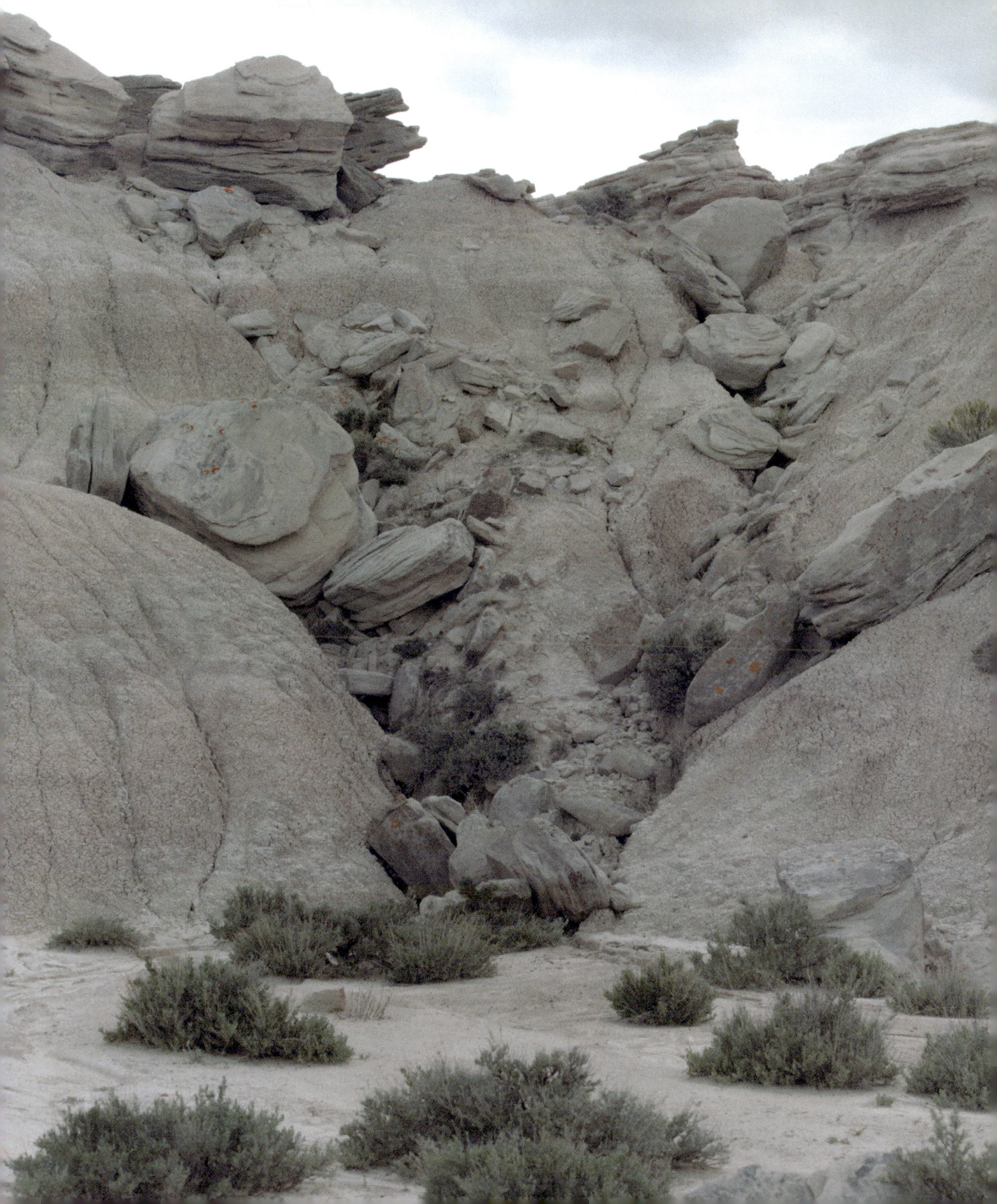

Labyrinth

It's a labyrinth

The eye is attracted

And then the mind is seduced

Led

Along a chaotic path
Farther and farther from those plants
Competing for attention.

Until the desired end,
A center where chaos subsides.

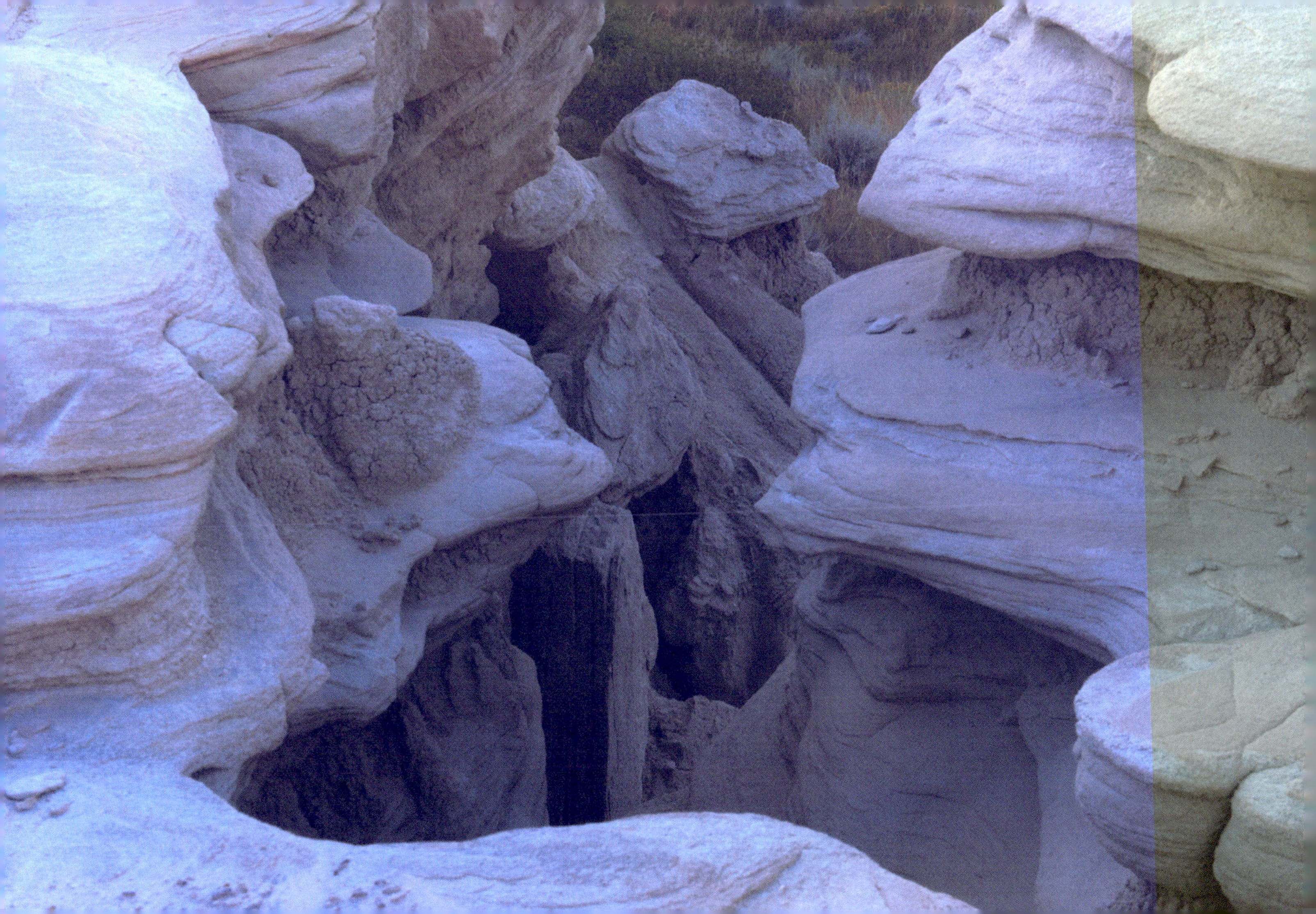

Trinity

Hills, water scarred
Rocks, water carved
Plants, water starved.

Nature's trinity?

If so, what about
The water?
Is it the source of all?

The eye may see a great deal.

But seeing is not understanding

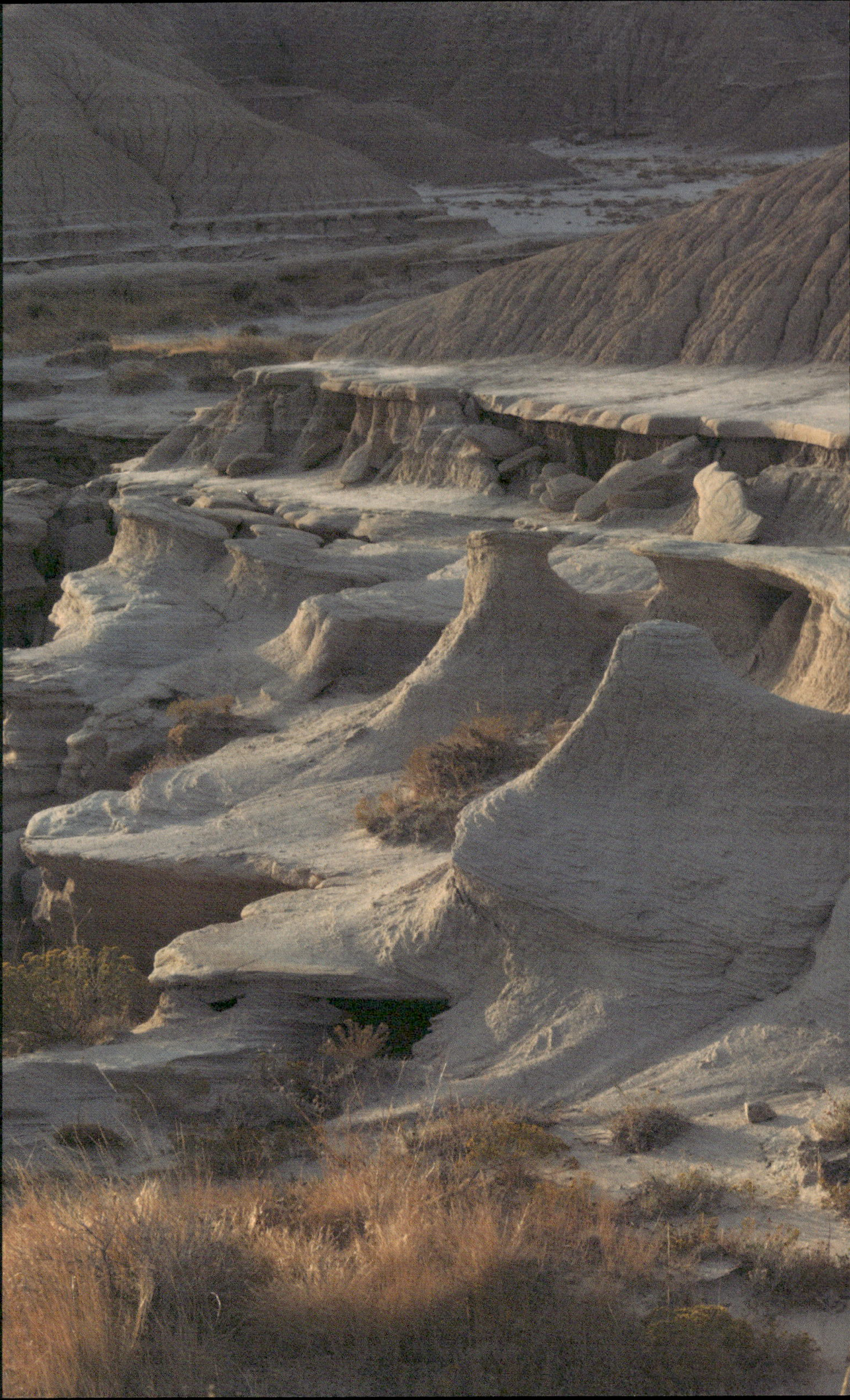

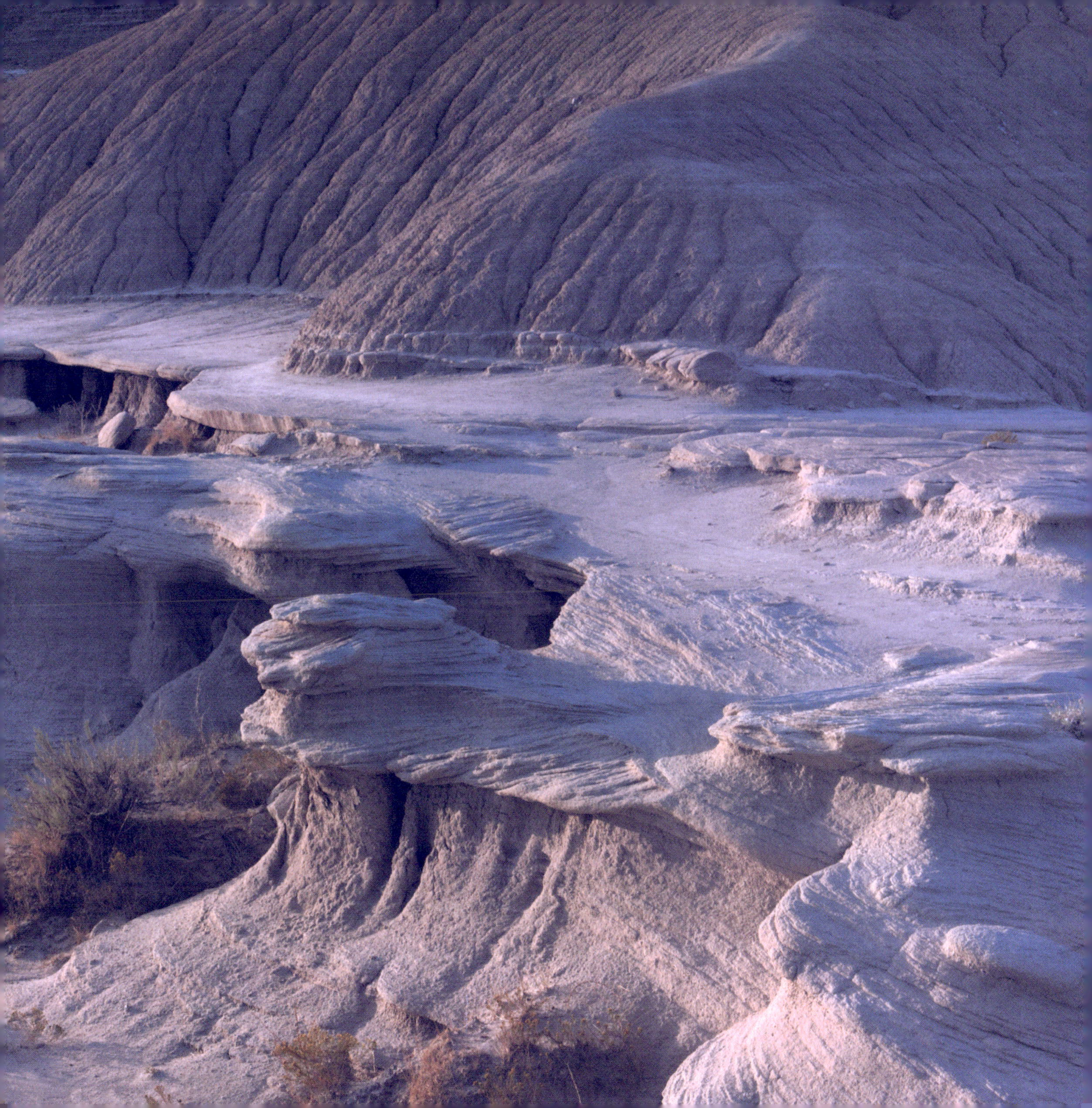

Broken Promises

Water flowed through here,
Leaving signs it had passed by,
But that`s all we have.
Promises made to the plants;
Broken when the next drought came.

The rocks are happy with what happened.
Water may support plants, but it eats rocks,
Carving them up and distributing their bits,
Leaving behind things for the plants,
Soil, protective recess for water to accumulate.

But the rocks had better look over their shoulders.
There may be little water to eat away at them,
However, the winds here are incessant,
Carrying bits that carve away at rocks.
Creating a bit of lithospheric irony:

Those bits came from other rocks.
Plants are smarter than rocks,
They don't self-destruct.

Promises made to the plants;
Broken when the next drought came.

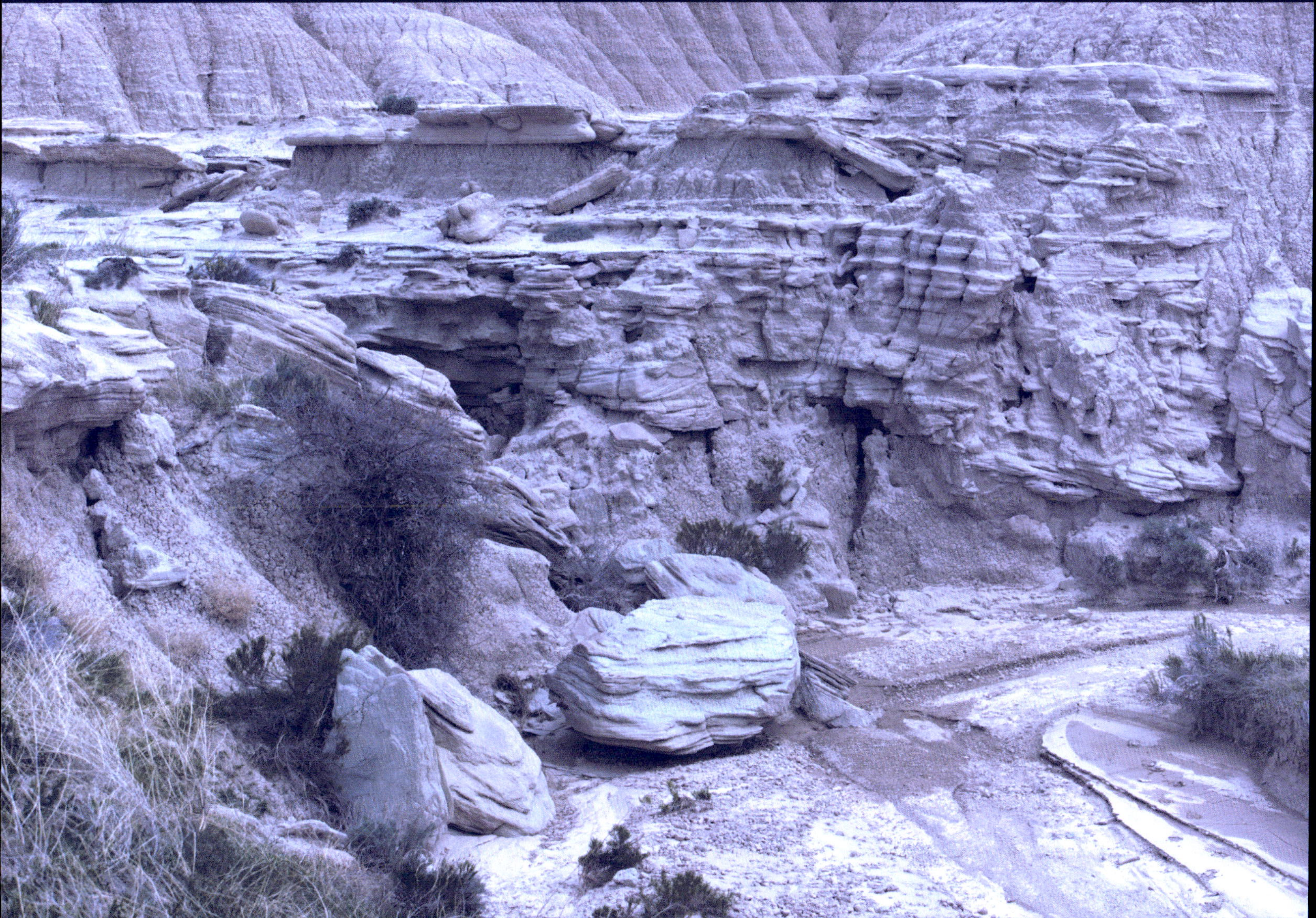

Disruption

A pile's appeared.
Layered rocks like those above
Soil in a small fan.
The symmetry's disrupted
The eye thrown into chaos.

Pretty straight forward.
The weight overmatched the support
And down it all went.
Likely inevitable
The chuckling plants don't help though.

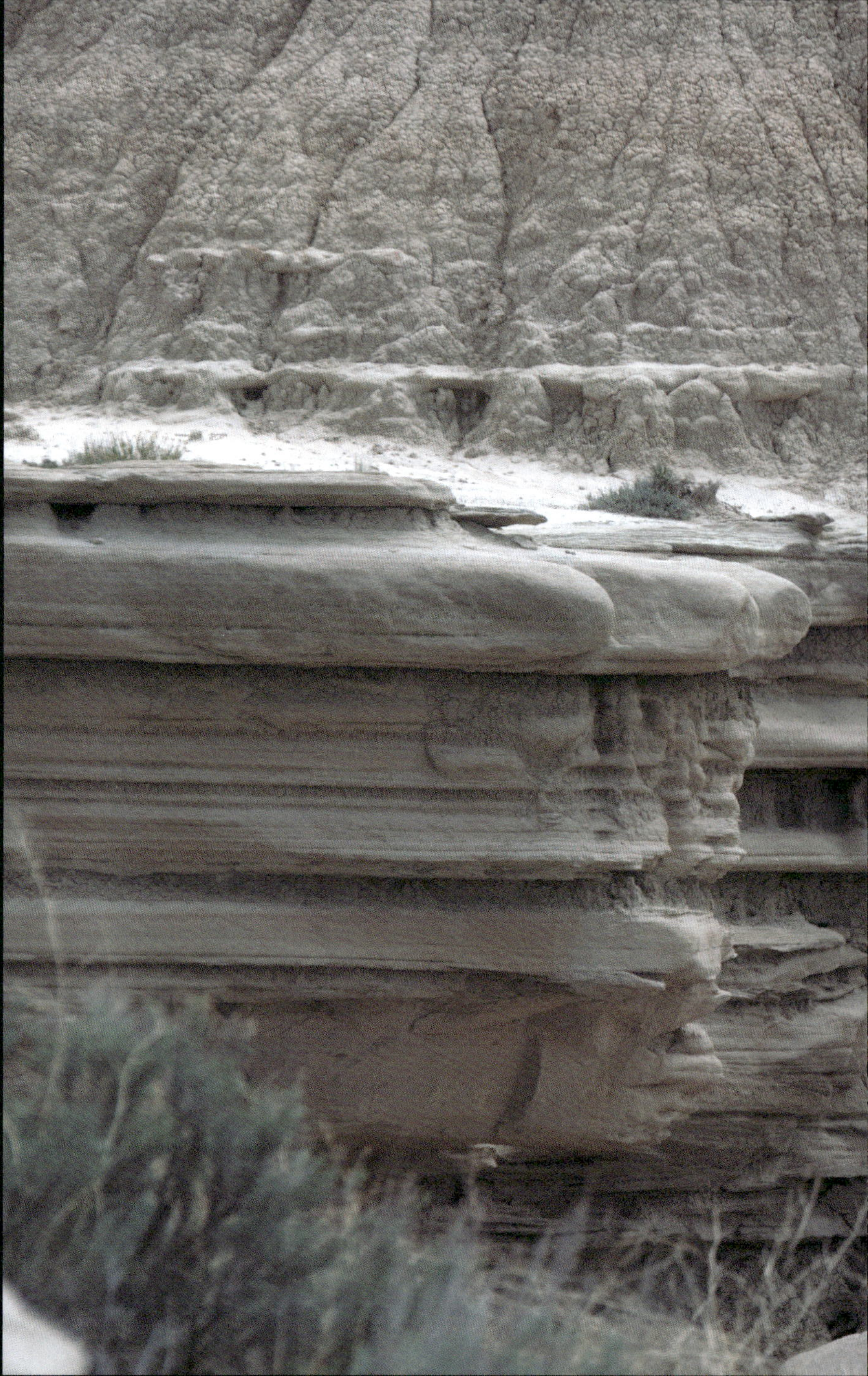

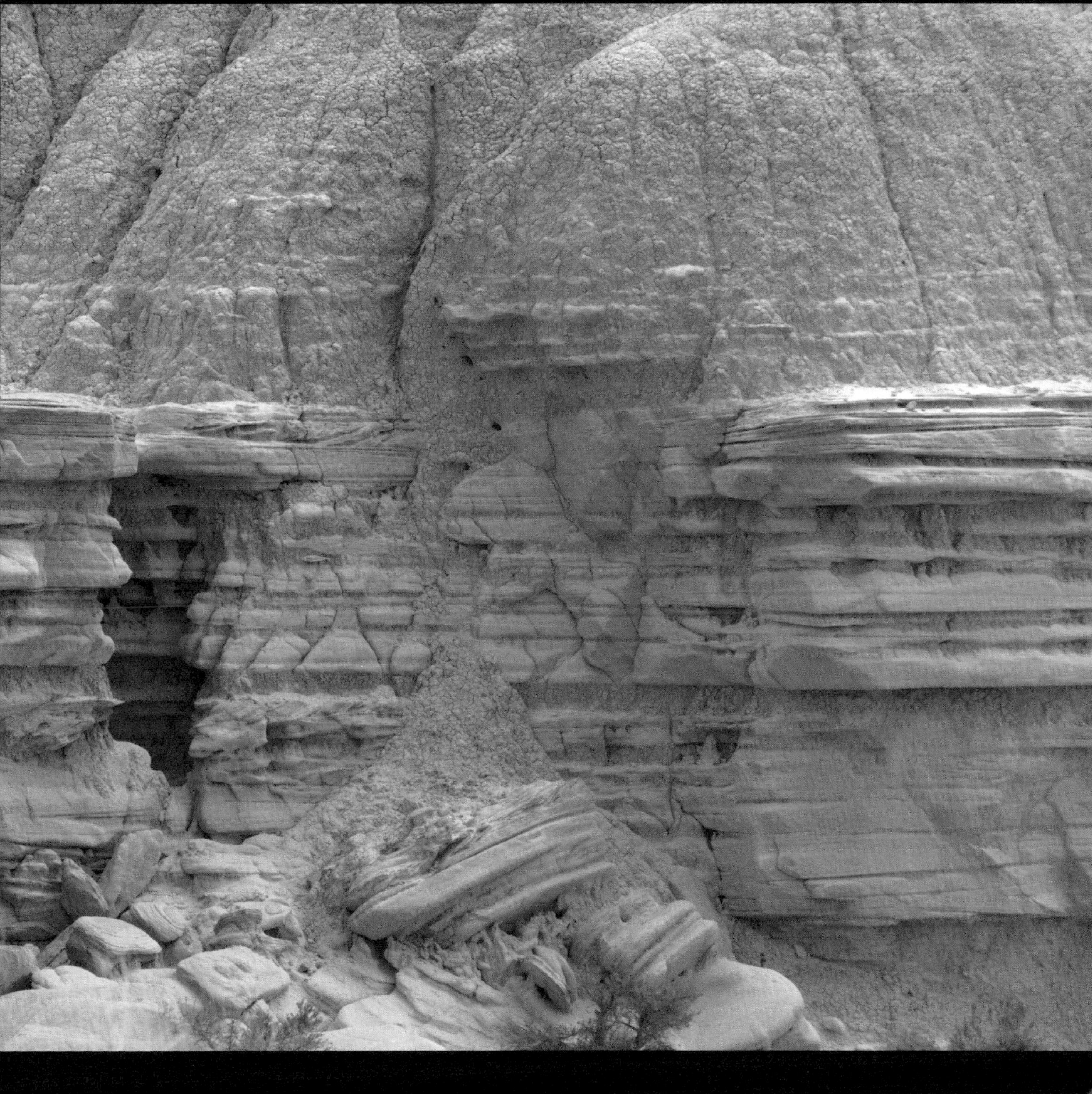

Contrast

Shallow depressions,
Sitting flat atop grey rock,
Sides gently rounded;
Smoothed by rain and wind-blown sand,
Surfaces that soothe the eyes.

Network of branches
Nestled below, borne on top
Niche-bound to soil;
Narrating their histories
Nourishing mind's reverie.

The steep hill looks down
Taking in the contrast and
Thanking the world
For the everlasting rock
And the ever-changing plants.

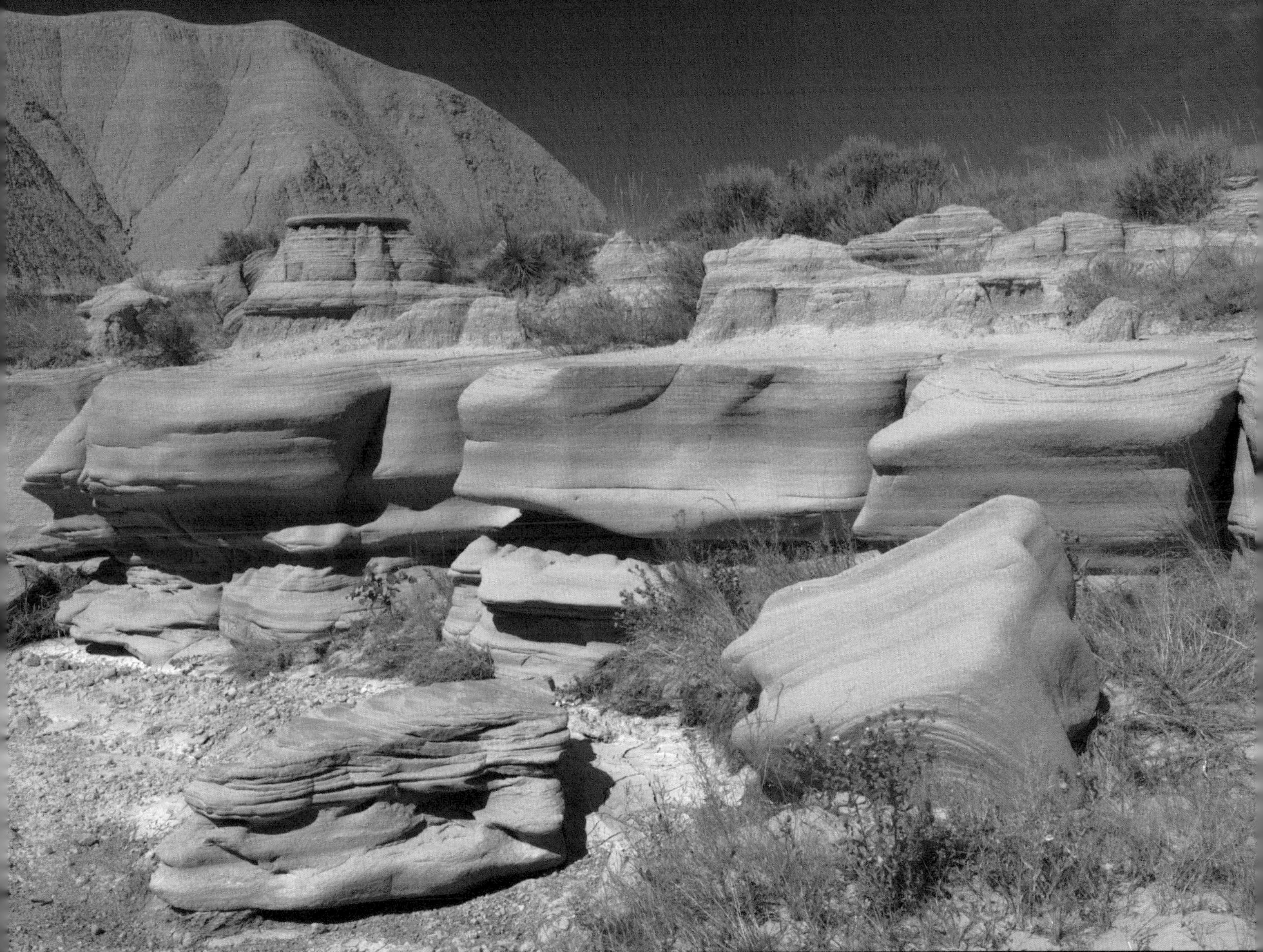

Exploration

There's a cavern here.
Maybe it offers protection.
Maybe it will trap water for us.
Maybe it will hide us from predators.

It's unwise to rush in without reconnoitering.
Get a couple sage bushes to volunteer
And that yellow flowered bush
And steel their courage with hard wood.

And maybe once the cavern's determined to be safe
Its aesthetic appeal will become clear,
Its complexity offering many different sights,
To satisfy the most persnickety.

What we have here is a plant's condominium
A plethora of sites,
Tranquil nooks and crannies
Where seasons can be enjoyed

Without great jeopardy.

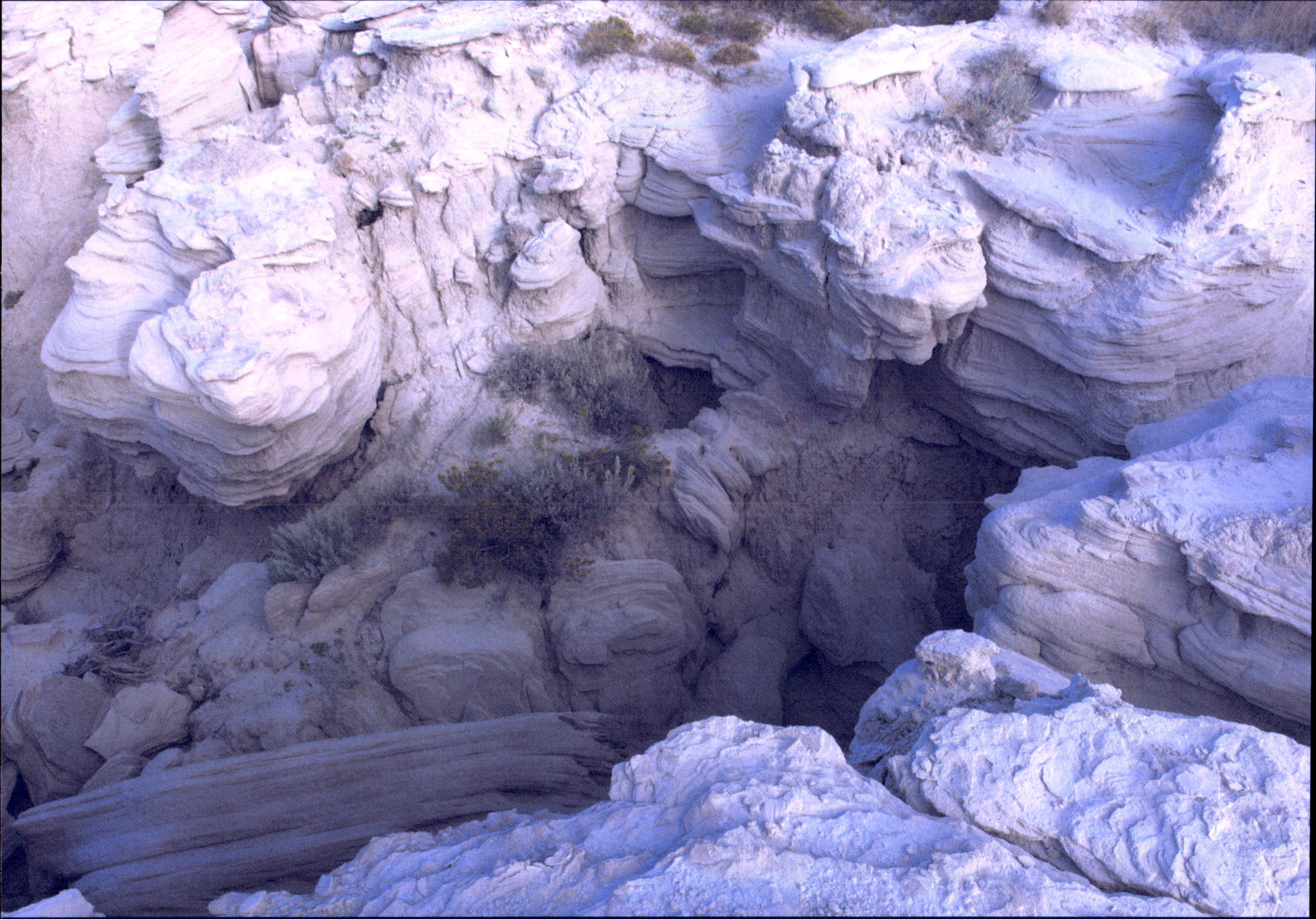

Where seasons can be enjoyed

Guardians

Pillars of compacted volcanic ash
  Layers exposed by erosion
Stand at the entrance
  Protecting the plants,
 Judging all who would enter.

But a price is extracted.
  The guardians sacrifice their bodies
To a higher calling,
  Pleasing the goddess
  By serving her plants.

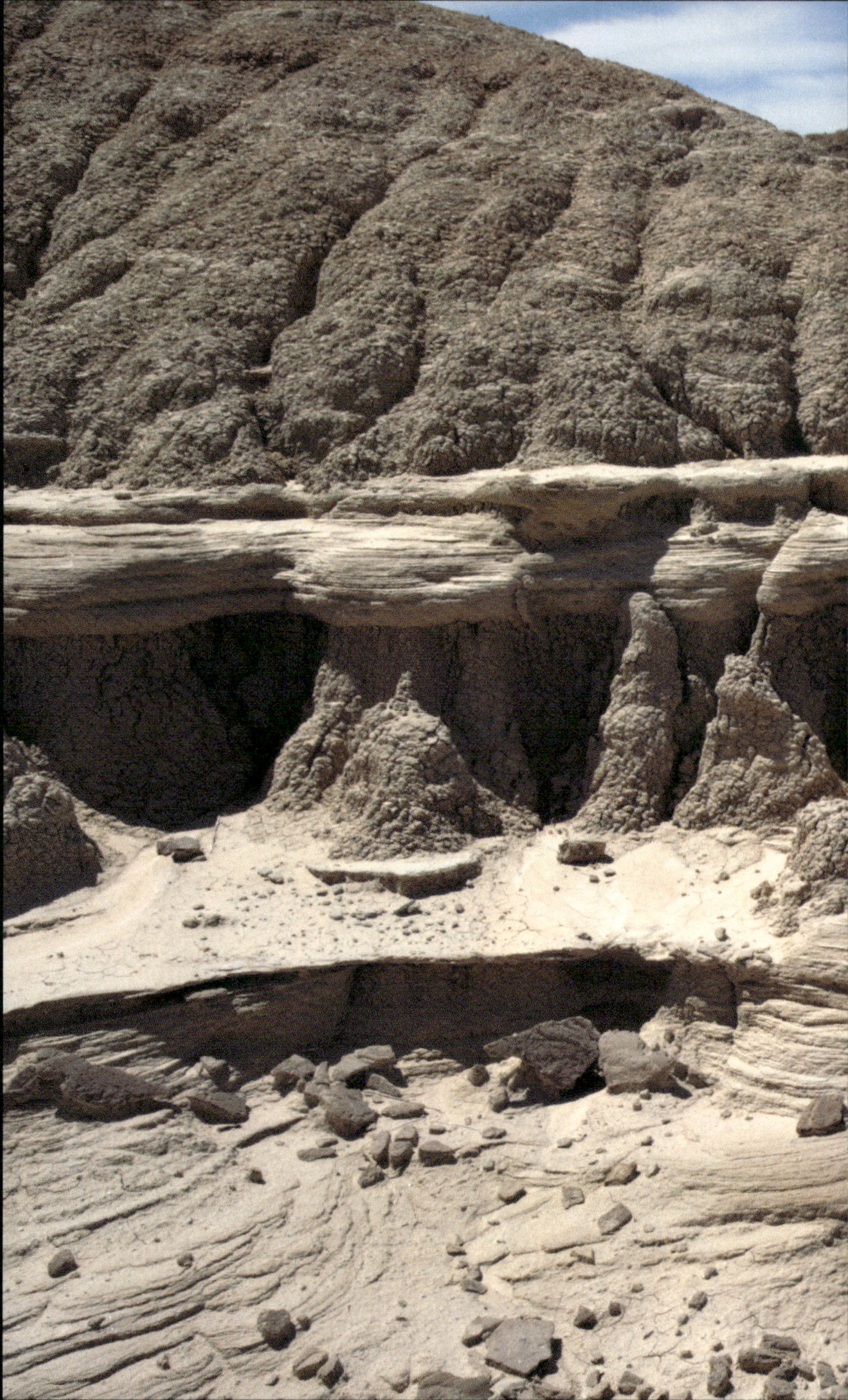

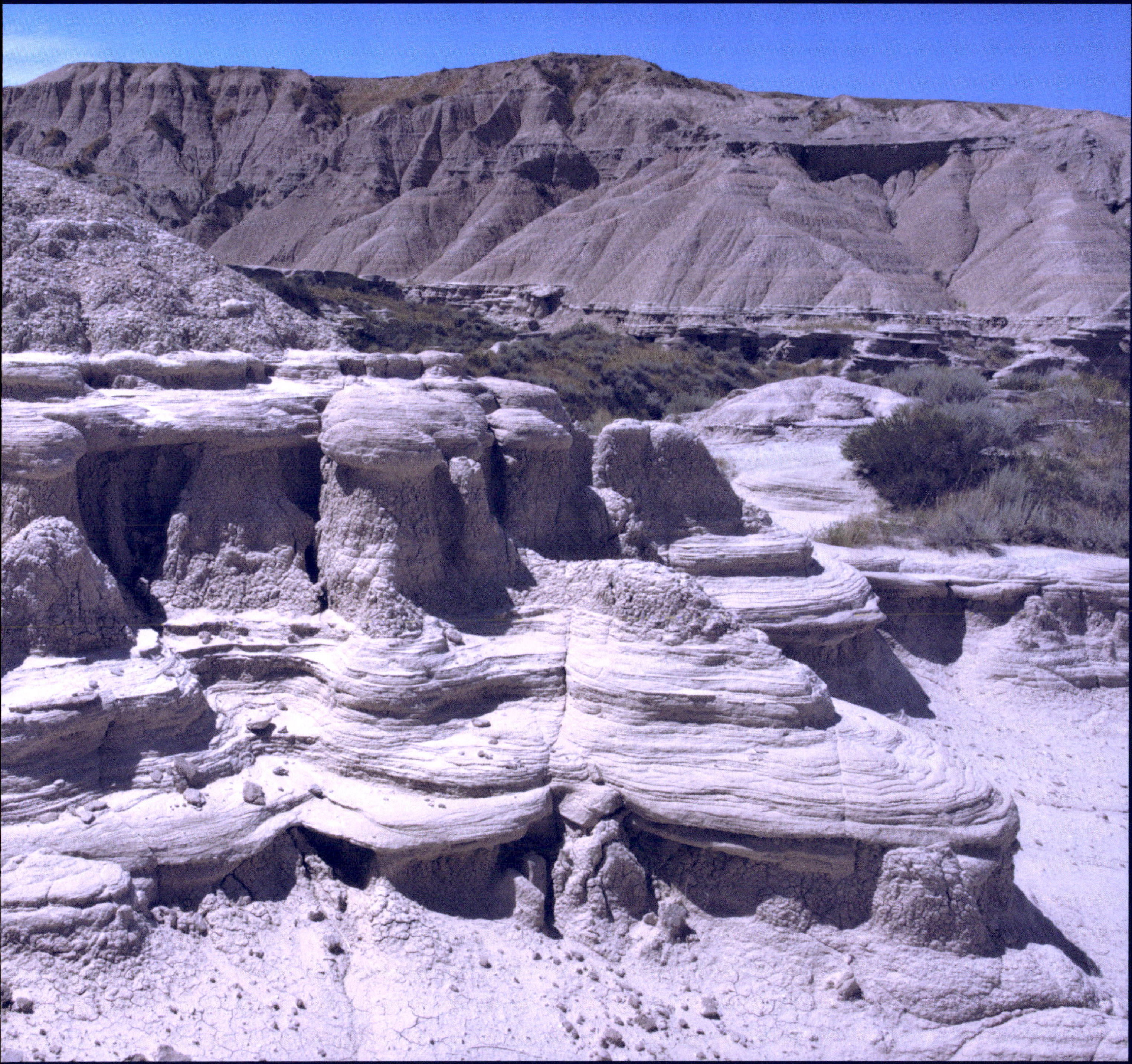

Haven

The water's been here
It's carved me a haven where
The sun can't find me.

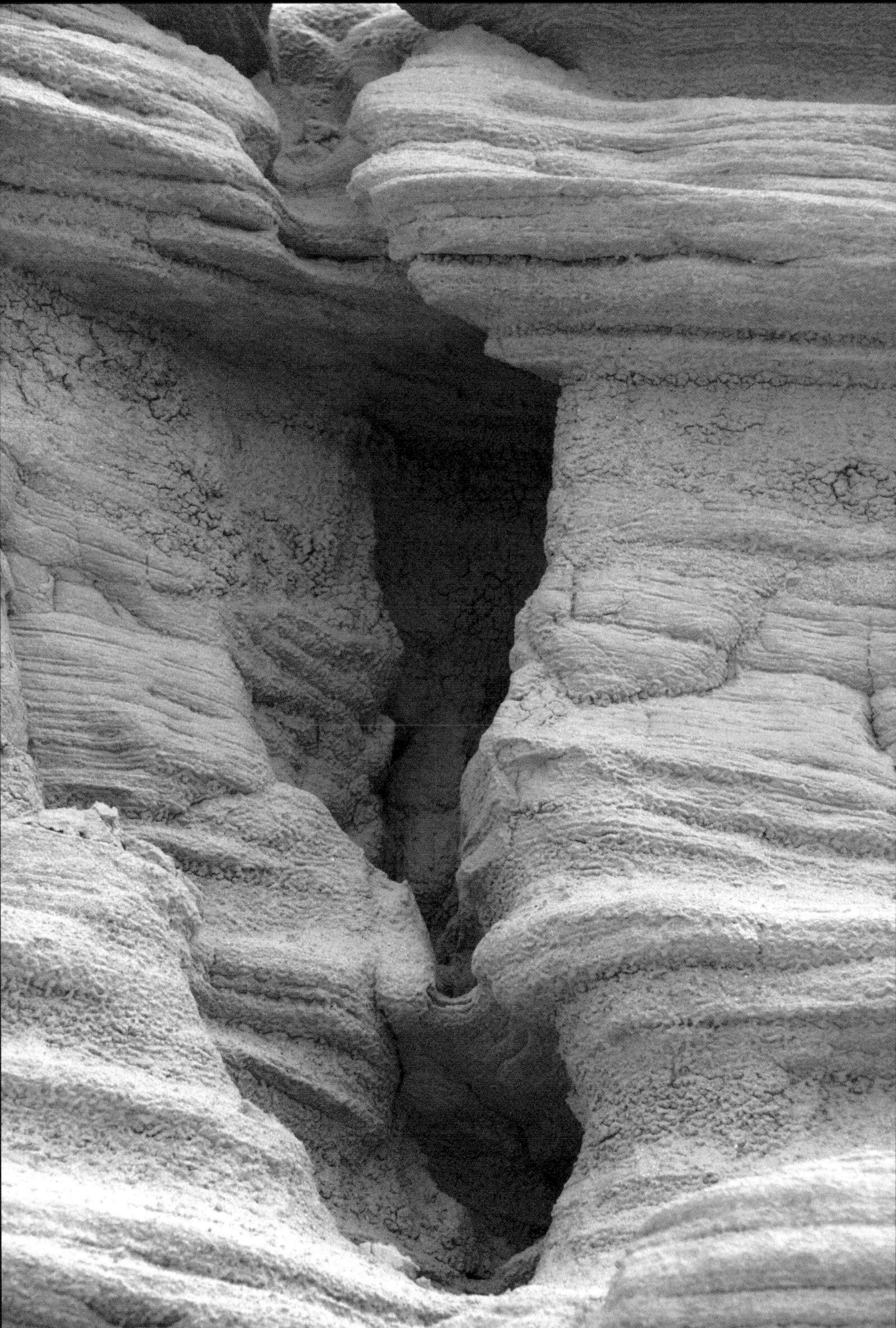

Hiding

I know you're there.
You're hiding from me
Moving within that complex,
Den to vault to cave to beneath an overhang,
  Even under a plant.

But now you can no longer escape.
I've got me here this focused beam
And I can penetrate your hiding places,
Trap you for mine own,
  For my amusement.

But it's not working.
My beam goes one way
I can hear you flitting elsewhere
My beam's strong, but too narrow
  And too clumsy.

And I fear it isn't you alone I hear..
There's a back-beat to sounds of scurrying,
Giving it a counter point
That perhaps is the most significant;
  The sound of the gods chuckling.

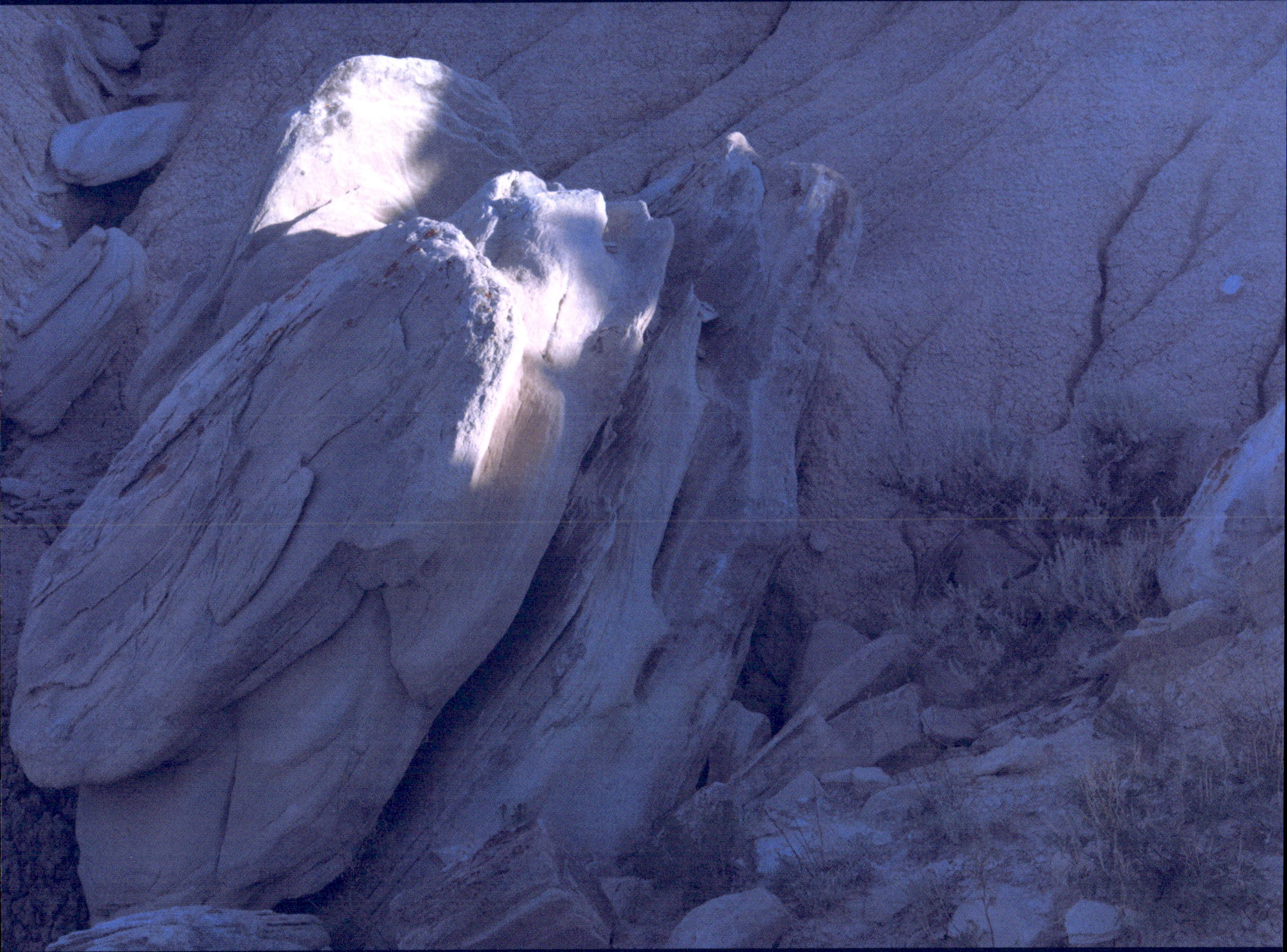

Safe Secrets

Starting at the top
You could pour all your secrets
Down this little gulch
And be confident that none
Would sneak out the bottom.

But should they try,
They'll never get by

The sentinel sunflower.

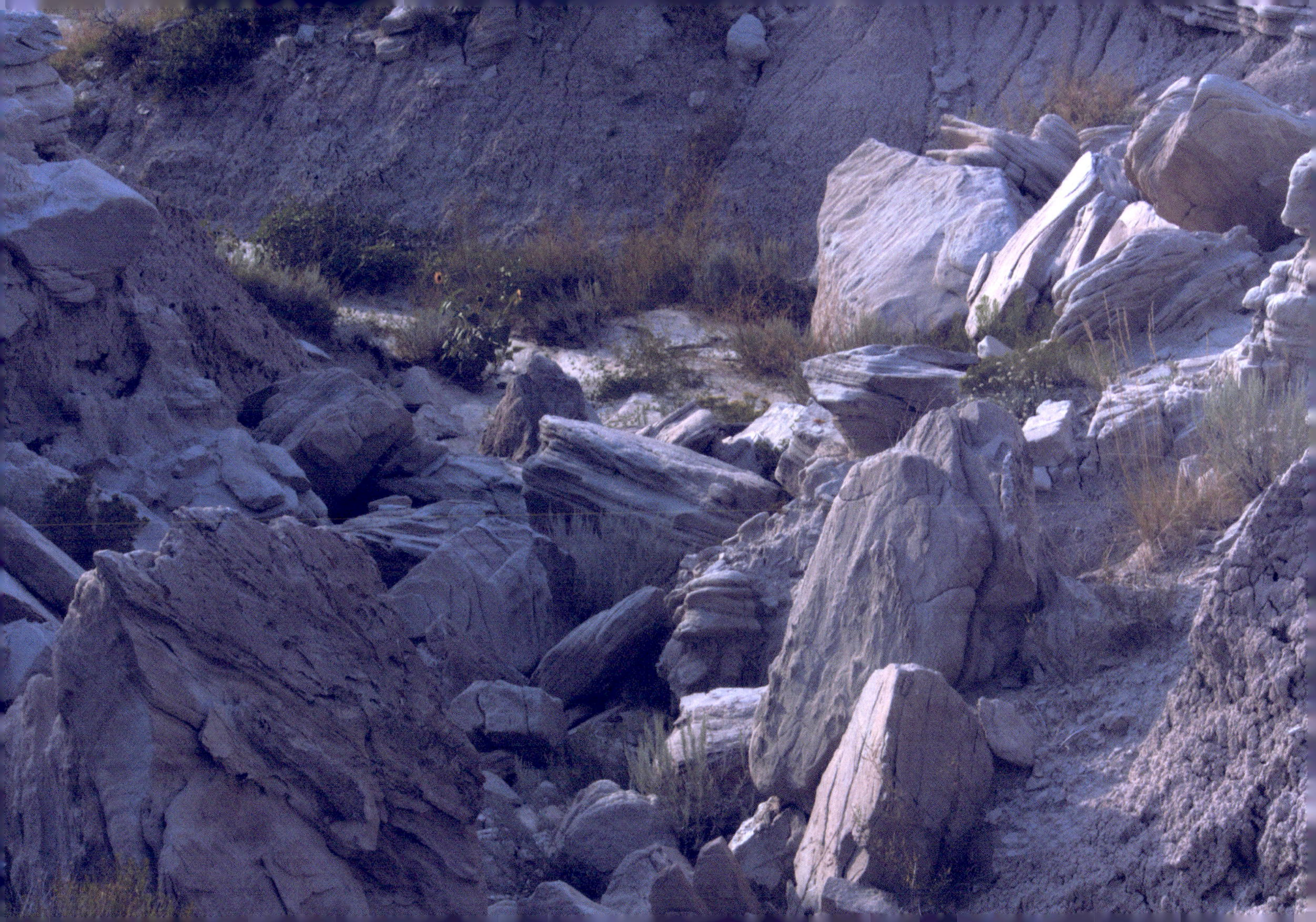

Connections

It's the edifice
White, against a pale blue sky
Connecting between
This place and the heavens,
Me and the universe.

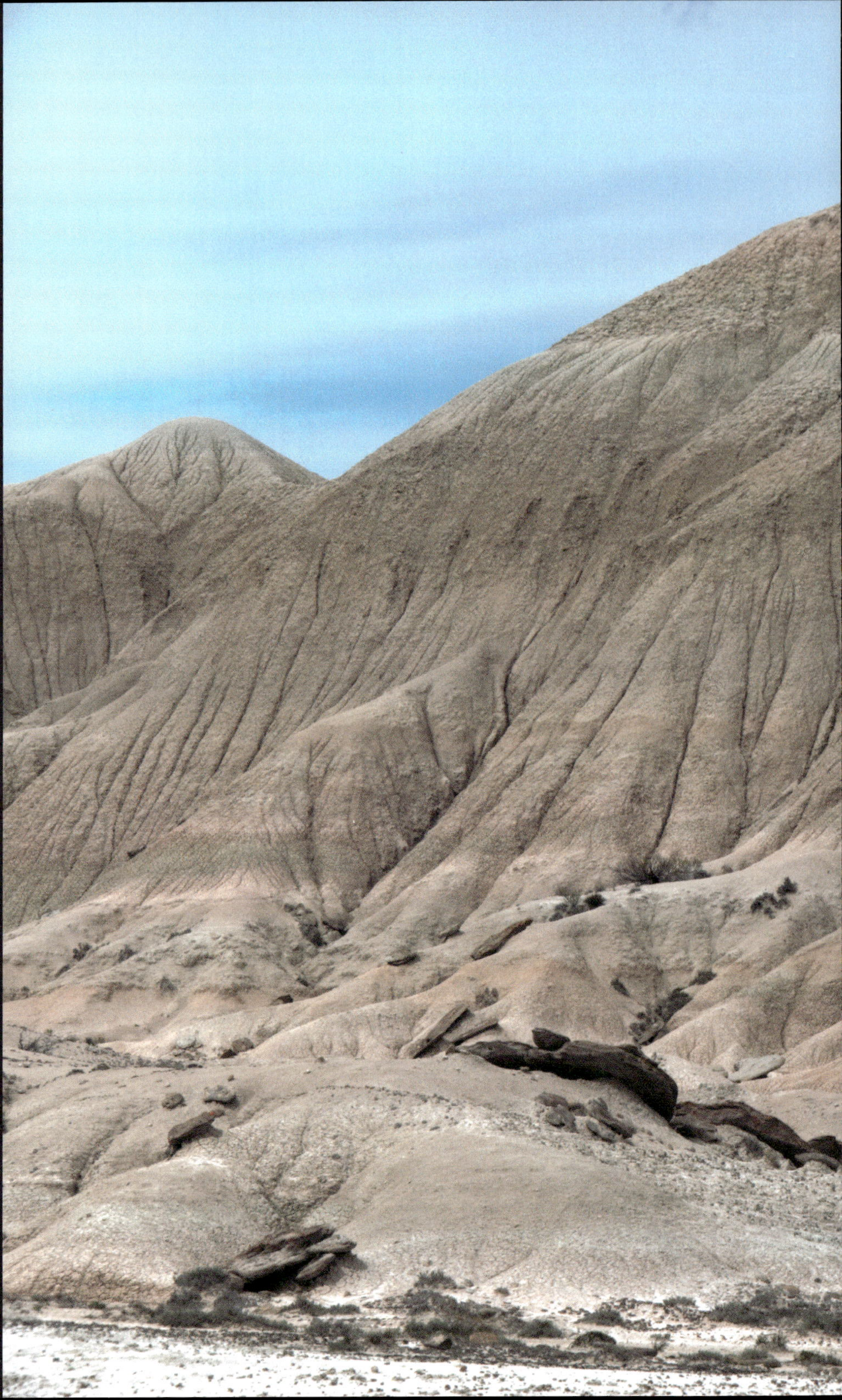

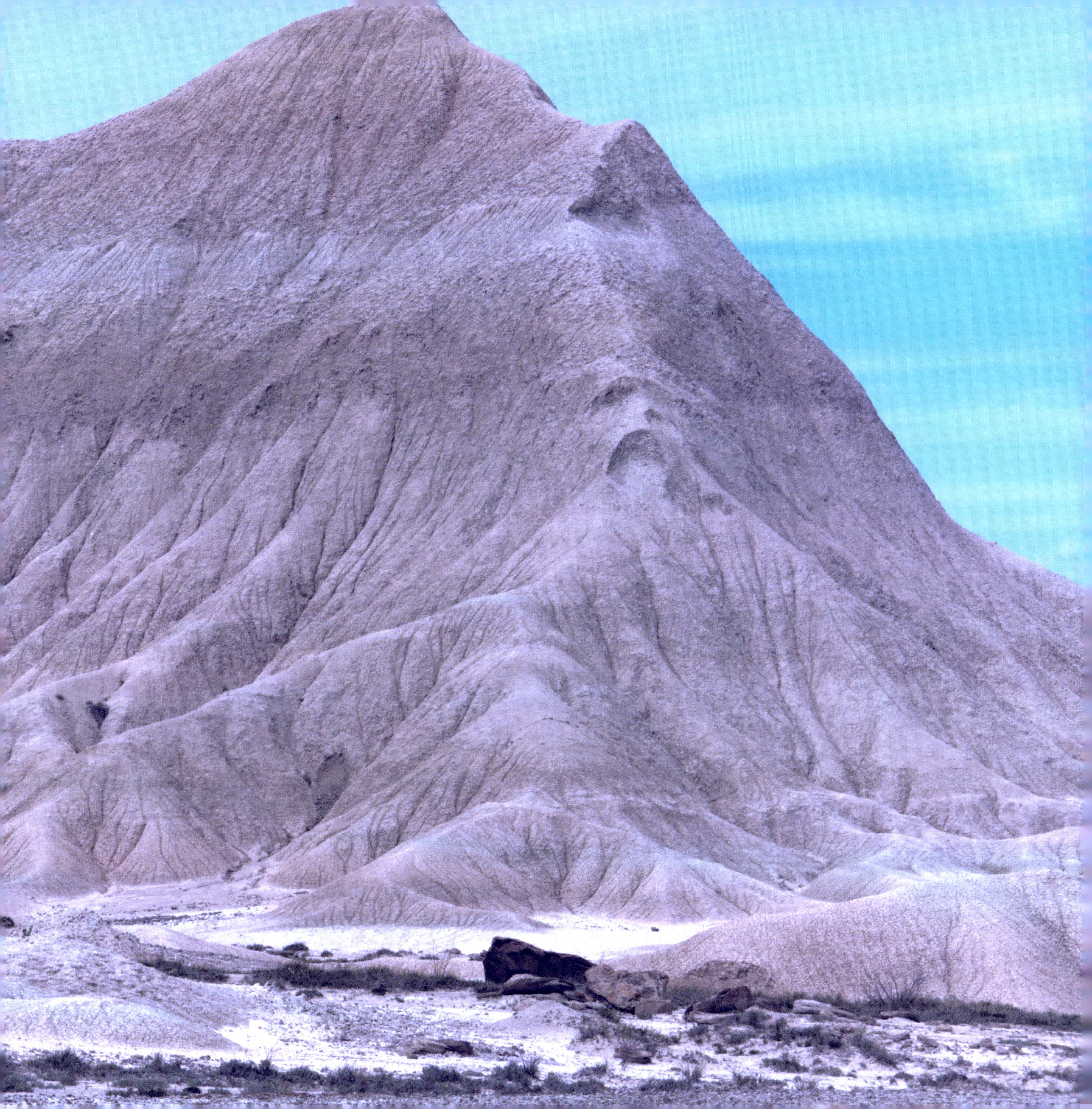

Respect

Don't give me no lip.
I'm on top of this here pedestal
Which means I'm in charge.

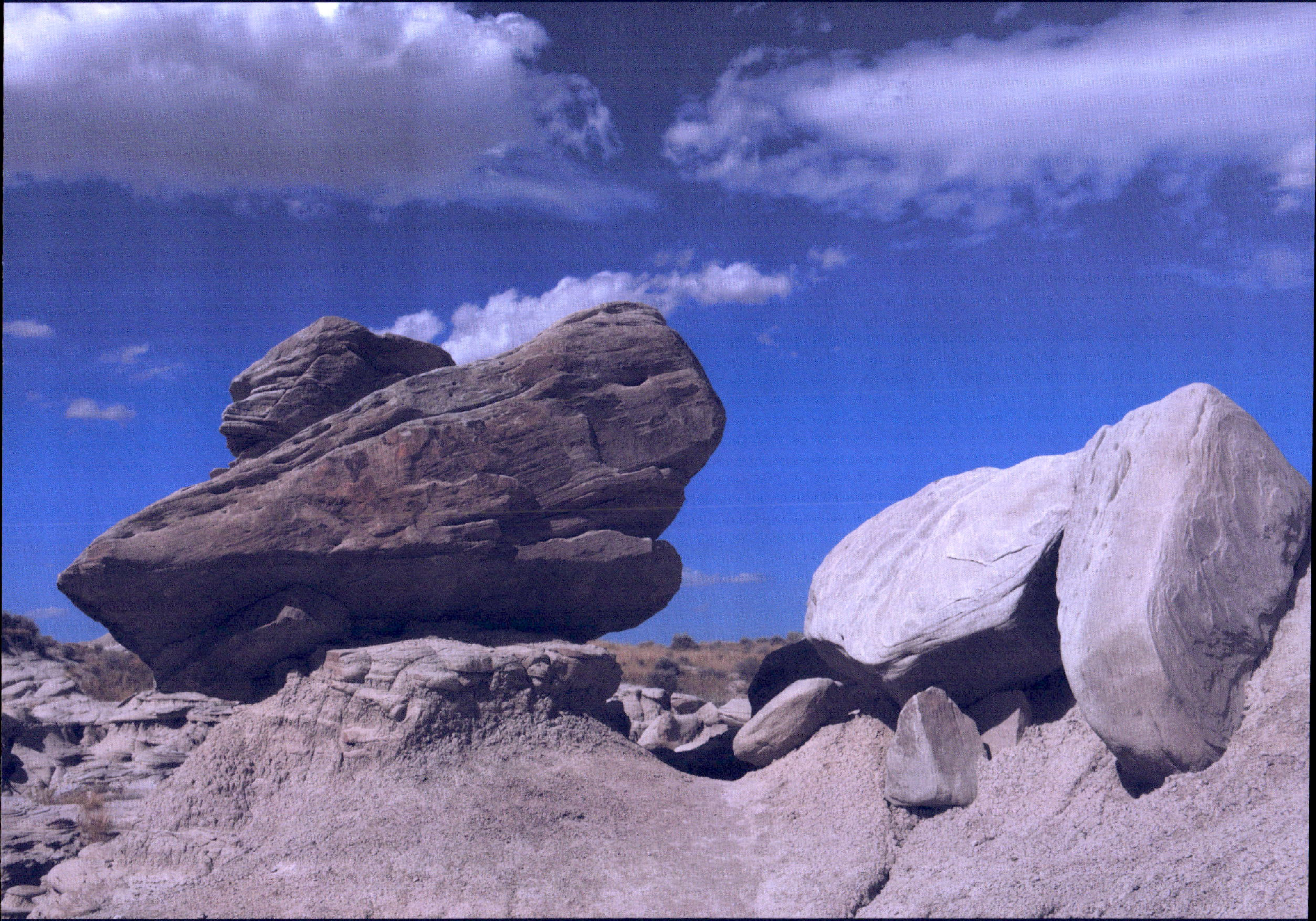

Dignity

See those little runnels on my side?

Each marks a path where, with each rain,
  A little bit of me was washed away,
  Carried down below
  To form soil where plants can grow.

It's a good trade.

I'm too steep to grow plants
  So I wash away
  So that my residue can

Leaving me, in my old age,
  Wrinkled and dignified.

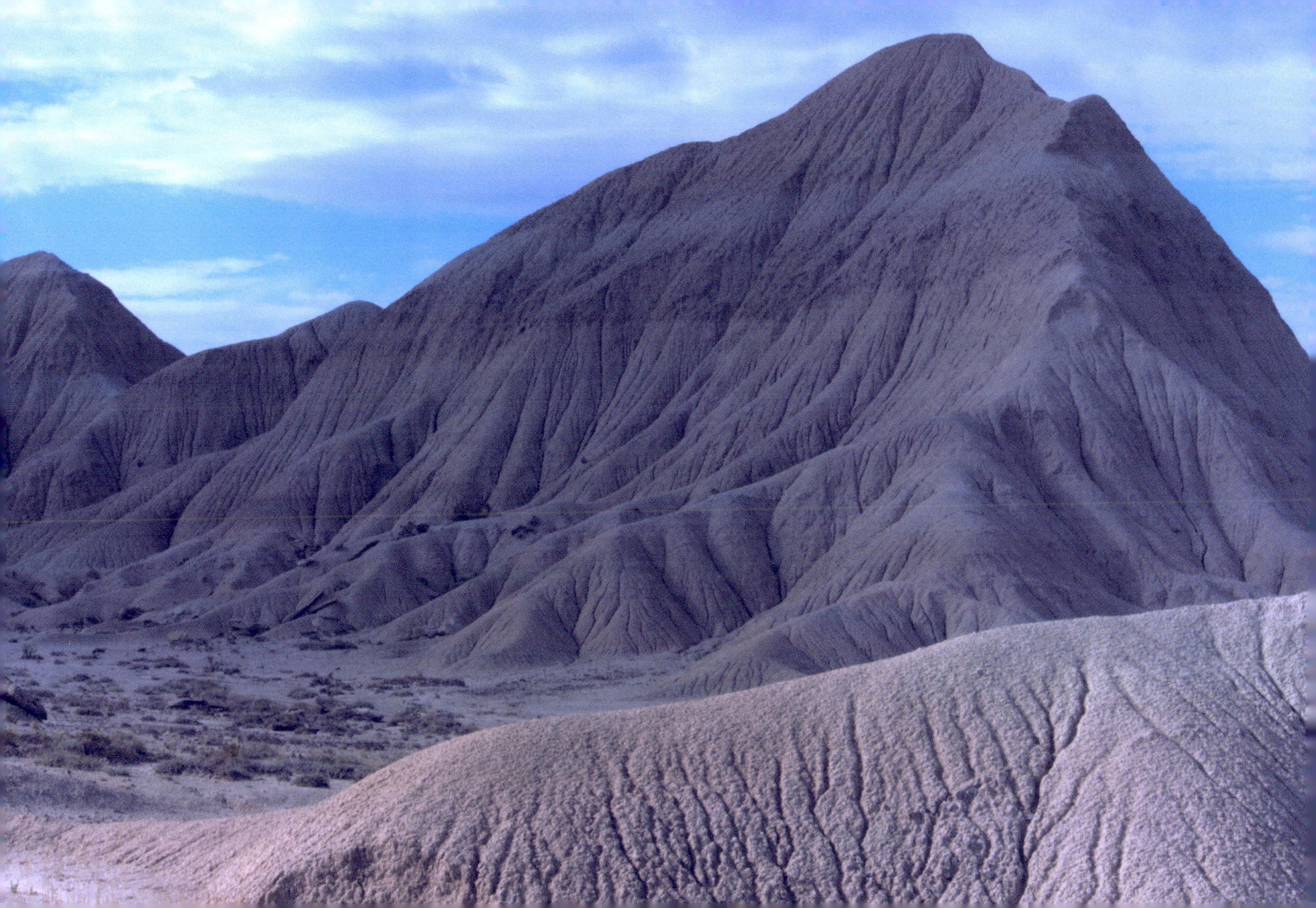

Snake's Wisdom

Those are my tracks you see,
  There, in the dirt on the road
    Left because of my responsibilities.

Every night I must abandon
  My sanctuary
    The place where
      I'm hidden from predators
      And can hide from my prey,

I'm driven out by knowledge there's mistakes on information signs
  Mistakes that lead human visitors to
    Do the wrong thing
    In the wrong place
    At the wrong time..

Those mistakes are of the product of the bumbling bipeds
  Who run this place.
  The ultimate of creation?

      HAH!

At least the mistakes are blatant enough
  They can be quickly corrected.

Allowing me to slither home while it's still dark
  And I can't be seen.

I can take the easy way
  Not through the grassy route.
    Concealing maybe
    But hard to pass through.

Saving humans from themselves
  It`s a dirty job
  But someone has to do it.

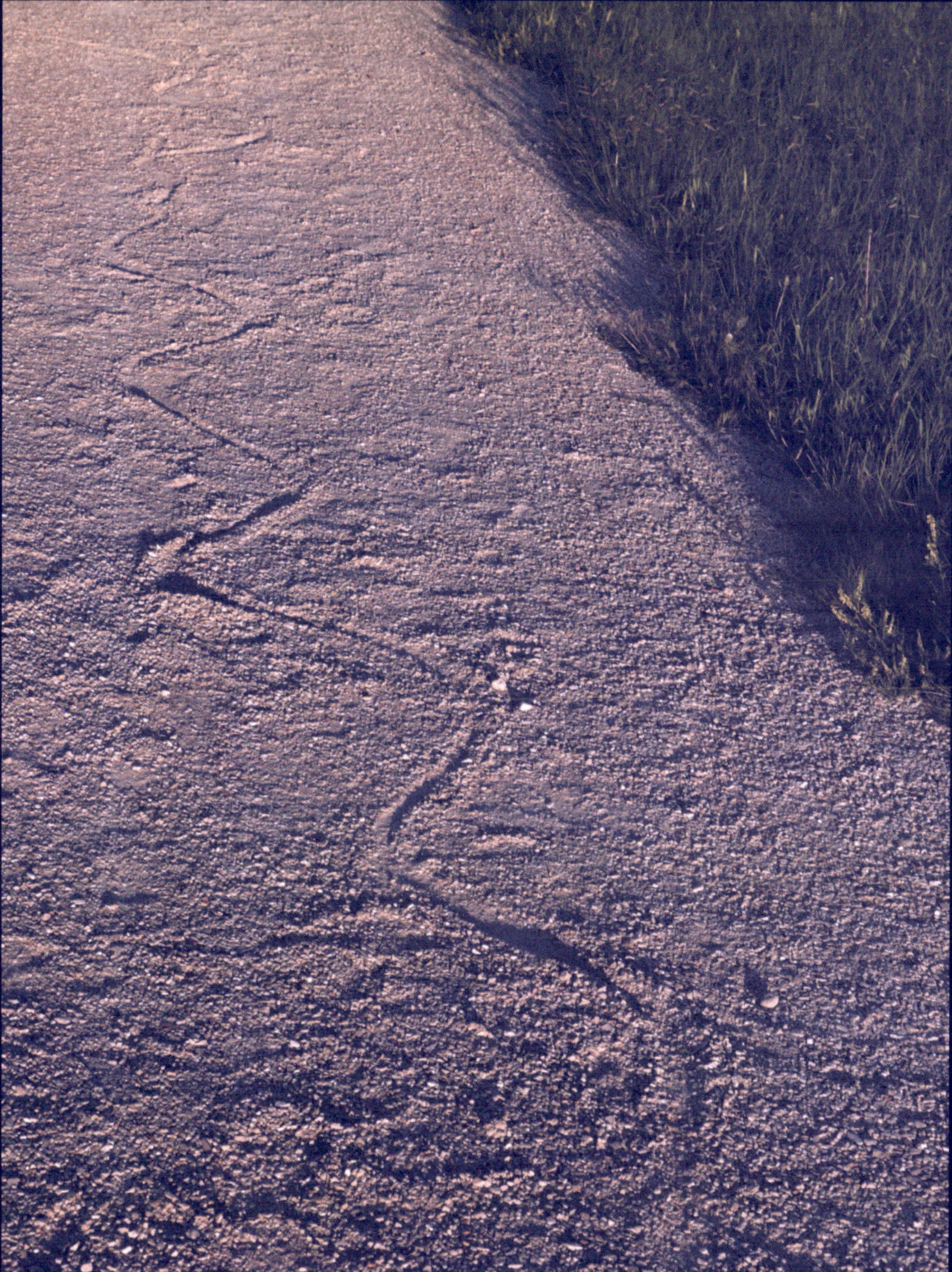

My Pretty

It was pretty here
In a rather gray drab way.
Oh there were carved slopes
With a ridge-top fringe of plants
Scattered boulders, some bushes.

But more was needed,
More than the shadows, more than
Dry leafless branches
And patches of grass, drought brown.
So it was left up to me.

I was a good choice.
I mirrored the slope's carving.
I played with shadows.
I used orange lichens as plants.
I offered up everything,

With just a bit more color.

I used orange lichens as plants

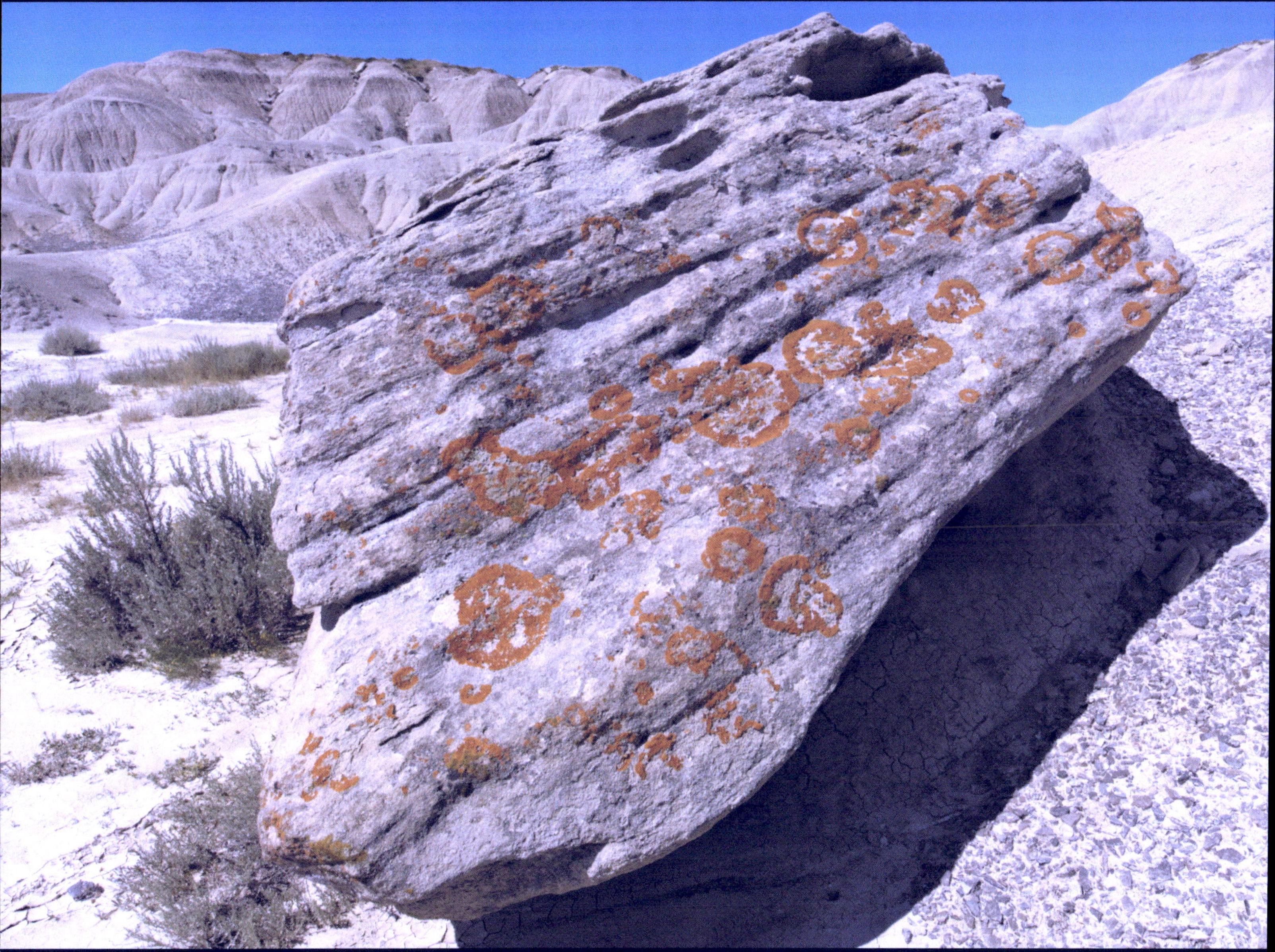

I offered up everything

Dependence

What have we here?
Steppe shrubs and prairie grasses
On the flatlands separating
Low white bluffs
With rocks instead of plants.

But they're not independent.
The plants get from the bluffs
Water,
Soil.
And a bit of protection from the wind

But the plants aren't free loaders.
They offer, in return
A way to keep water and soil in place.
And beauty
To enhance the existence of bluffs and rocks.

Neither are humans freeloaders,
If they're careful;
Treat the steppe and water with respect,
Treat their history with respect,
To enhance their heir's existence.

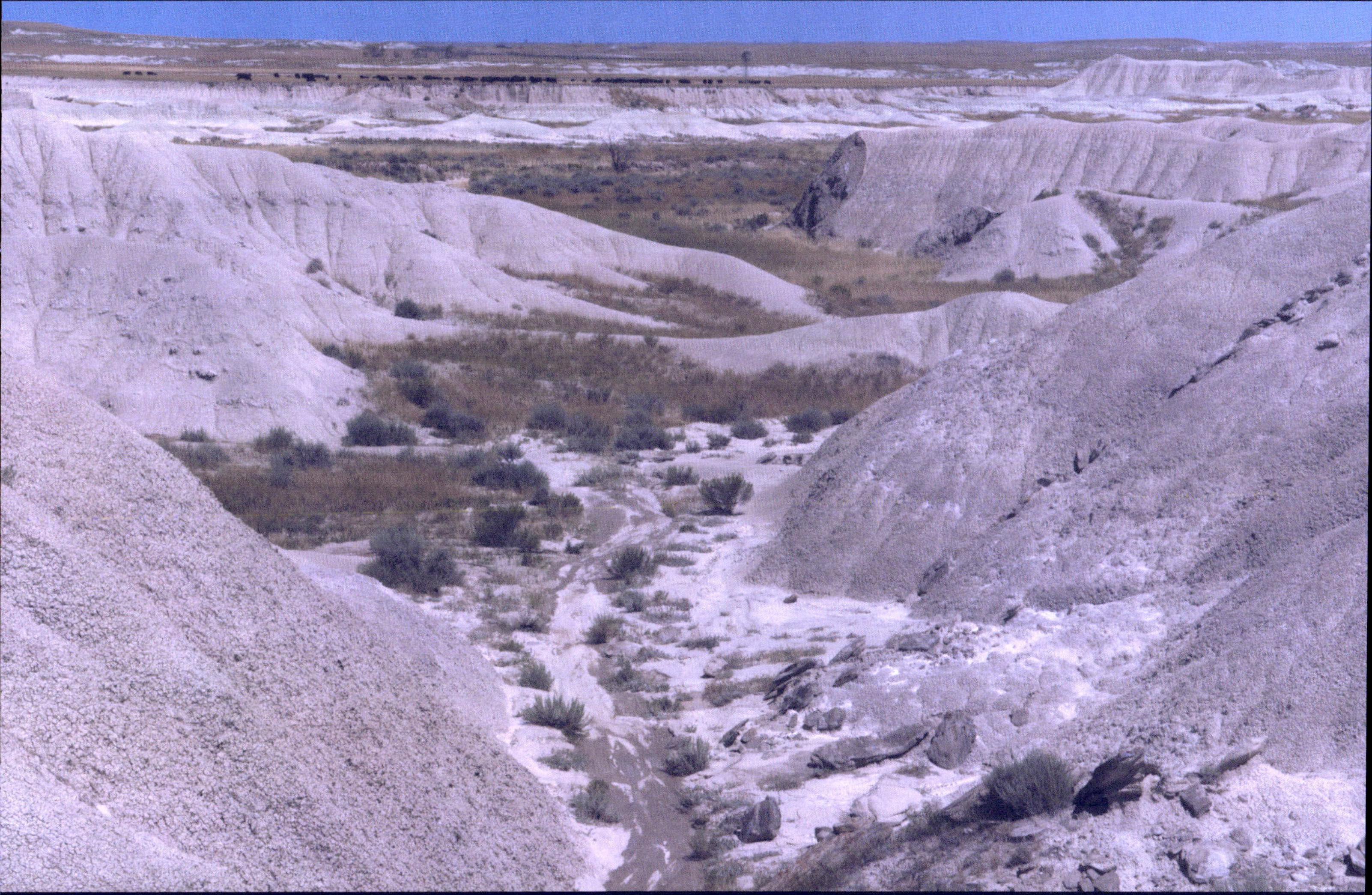

Shrub and Rock

Shrub and Rock - I

Complex and massive
But the same, year after year.
Shrub, renewed each spring.

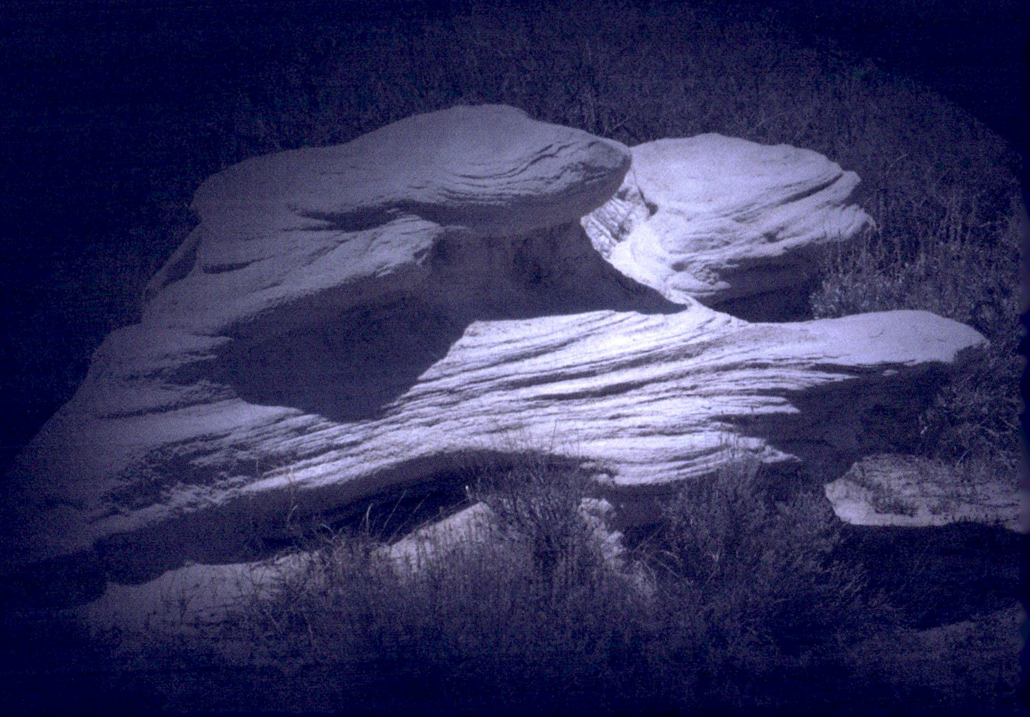

Shrub and Rock - II

That rock can be picked
Or one of the shrubs since both
Will hide a rabbit.

Shrub and Rock - III

An intricate rock
Large, white, with many contours.
Can't compete with shrubs.
It has size and persistence
But's static, spring to summer.

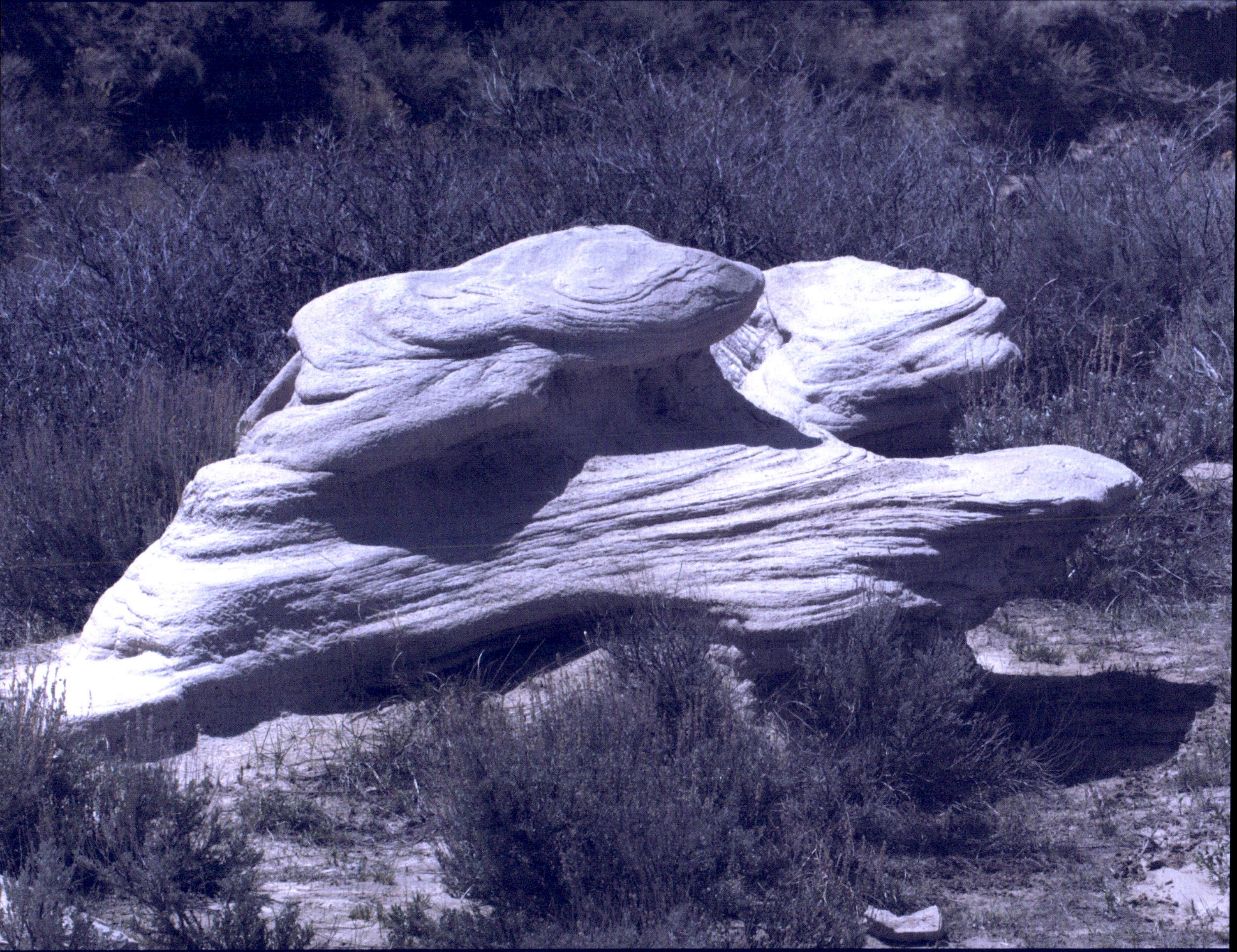

Toadstool Knoll

I sit very still on a knoll
Surrounded by grass and shrubs
In a midday sun.

Then take a careful glance up;
Hopefully seeking company,
Buzzards I expect to see circling overhead.

Because I've not moved
They'd have identified me as
A potential meal.

Should these soaring birds appear
They'd add to the pleasure of sitting
On a Toadstool knoll.

They'll ride the updrafts
That carry the fragrance that
Marks a Toadstool knoll.

Fragrances from sun's heat
Teasing odors from the plants;
Dry grass, sage, bushes.

These odors connect
The sun, through the plants to
Buzzards overhead.

I'm not relevant
To the story. I'm here as
The luck of the draw.

Fragrances from sun's heat
Teasing odors from the plants;
Dry grass, sage, bushes.

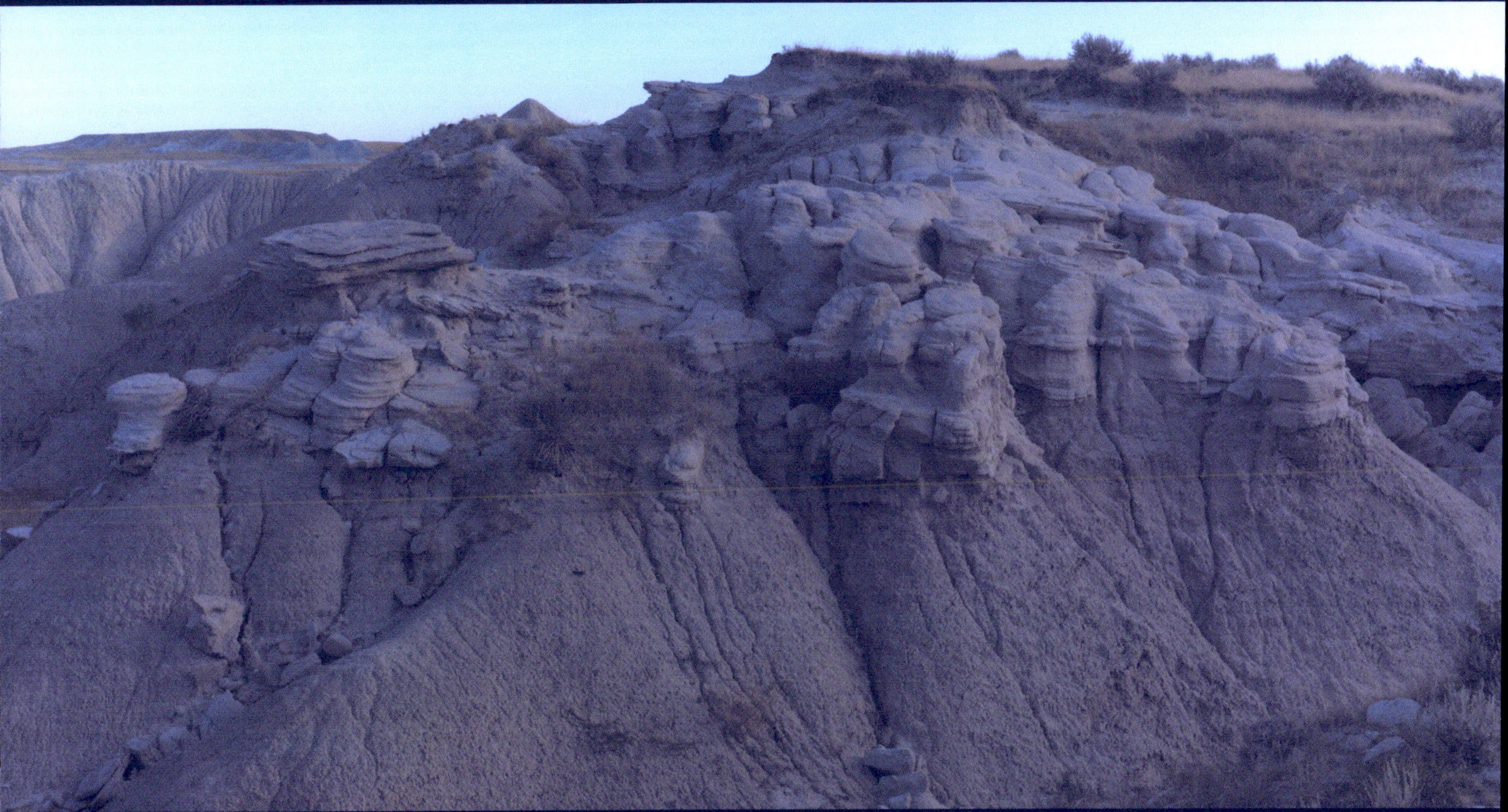

Responsibilities

What have we got here?
A few boulders, loosely strewn,
Dirt easily moved,
Layers of rocks, bushes, grass.
Who will hold all this in place?

The boulders, too loose.
The dirt, friable, no strength.
Layers of rocks are it.
But what does Nature wish?
Since plants are her favorites

I'll bet they're the most critical.

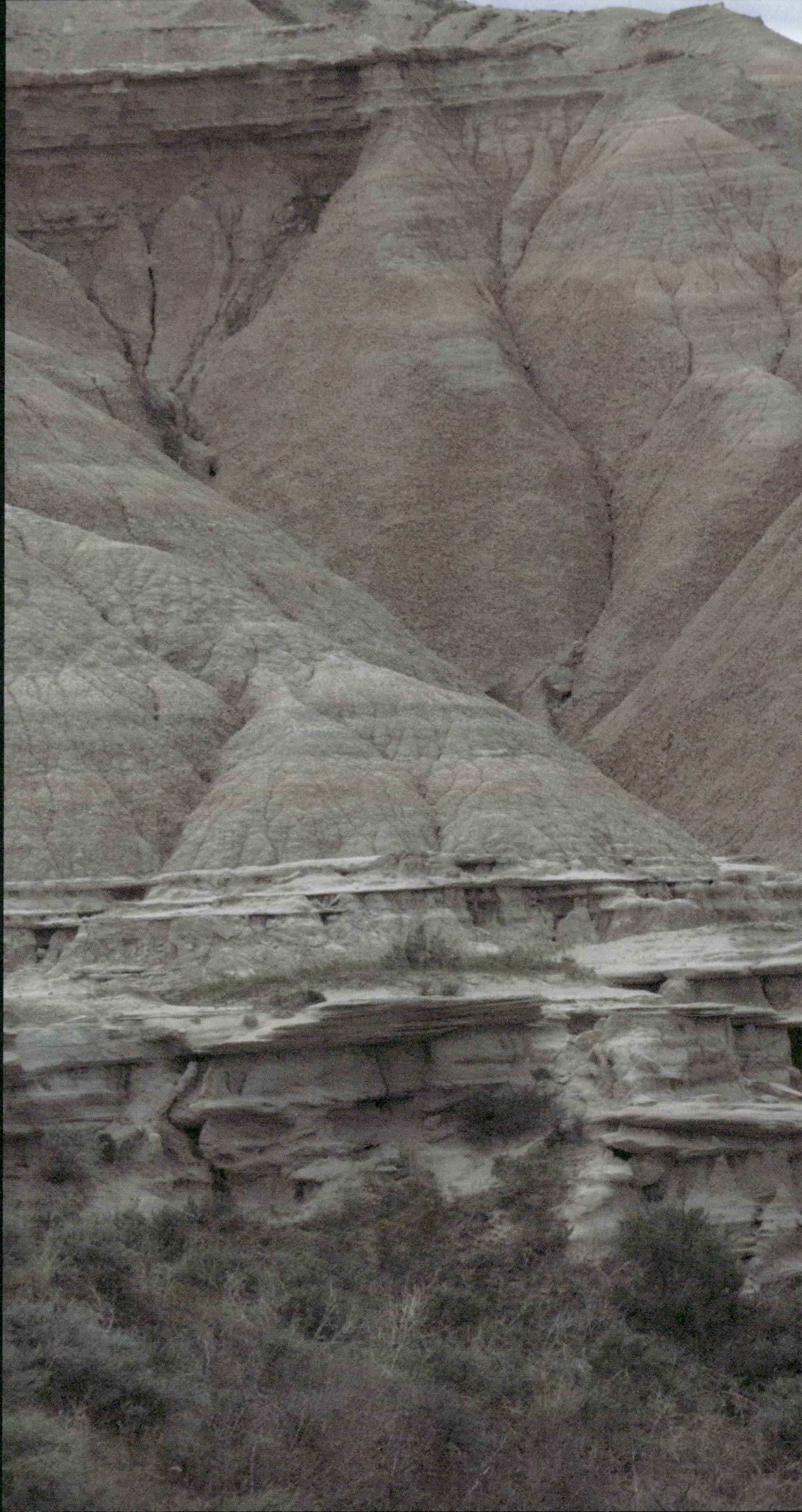

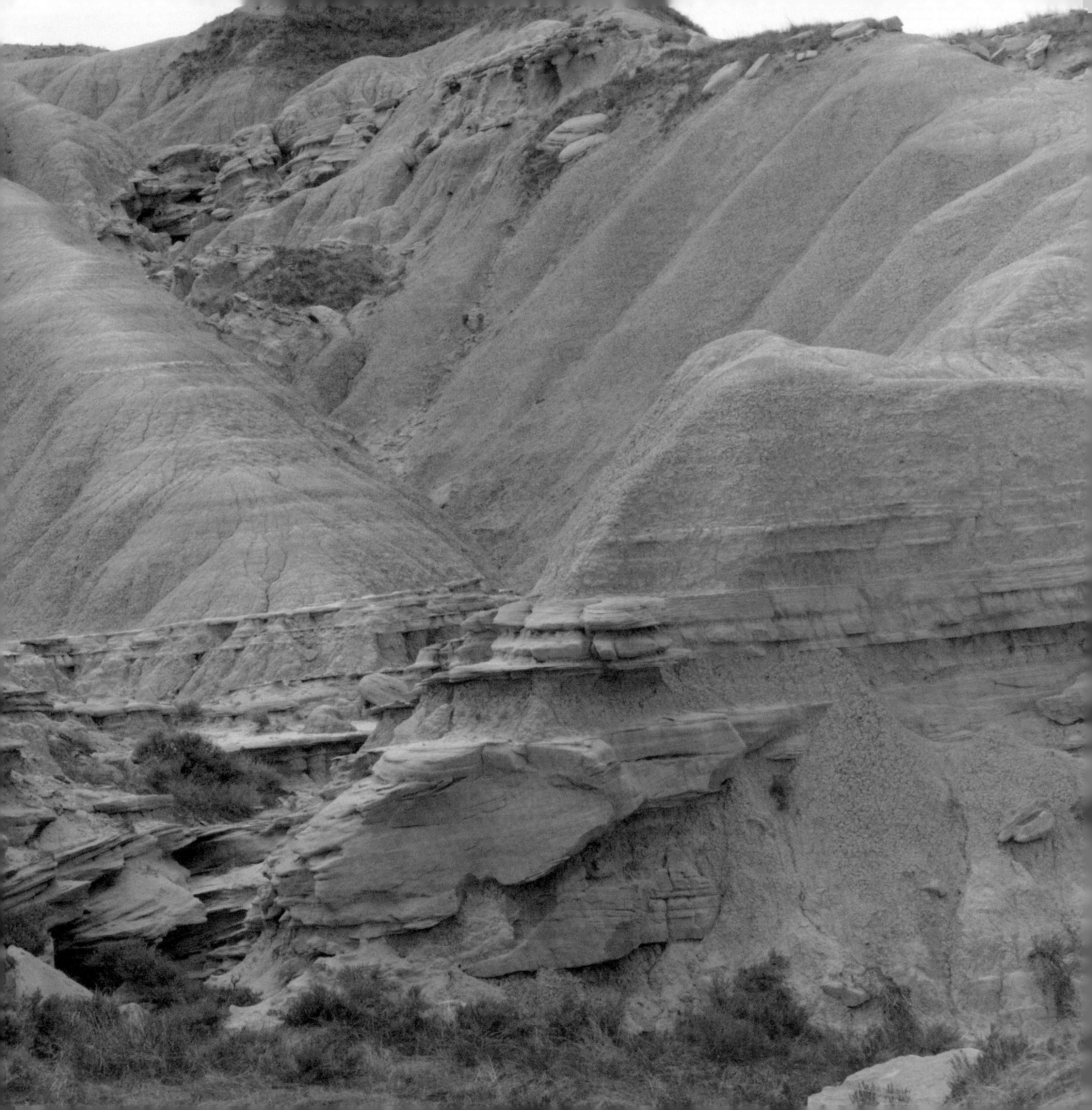

Seasonal Distinctions

The plants are scraggly.
  Beaten down,
  Dried out,
  Barely hanging on,
  Not much for the eye
    Or nose.

The rocks have a majesty.
  Formed in layers,
  Different designs,
  There for eons,
  Sculptures gray and easy on the eye
    Still not much for the nose.

Come back next spring.
  The rocks, the same.
  The plants, wouldn't know them.
  Green, vibrant
  Kidnap the eye
    And saturate the air with the odor of growth.

Just gotta plan your visits right.

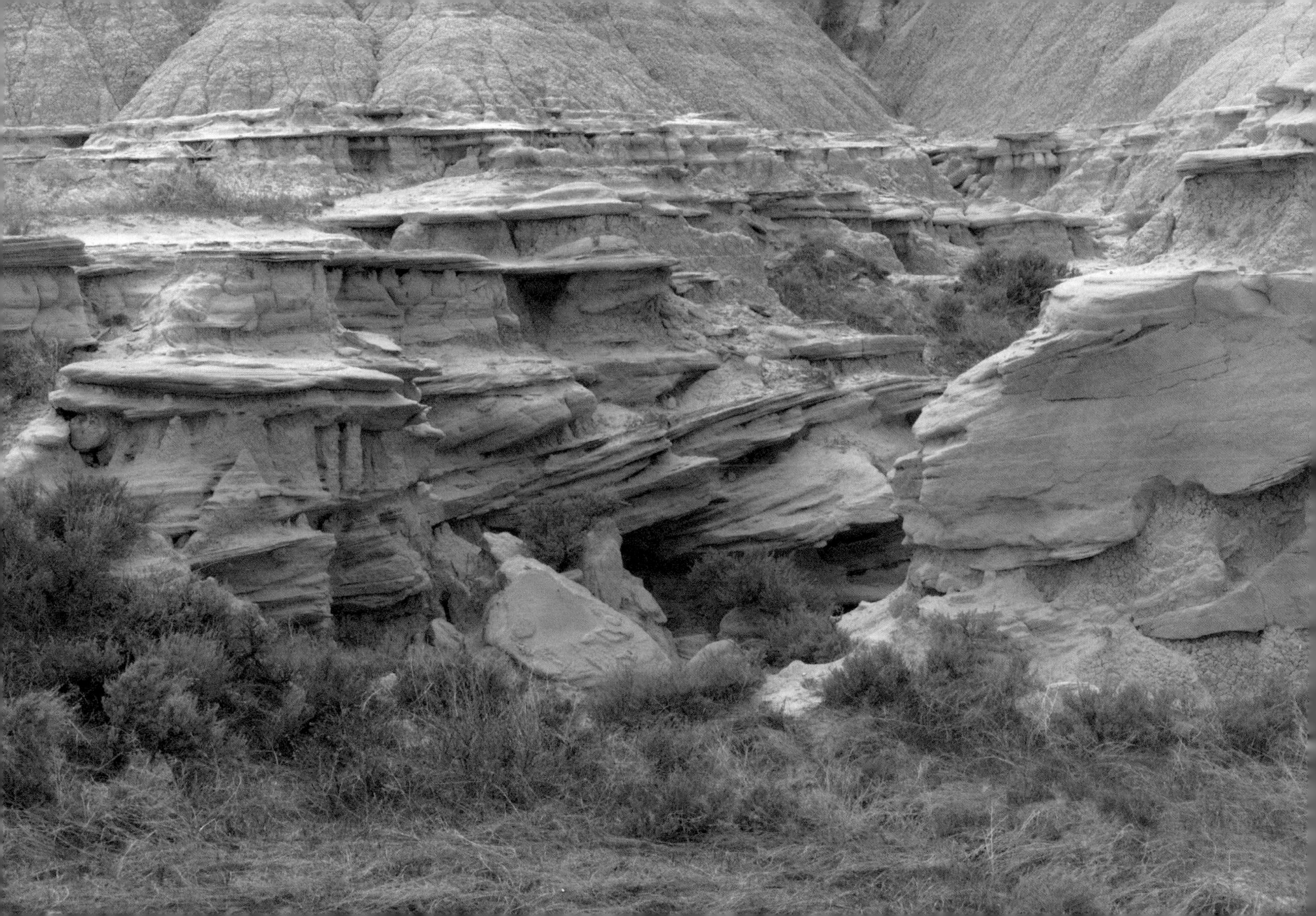

Lichens

Rocks reflect the sun
Lichens too, but first
They alter the light.

Lichen's Dawn

Rocks are a mirror of nature
Especially when they capture and then reflect dawn`s light.

Lichens growing on the rocks mirror nature too
But differently.

They take in the light
Transform it to a different plane
And then project it back.

Together they move the dawn to a higher level of being.

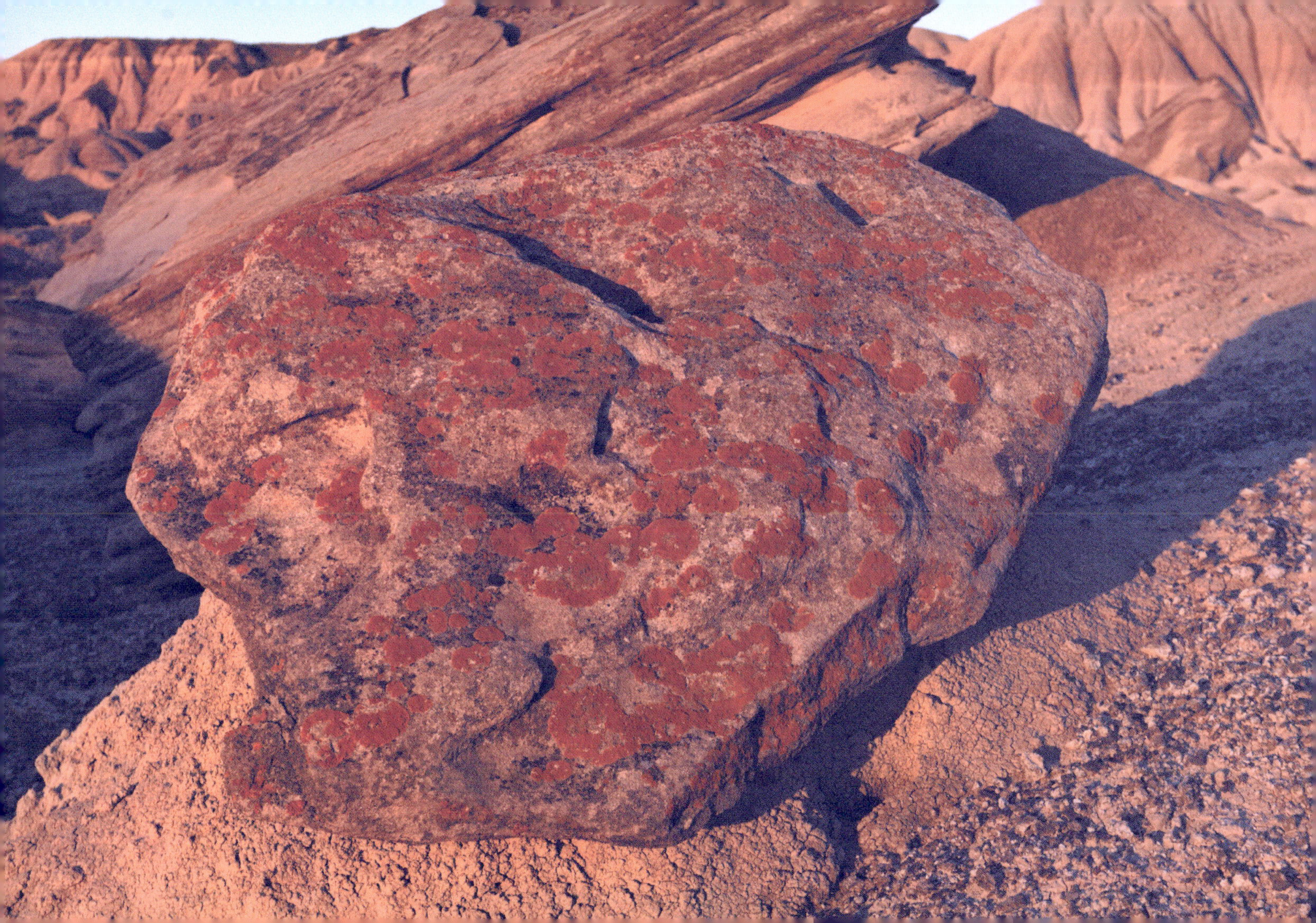

Wind Dancers

Unlike the antelope
  We can't race before the wind
  We're anchored here through life.

But we have our ways
  Of celebrating the wind,
  Of showing our appreciation.

Dance!
  Translating the winds energy
  Into moves sensuously

Showing our joy of life.

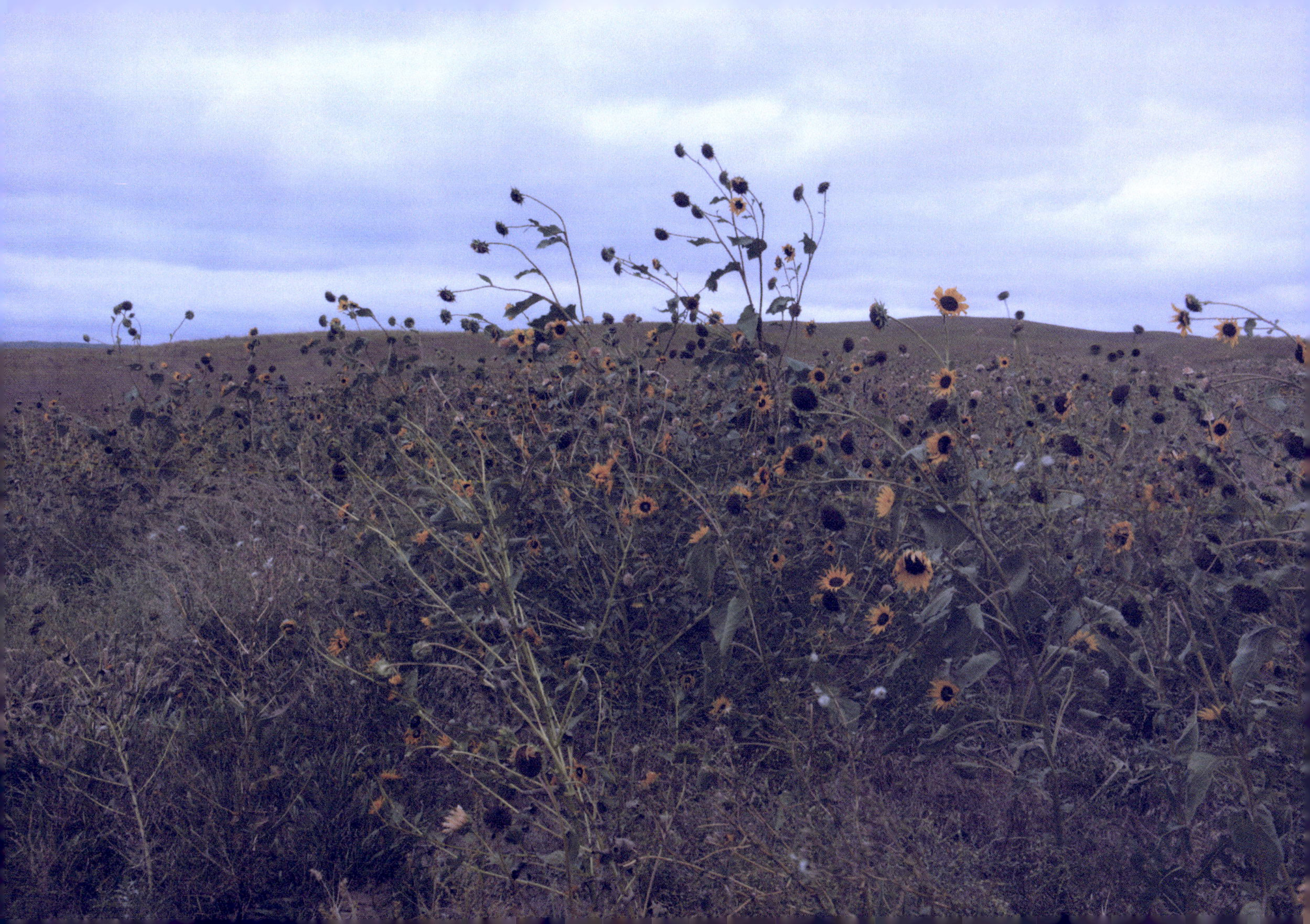

Graceful

Antelope float across grassland
Effortless motion transforms
Animal into graceful flow.

The grasses over which they run
Undulate in waves
With the arrival of a breeze

Summer's downpour strikes the earth
Rills form
In the ridge the antelope pursue

Everything flows
Different rates and different ways
But everything flows

All captured in an afternoon
Image at Toadstool.

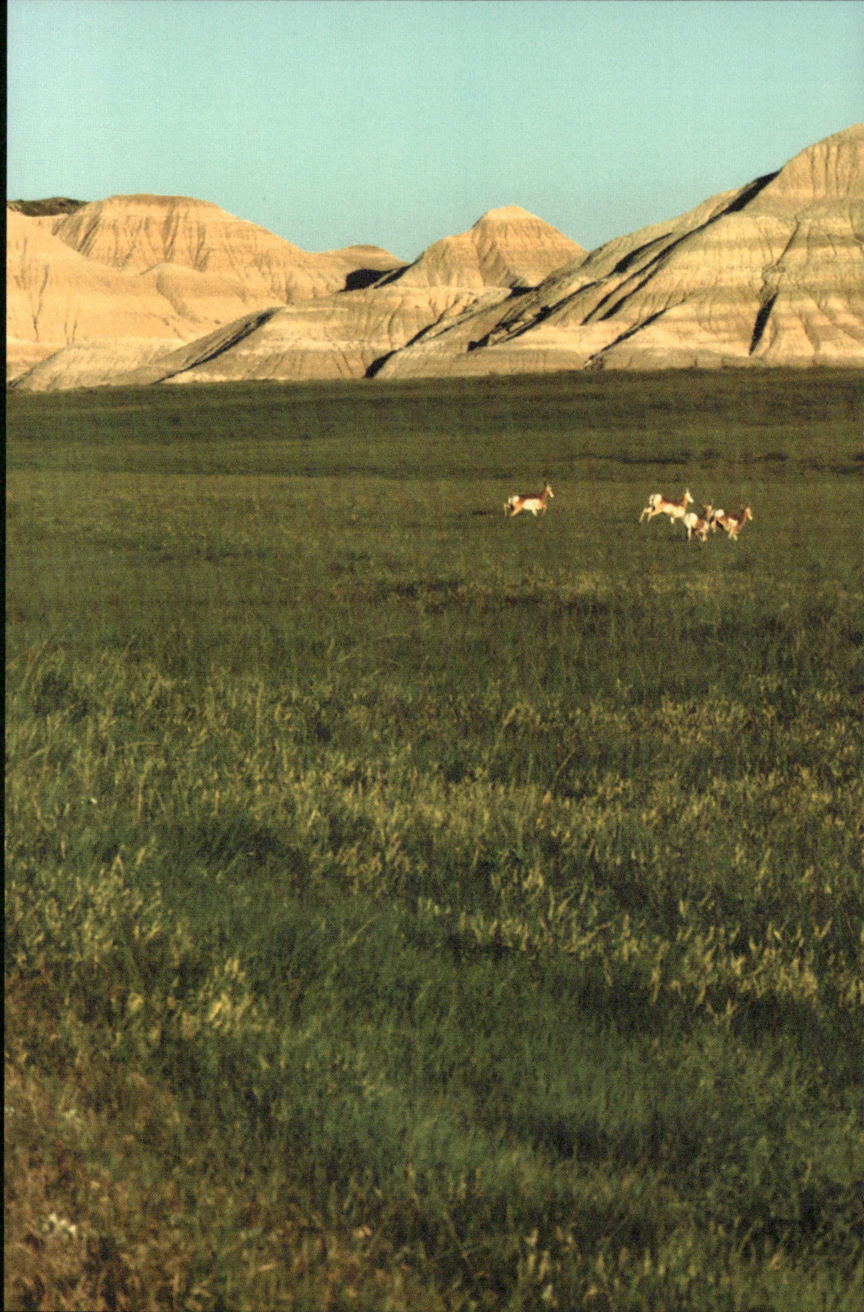

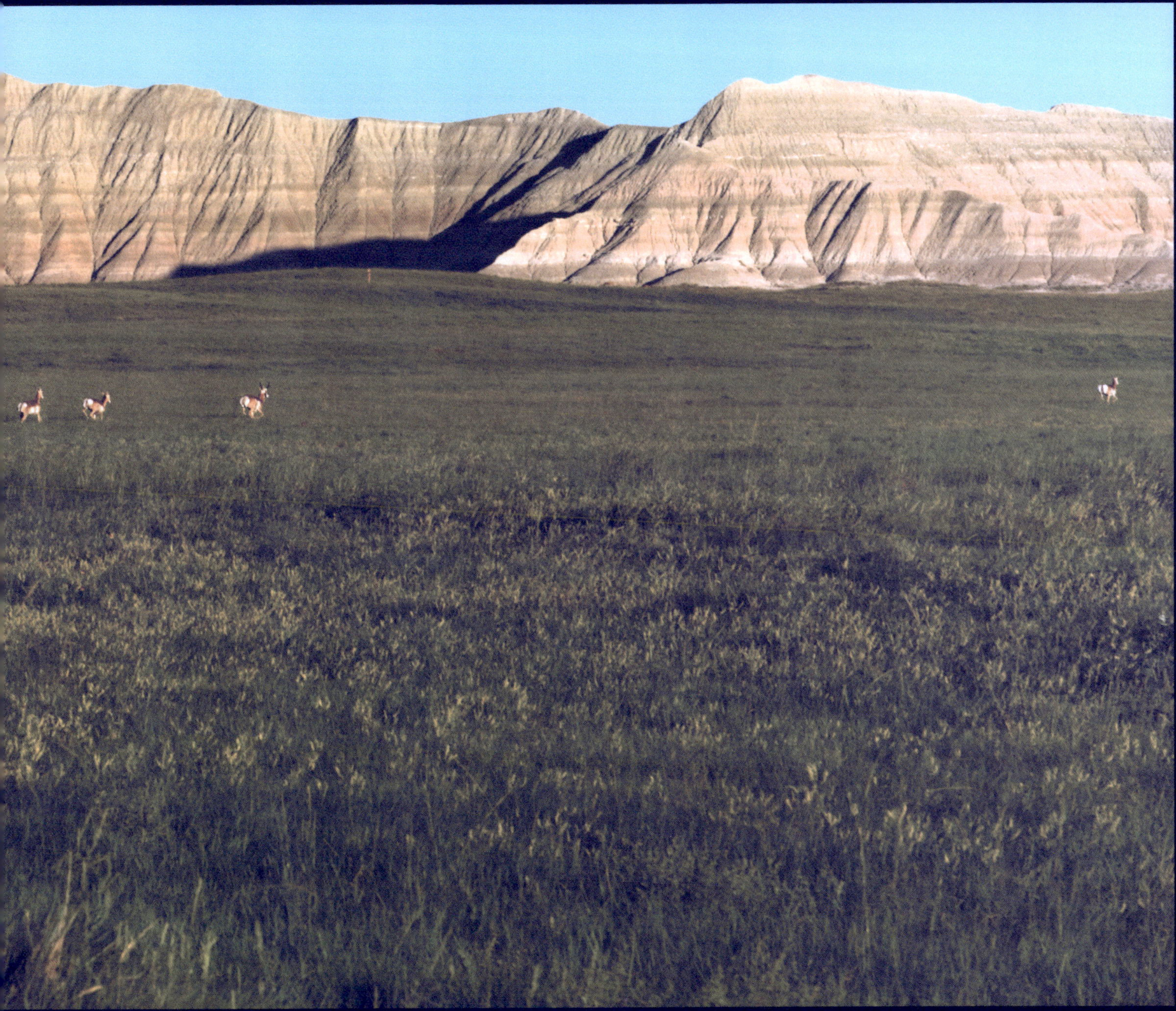

How?

How does it do it?
Relaxed, yet still posed for flight
In the blue light of dawn
One ear catching the new sun
Survival's promise.

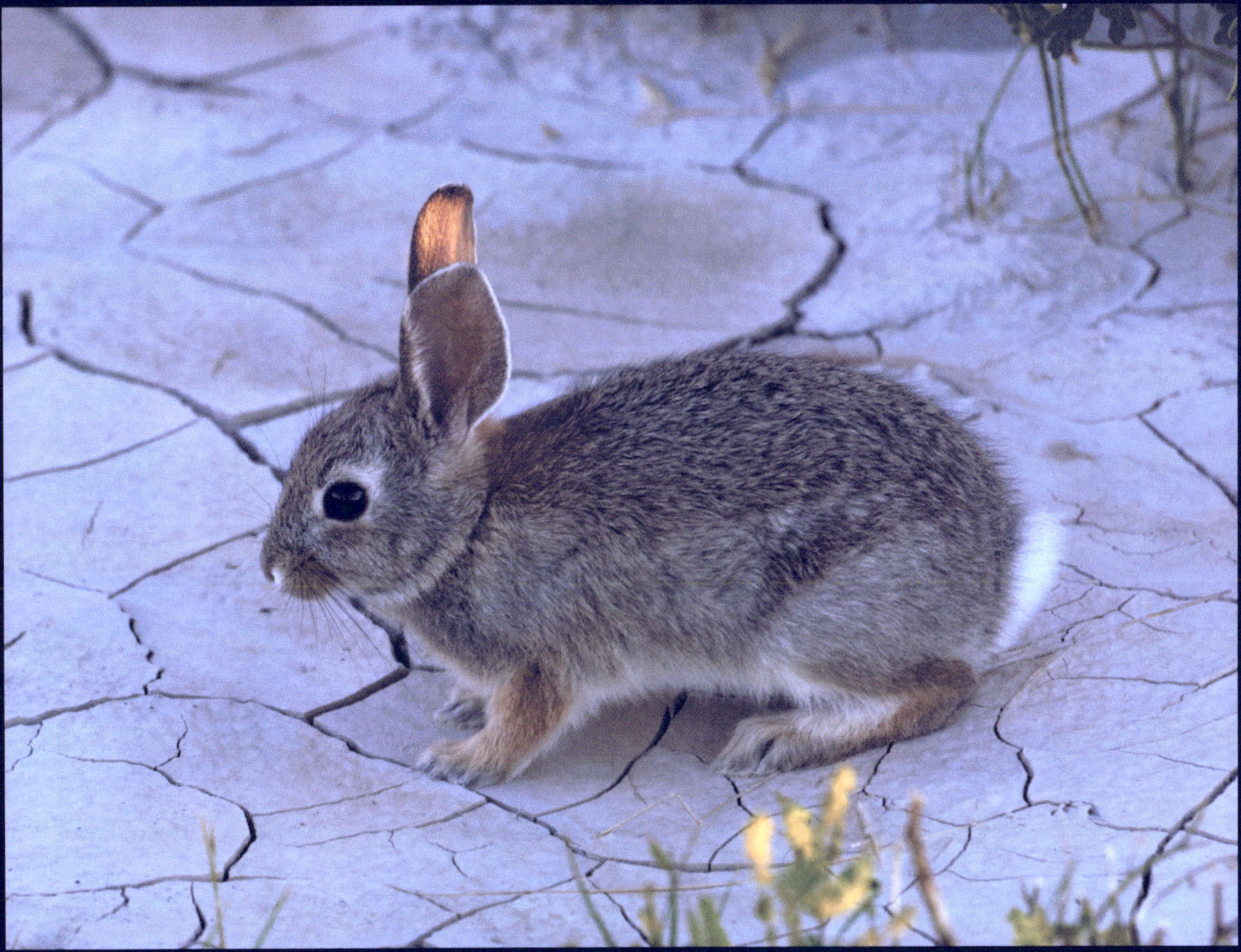

Intruders

It was all designed.
Layered rocks had been exposed,
Columns outlined bluffs.
There was a serenity
All camouflaged with drab gray.

But some things snuck in.
Likely they came from that crypt
There in the shadows
Where they'd waited patiently
For a place they could survive.

Now they're everywhere
Soil's accumulated
Changing day by day
They spread farther year by year
In many different phases,

With spring's arrival
They make themselves from nothing
Rising from the ground
Trimming the tedious gray
In a way the rocks never could.

There was a serenity

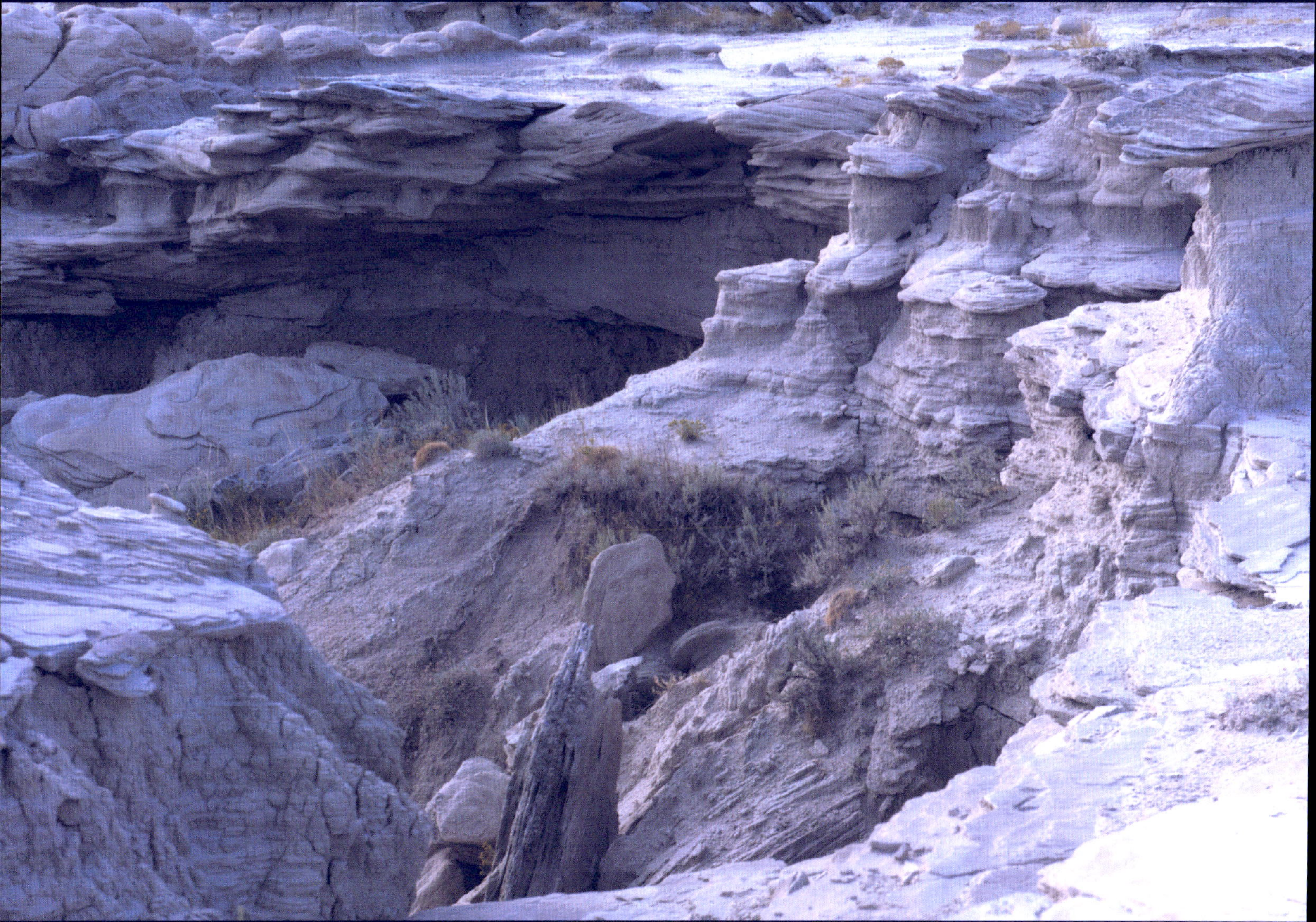

All camouflaged with drab gray

Options

That row of jagged hills
Points into the distance
With a goal in mind.
Perhaps the distant sunlight
Reflected off scattered clouds?

There's some flatland steppe
Along that row of steepened hills
A bit of prairie.
Shunning the dawning sunlight?
Dodging that distant mountain?

There're those flattened rocks
Aligned along a low ridge
Steering their own way
Toward neither sun nor mountain.
Nature has her options.

There's some flatland steppe
Along that row of steepened hills
A bit of prairie.

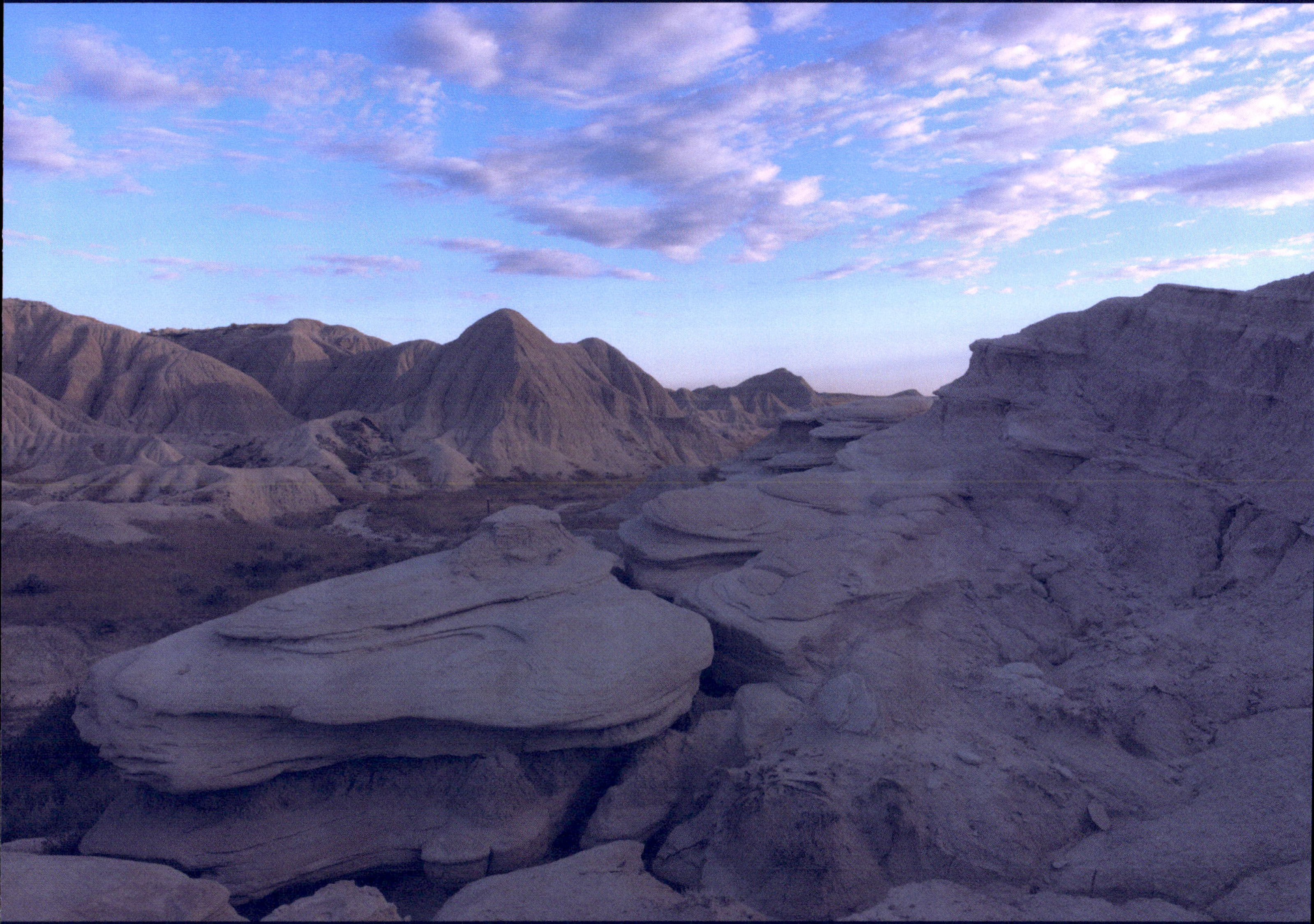

Parade

The crowd stood and cheered
The yearly river flow
Then forgot to leave
   When the flow ended

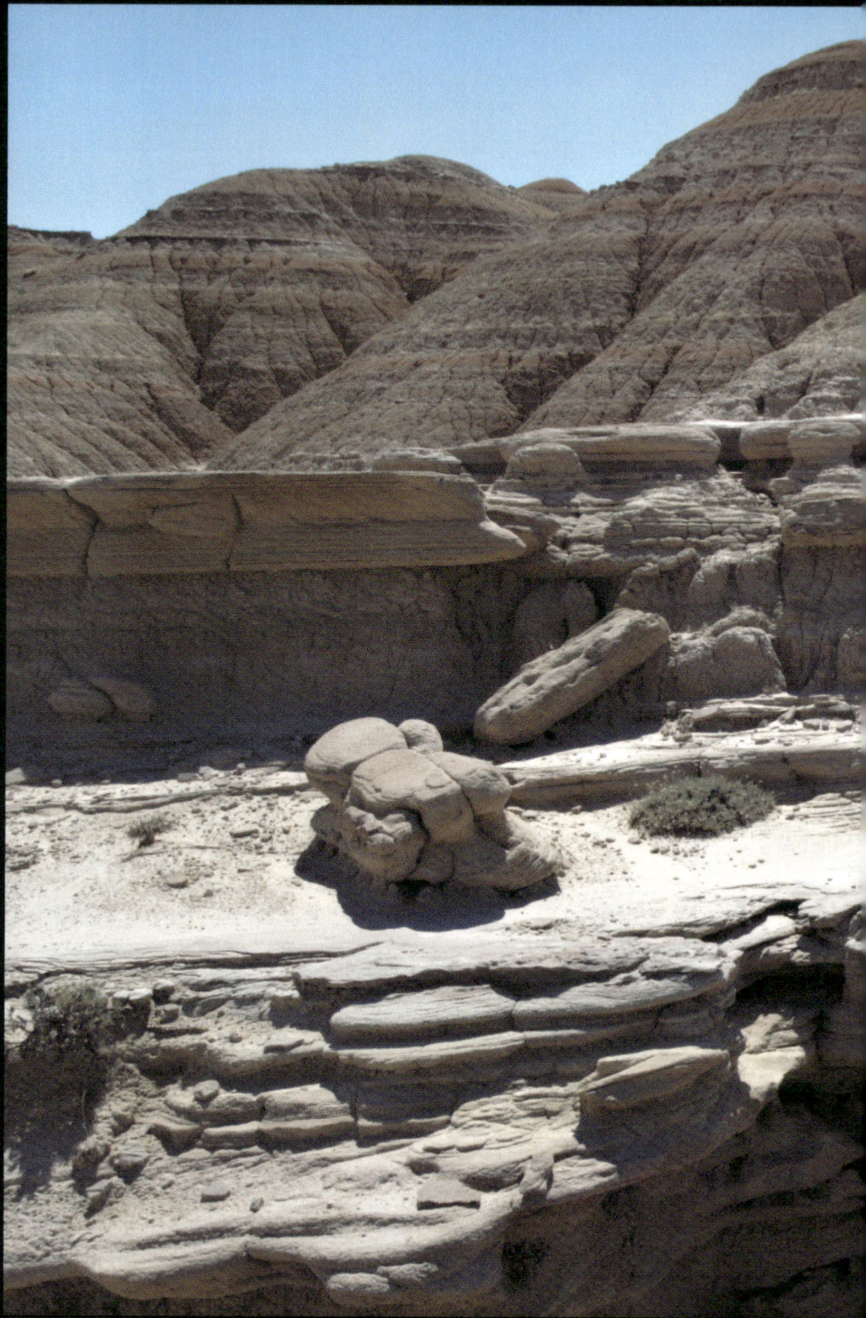

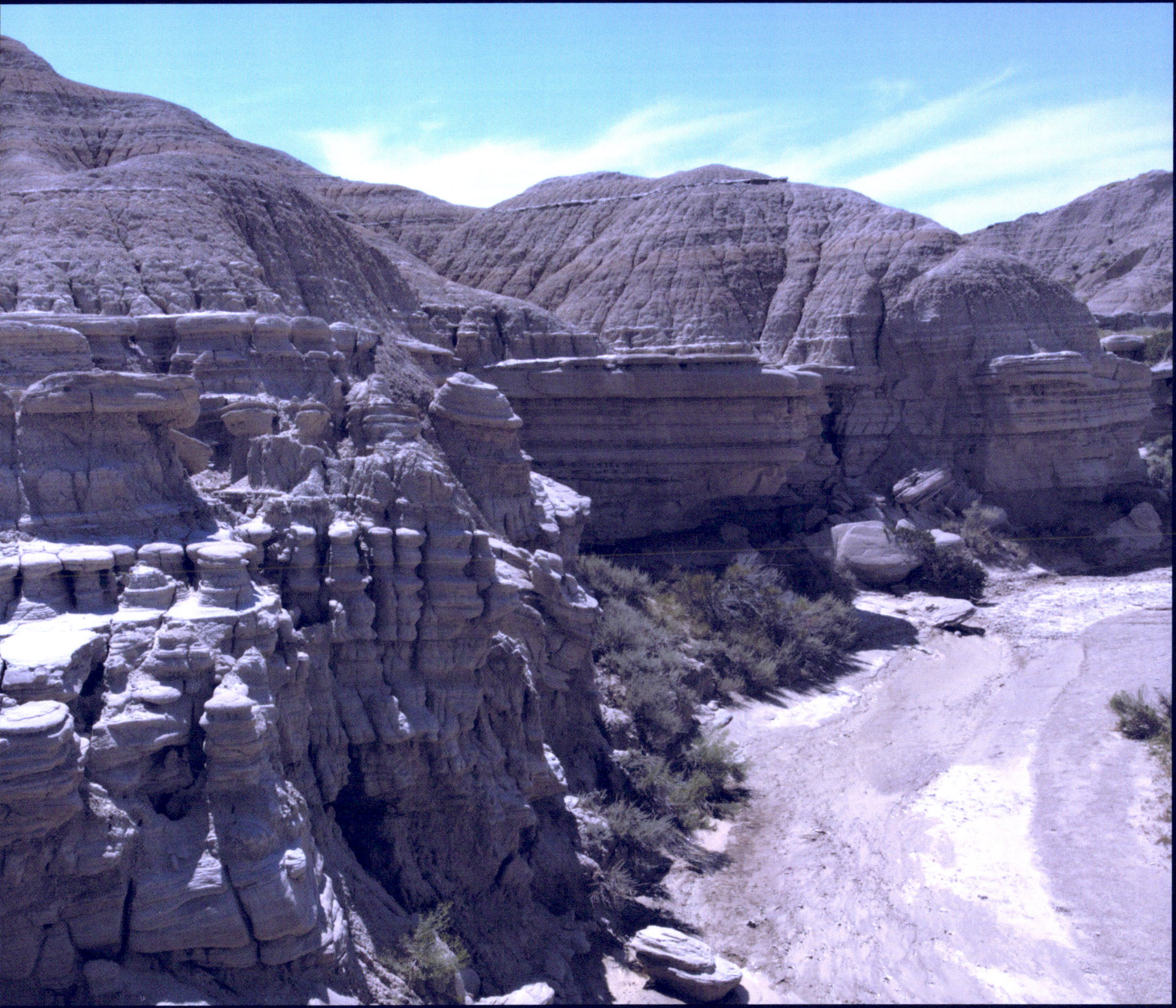

Thwarted Romance

Rock varves look down on
Pending romance thwarted by
A stone barrier.

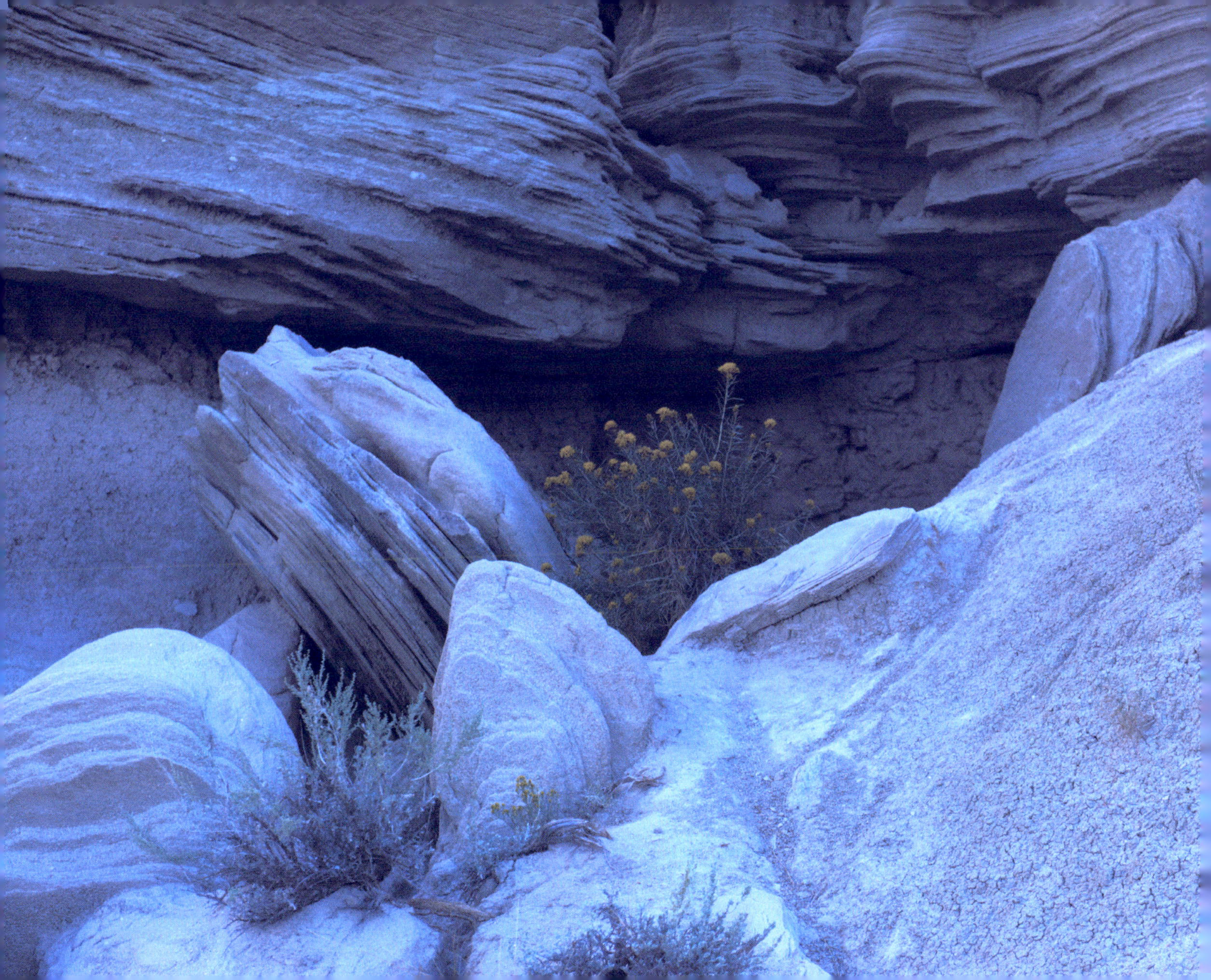

Holding On

I can hold on here.
Slopes are steep, soil's loose
And washing away.
But I remain confident.
I have the tools to hold on.

Roots, from the origin,
Defy the devious ground.
That's not surprising.
Soil lacks my advantage
Memories of survival.

Histories restored
With each threat to survival.
They're not always successful
But this is a game of odds
And dumb dirt don't stand a chance.

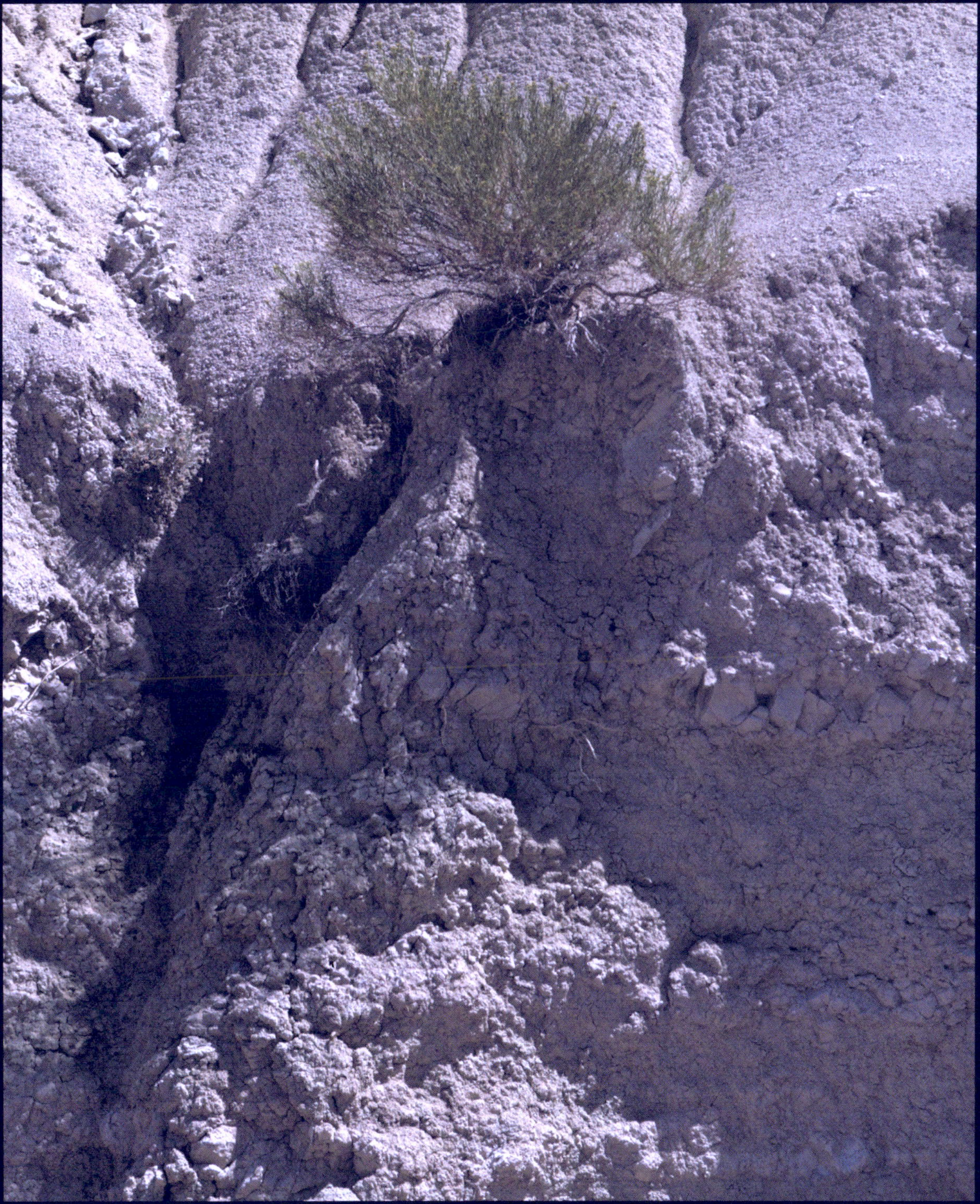

Mentzelia

We've made it here.
Coerced what water's available
Into a holy alliance.
We get to grow and, in return,
Keep some water in this place.

We've donned our protective garb
To keep four-legged water thieves at bay
And added chemical inducements
For animals to seek moisture elsewhere;
We're a pair to be reckoned with.

But not all animals are enemies.
We use our white flowers
Not to repel noxious animals
But to attract nocturnal fliers
Seducing them into a relationship.

They get food so they can survive.
We get pollen for seed
So next year the story's told again
And old friends can be revisited,
Like that ancient one behind us there.

We've added a lot to this place.
Were it not for us there'd be no more,
Than some friable white soil,
The odd animal passing through.
Life's meant to be more than that.

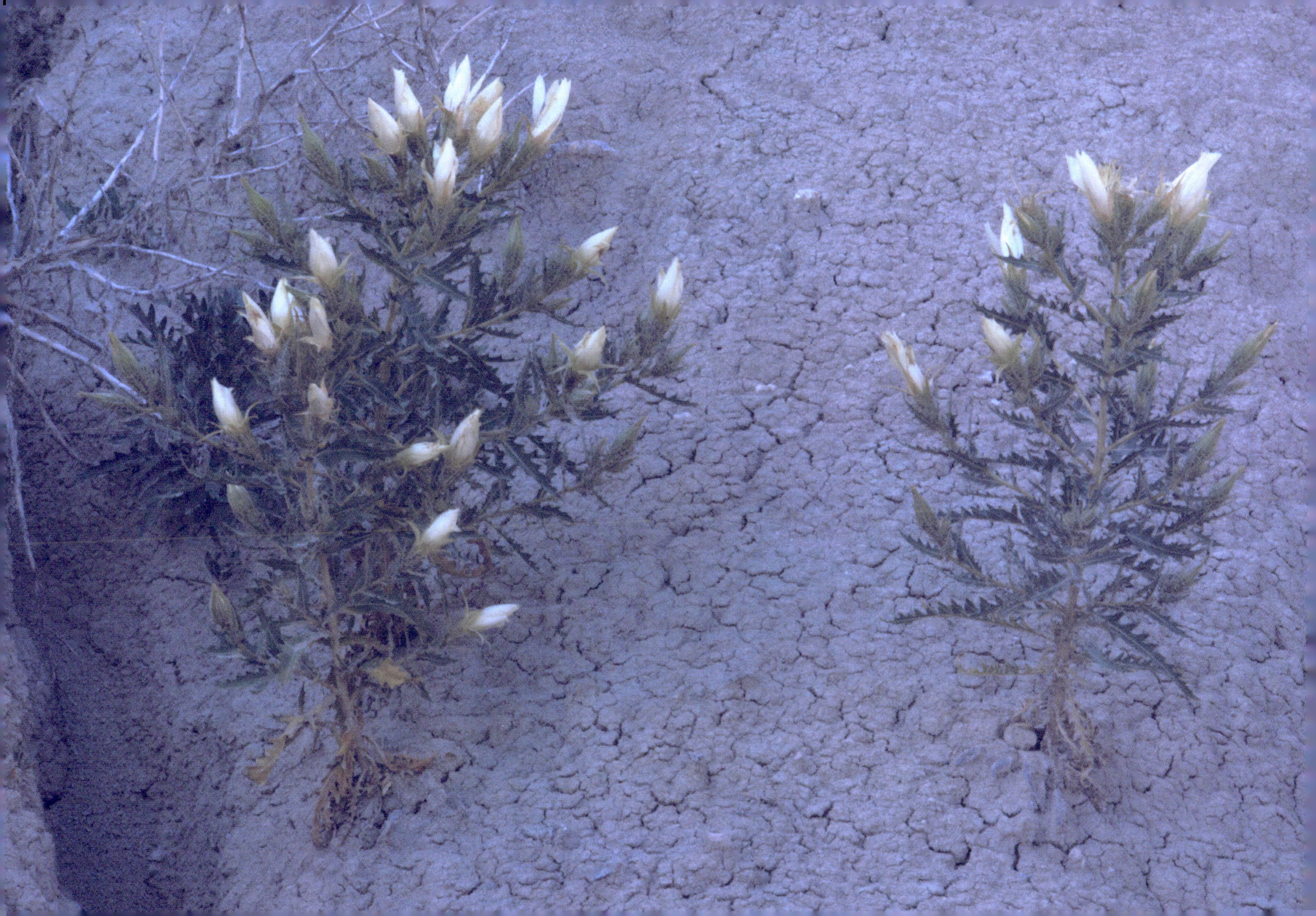

Release

Hills scored by water,
Rocks layered by wind,
Dictate where the shrubs can exist.
But look!

There's an opening!

If the shrubs get that far
They're free.
To follow the clouds east
And meet their kin.

Who've established themselves
In new homes;
They'll be free to explore
nothing to shade them.

And they can play in the sand.

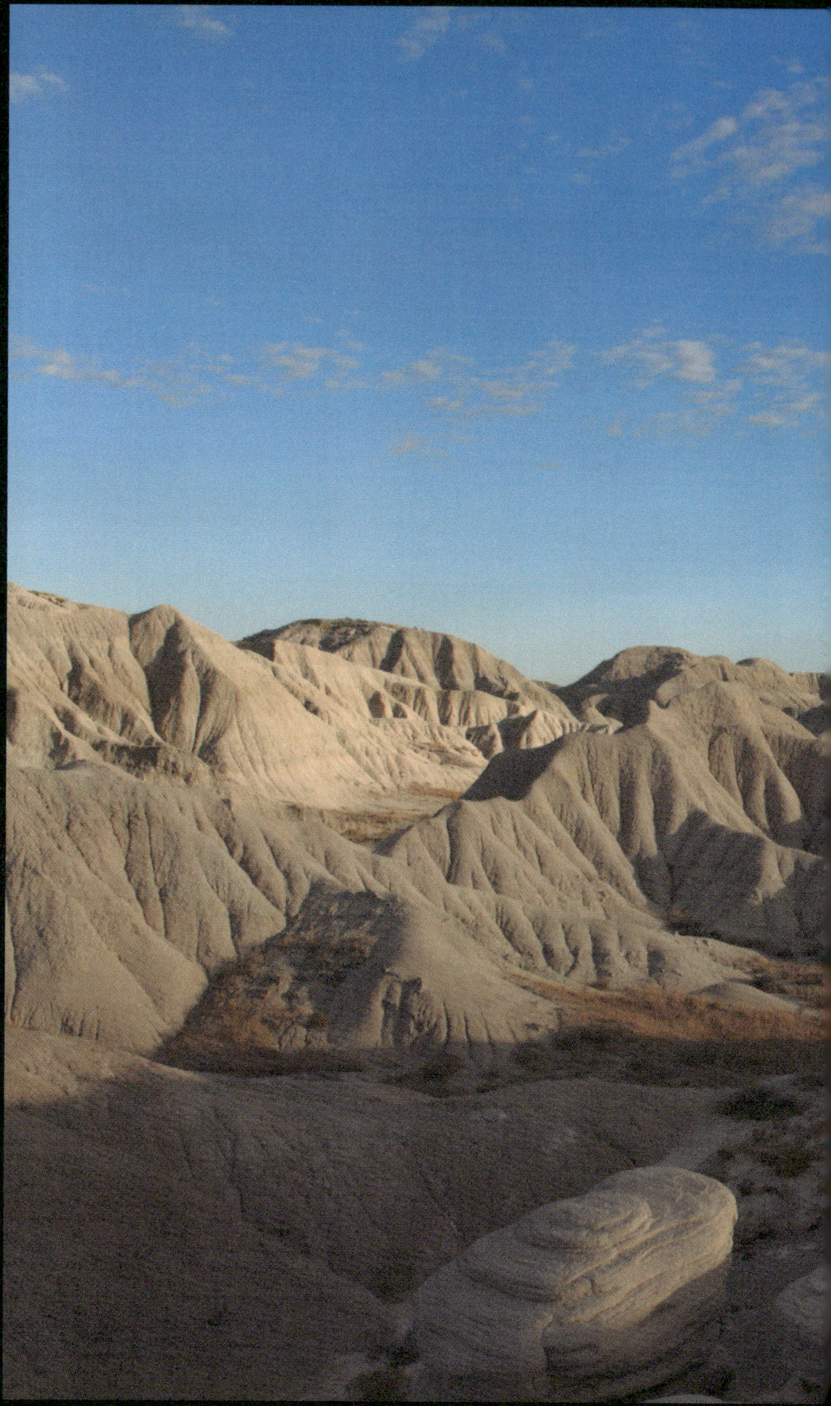

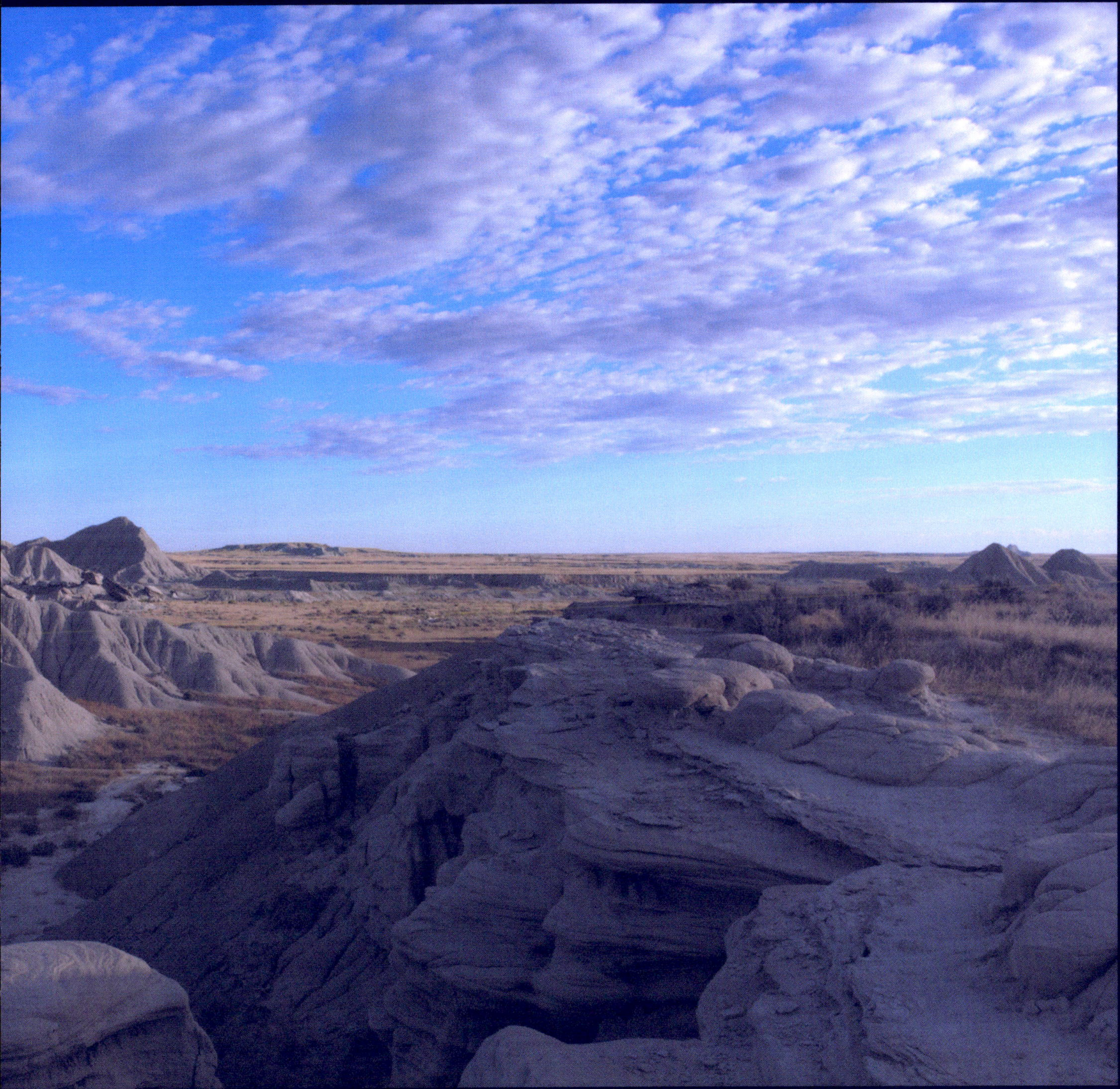

The Gift

It was rather bleak.
Soil, rocks, all dismal gray;
Twas monotonous.
Then a surprise gift arrived.
A bit more color, more complex.

Soil gave a home.
The rocks opened up their arms
For security.
All had existed as form
With substance came a new grace.

A surprise gift arrived.
A bit more color, more complex.

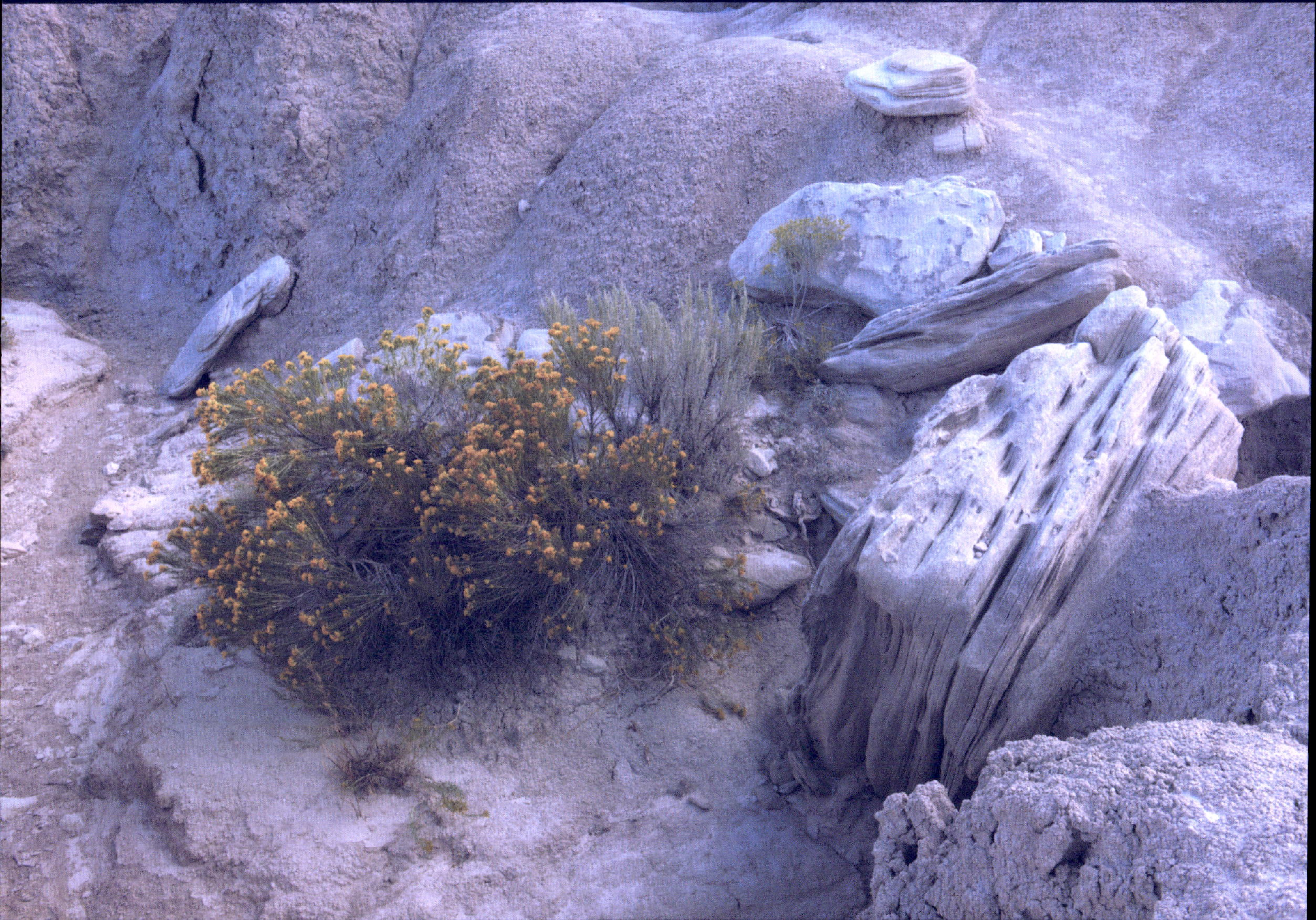

Late afternoon

The sun is setting,
Shadows lengthen in the canyons
Revealing details
On hillside surfaces
Uniform in noon sunshine.

The day's heat has freed
The smell of dry grass and sage
Flooding the air
With memories of the day
And promises of night's rest.

The hills don't need to sleep
They stand at ease, unchanging day to day.
But not so the steppe.
Life has extracted a levy.
It must if it is to survive.

Parts are grazed away
Is the price that's wrung
Overnight the next day's ante is made.
Dawn brings renewal;
Steppe regeneration.

And with the morning
The daily cycle begins anew
Rejuvenated steppe
Will, again, respond
To the day events.

Once again sunlight
Will be trapped as parts of plants
To be presented
To grazers so they survive.
And do the plants benefit?

Not really.
They're just altruistic.

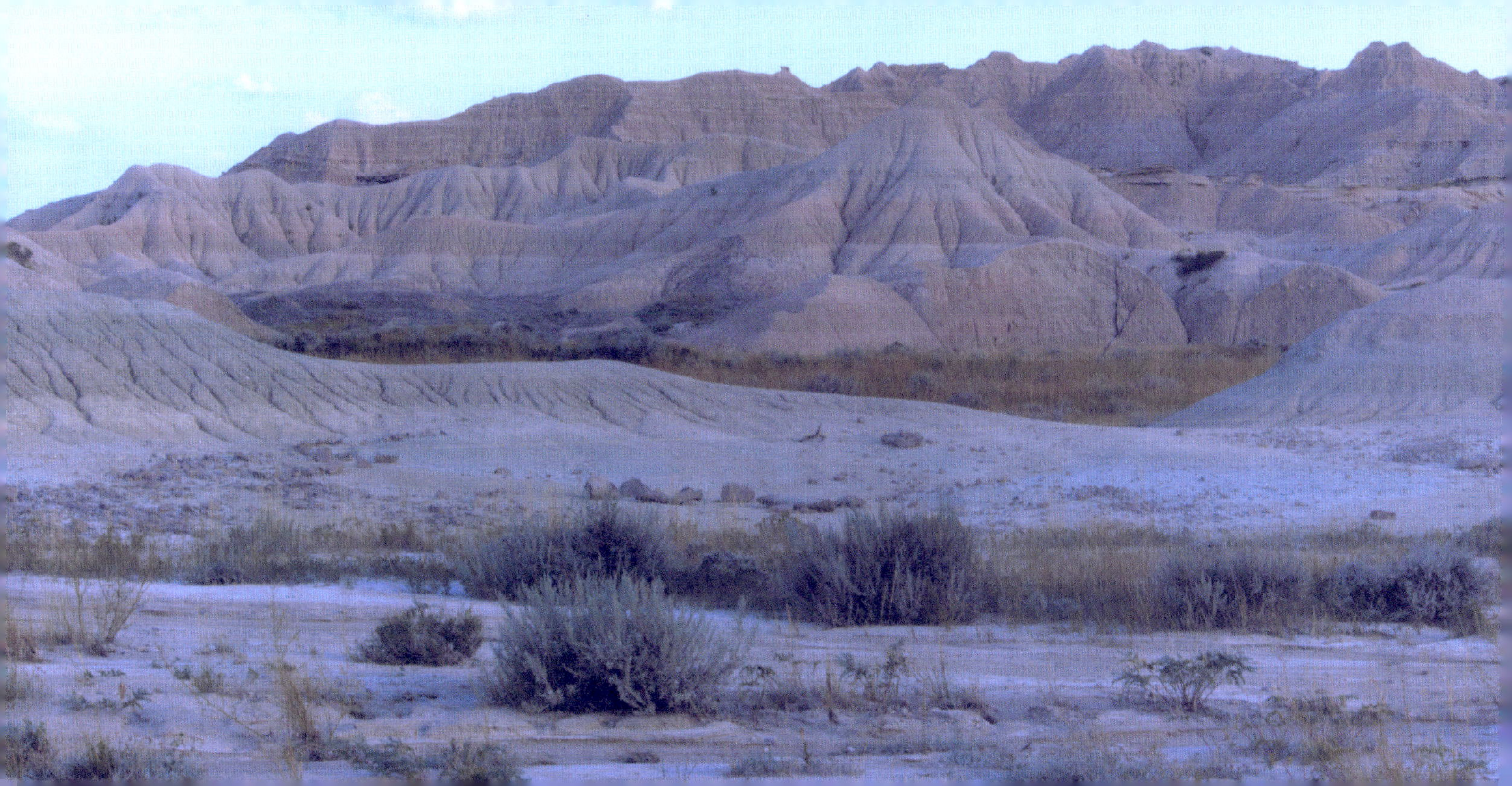

What If

How would this place be
  If plants could grow on these slopes?

There'd be no
  Little gullies cut by water
  Reflection of the morning sun
    Highlighting surface texture
  Welcoming beacon for a wanderer
  Nothing to contrast with
    Grasses and shrubs below
    Bushes above.

I like plants
  But on these slopes they have no place
    They mute the voice of the terrain
    The echoing whispers that envelop the watcher
      Encouraging immobility.

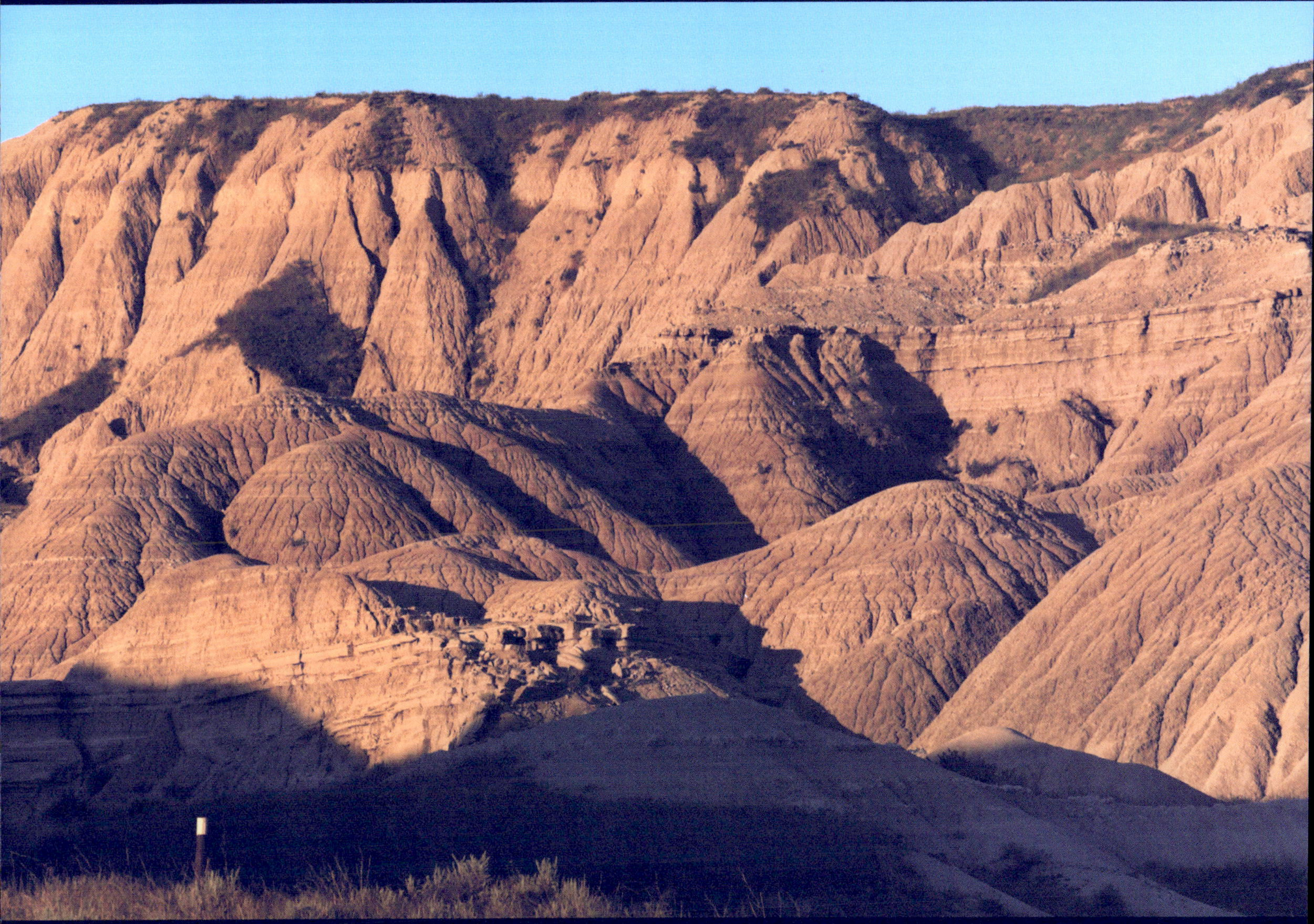

Plants Seeking

There're open lands on the hills up above.
  Ecologists call it an "unoccupied niche".

The plants could see the open lands,
  New space available to them.

Explorers were sent to seek out paths
  Leading to the open lands.

But the hills didn't want the plants
  Messing up their pristine slopes,
    Hiding the runnels and strata
      That decorate their surface.

Fortifications were built,
  Buttressed by rocks,
    Forming a picket-line of defense.

Soil was loosened
  So rain would wash it away
    Denying the plants a root hold.

I doubt the plants will be successful
  In their bid for the open lands
    To occupy a new niche;

The defenses of the hills are daunting,
  Well planned.

The hills will be pleased.

The plants will be disappointed.

But what about the ecologists
  And their "open niche"?

The hills likely don't care,
  Nor the plants.

And if they don't,
  Why should I?

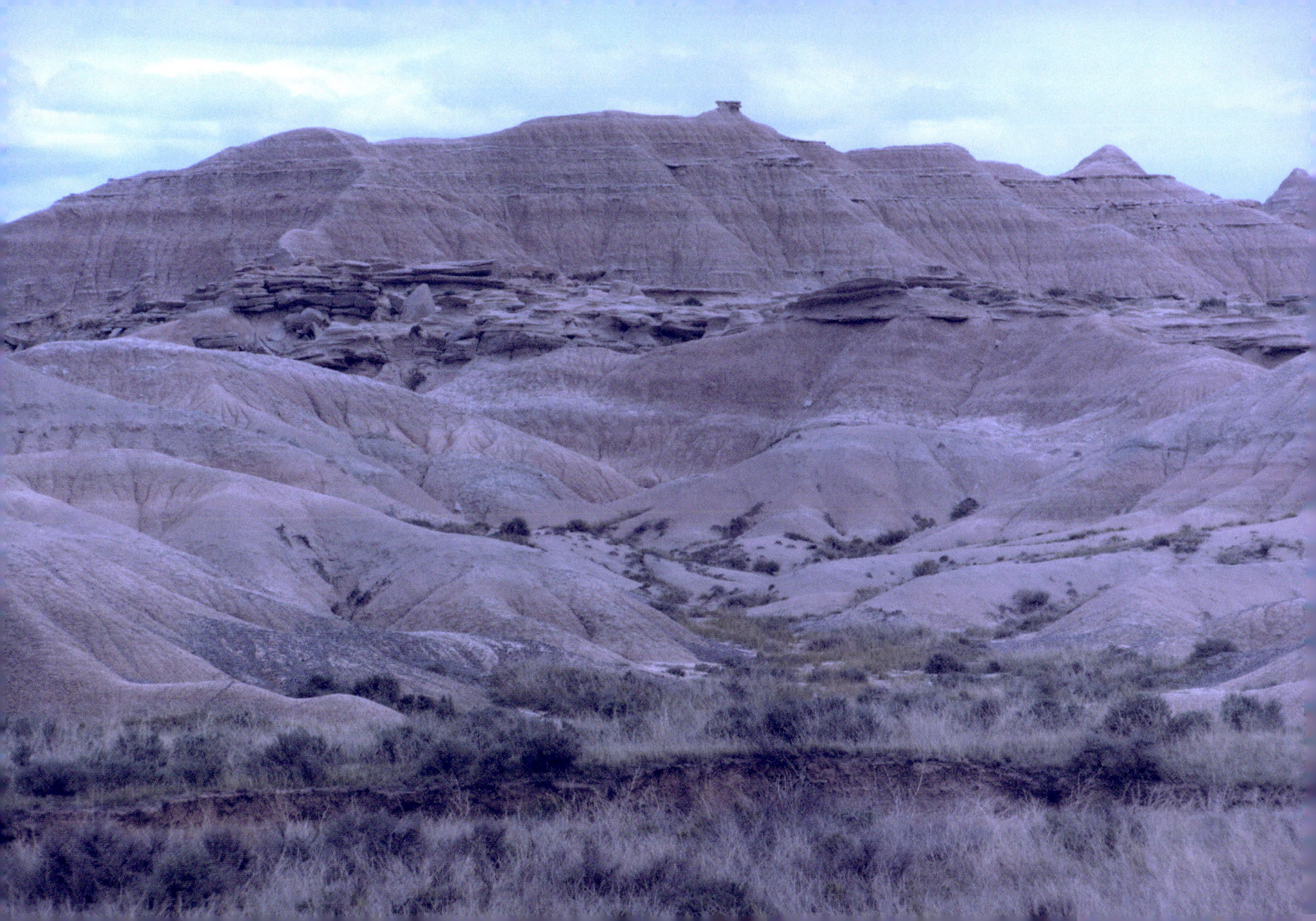

Desert Hillside

Desert Hillside

I don't understand
Soil washes down
But not color,
What maintains that contrast,
Peak to vale?

And why the contrast
Look closely and see subtle
Grey and red.
And different textures are there.
Some softer, some harder.

If we knew enough,
Or could stand here for eons
Would we see the colors appear
And the different textures develop;
This hillside unfold before us?

Look below that colored slope.
To that flat land there below,
Formed by flowing water
There plants can explore for sites
Where they can stay, to grace the countryside.

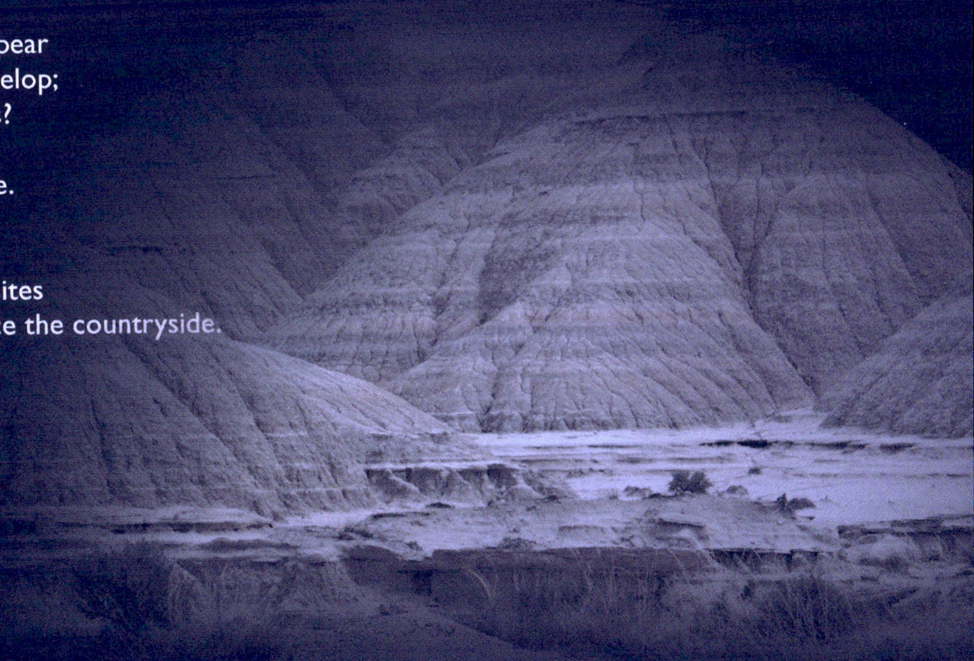

Seeing

That slope catches the eye.
Bands of gray and red
Tied together by many small runnels.
Woof and warp
Weaving a subtle tapestry
To drape on a desert hillside;
Decoration to atone for a lack of plants.

There's a trap for past climates,
Wetness and iron oxidized red.
Dryness and a soil that's gray.
Rain on that slope carrying away soil
Unprotected by plants.
There's a history there
A story to tell.

You can sit and watch the sun and soil
Play off against each other
Never the same,
  Hour to hour,
  Day to day,
  Season to season.

You can sit and watch history and beauty
Play off against each other
One there, one emerging
  Hour by hour,
  Day by day,
  Season by season.

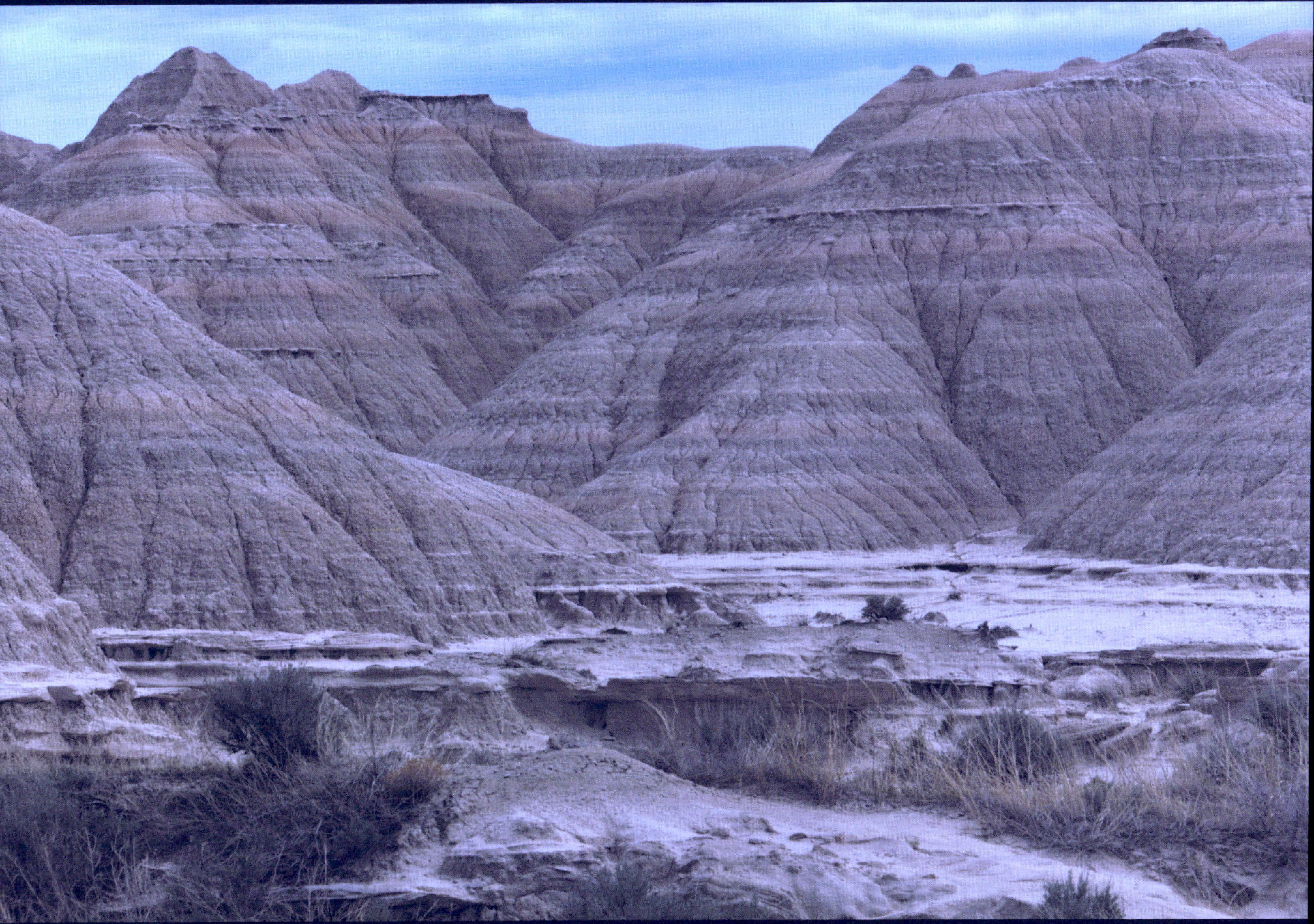

Hill's Gift

Glance once, not much there.
Look again, open your mind,
To delicate hues.

The gift from the hill.
Soil carried down, leaving
Small gullies behind.

More than soil flowed.
Blue hues flowed downward as well
So colors were shared.

There's fruitfulness too.
When the blue hues flowed downward
Lowlands were enriched.

And from enriched lowlands
Plants could grow so the hills
Would be entertained.

And we could appreciate subtlety.

The gift from the hill.
Soil carried down, leaving
Small gullies behind.

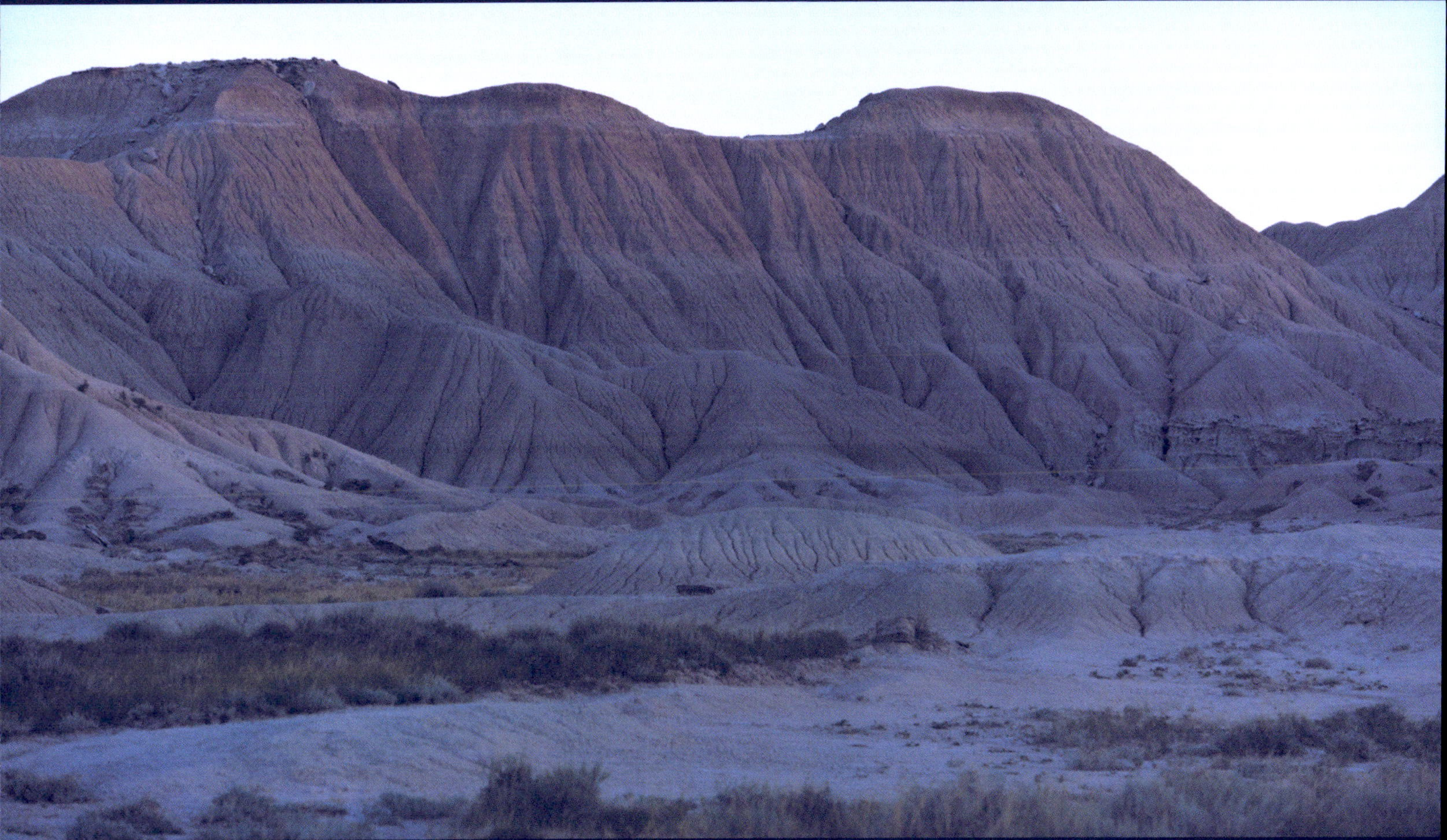

A Good Place

This is a good place
The hills deliver water
And don't block the sun.

It is a garden
Plants are growing there, and hills
Offer protection.

It's a place to rest
Surrounded by hills, with
Shrubs to perfume the air.

What do we have here?
Sand, hills, rocks, little gullies.
Yes, and spring's promise.

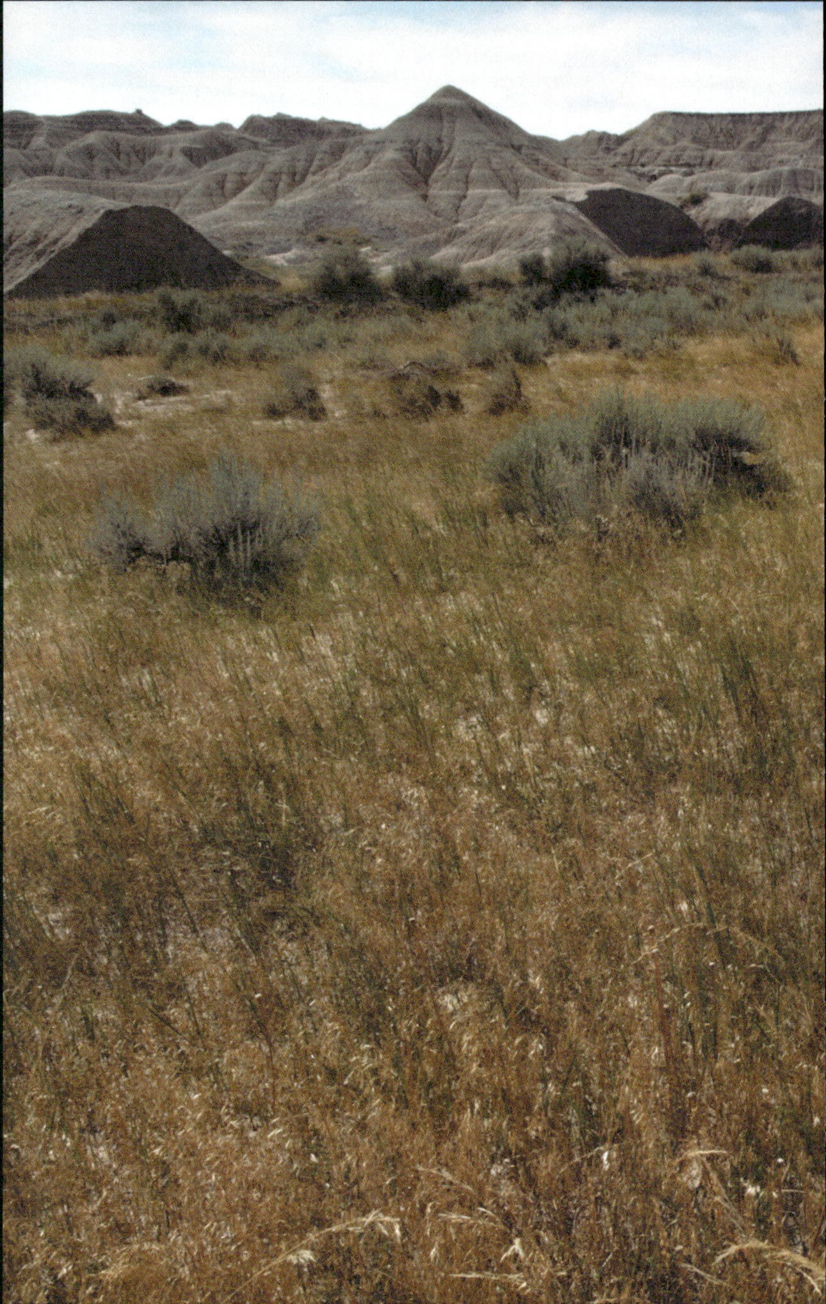

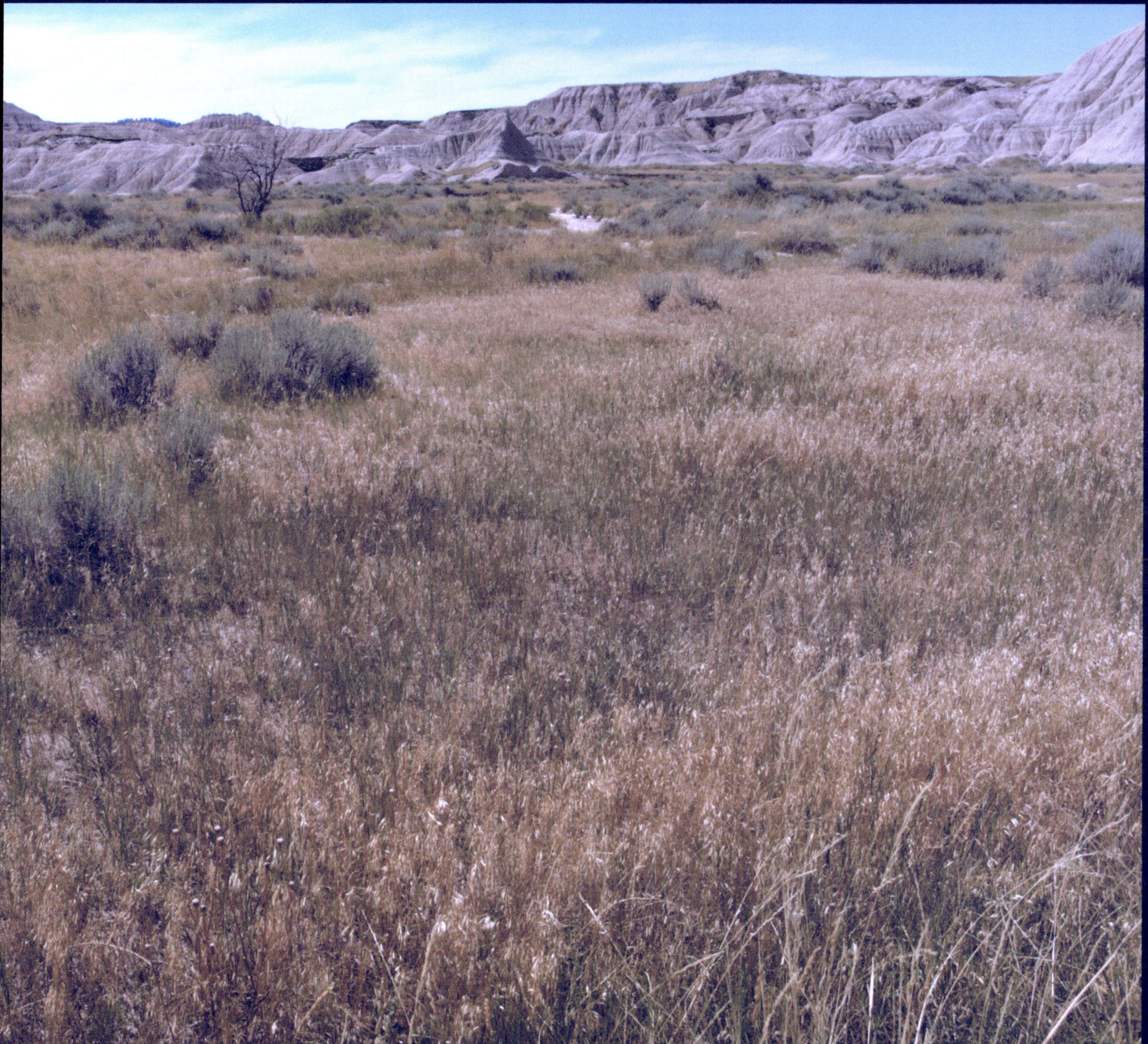

What's That

What's that over there?

The mighty hunter
  In his deer-stalker hat
  With his trusty piece?
That bothersome brother-in-law
  With his inane chatter
  And attempts to sell snake-oil?

Both can be avoided.

Between the two of them you'd discover neither
  Two neurons
  Nor one functional synapse.
A couple of hops, two side steps
  And they couldn't find me
  With radar, GPS, and a pack of blood hounds.

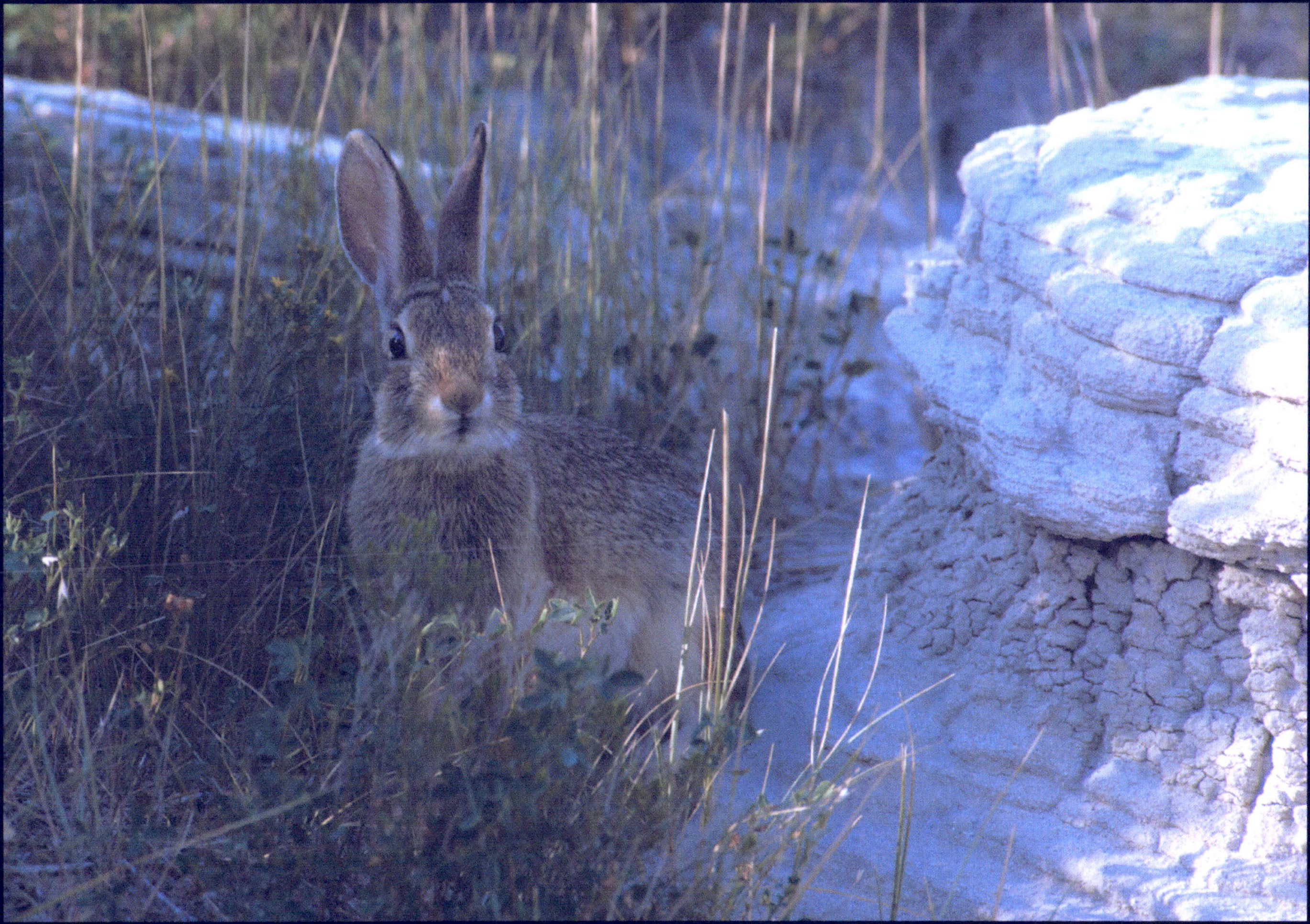

Choices

Where do I go?

Narrow my focus to the head of this draw
  Luxuriate under these bushes
  Feel their protection
  Take in their fragrance?

Move down that draw
  Guided by low ridges
  Along a route unencumbered by plants
  Following an old water course?

Venture out into the grassland
  Explore between the dense stems
  Sense their wiry toughness
  Breach in their crisp cleanliness?

Move beyond the grassland to that low ridge
  Bleached by its history and the sun
  Devoid of vegetation
  With protecting ravines cut by erosion?

Think I'll go with the ridge.
  It's simpler but still pretty
  And when the ridge's attained
  Limits dissolve.

And more peaks
  And more ridges
  And more grassland
  Are all revealed.

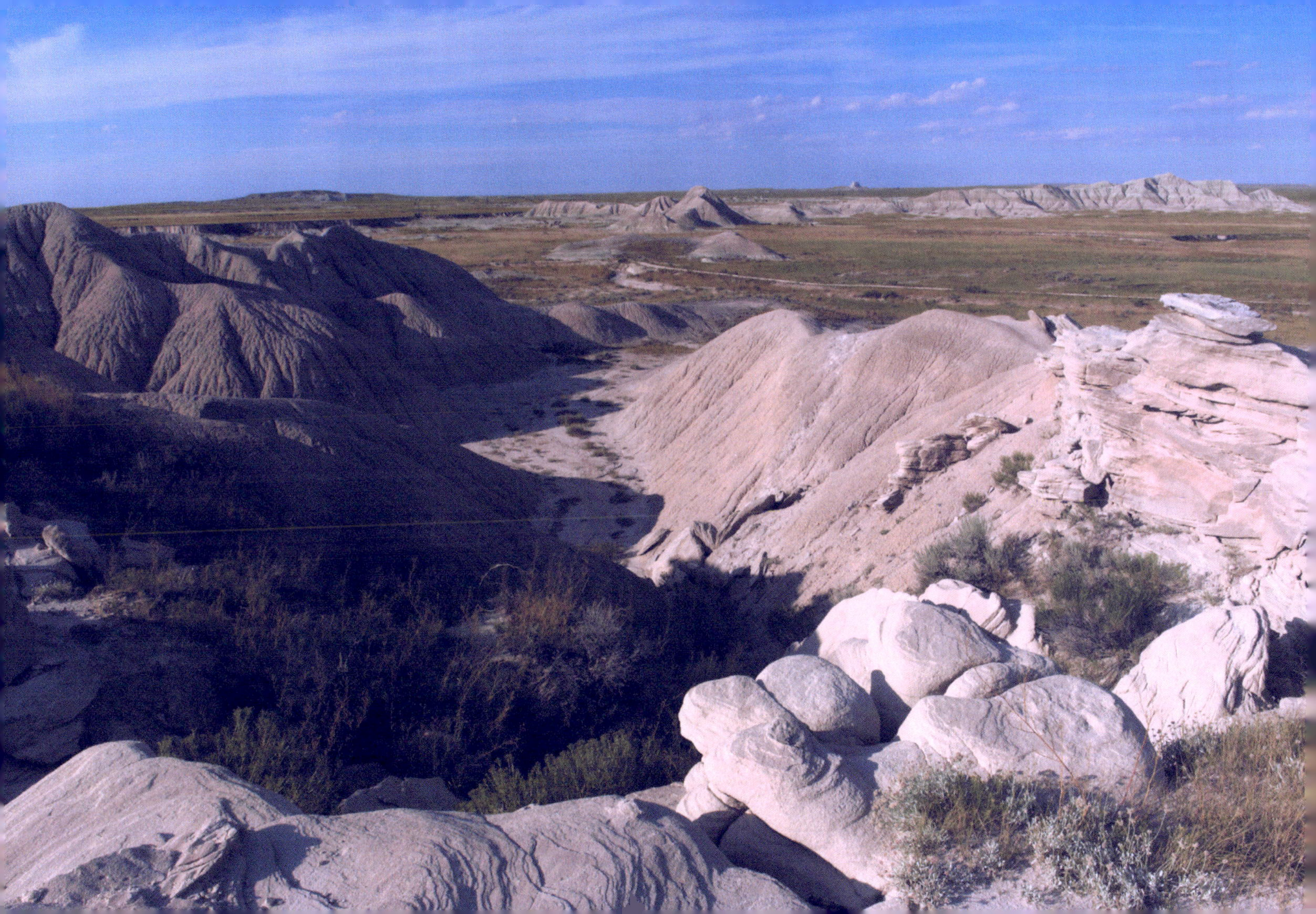

Don't Fret

It appears to be an unhappy scene
It's dry
The plants look dead
But looks do so deceive

Now it's dry, yes
But water's flowed in the past
You can see its path it left
When it flowed down the hills, across the valley floor.

The plants may look dead
But they're alive
You can find yesterday's history, tomorrow's potential
Within their bodies.

No goddess would abandon her creation to death
She's sent her emissaries,
Clouds to evaluate and report
So she'll know when it's time to act.

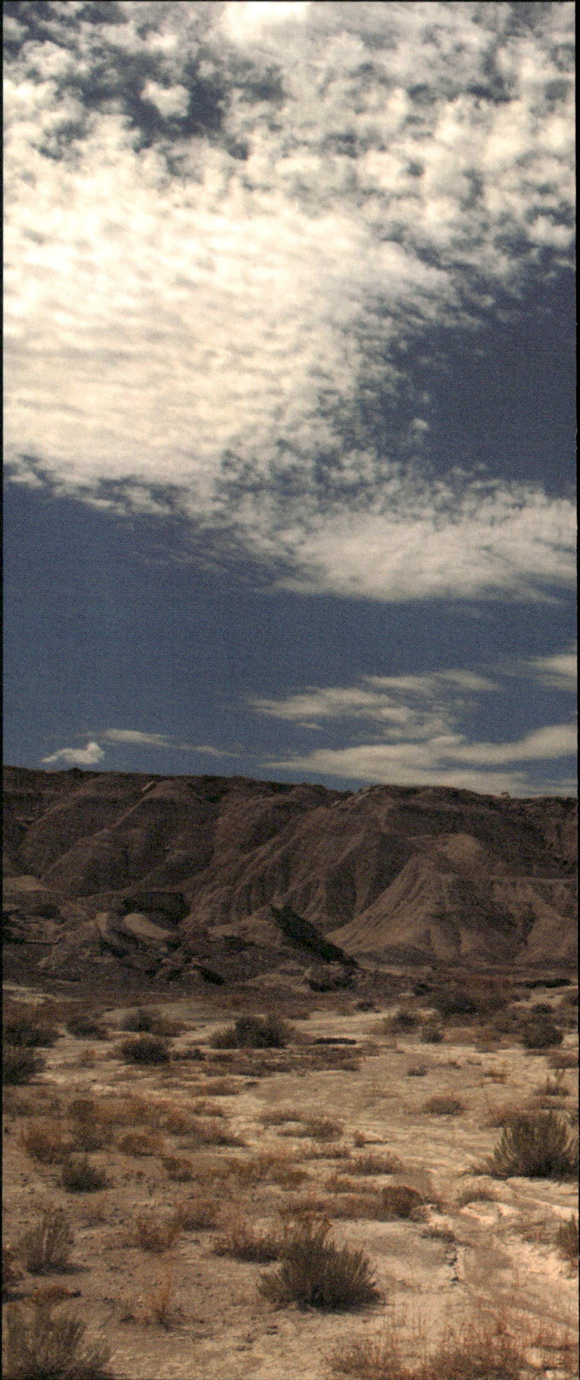

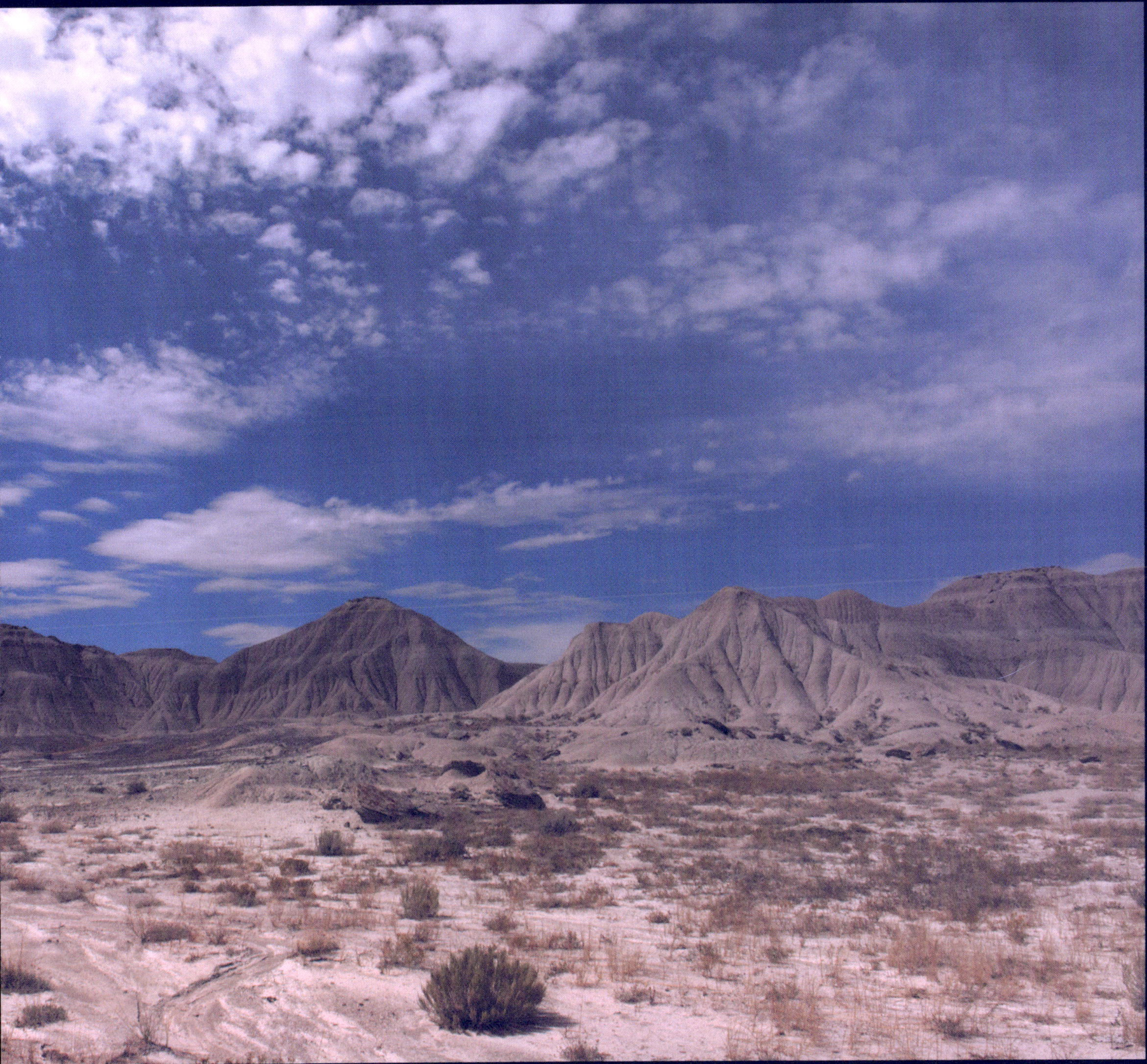

Why the Sage is Gray

Sagebrush wasn't born gray.
No, it started out green
  Like all other plants.

But then it started to wander west
  Until it came to this place
  Where it wanted to stay.

So it asked the hills' permission
  To enjoy life here.

The hills were pleased with the company
And asked that the sage to take on some of their color
  So other wanderers would be attracted.

The grasses then came

And the steppe was formed.

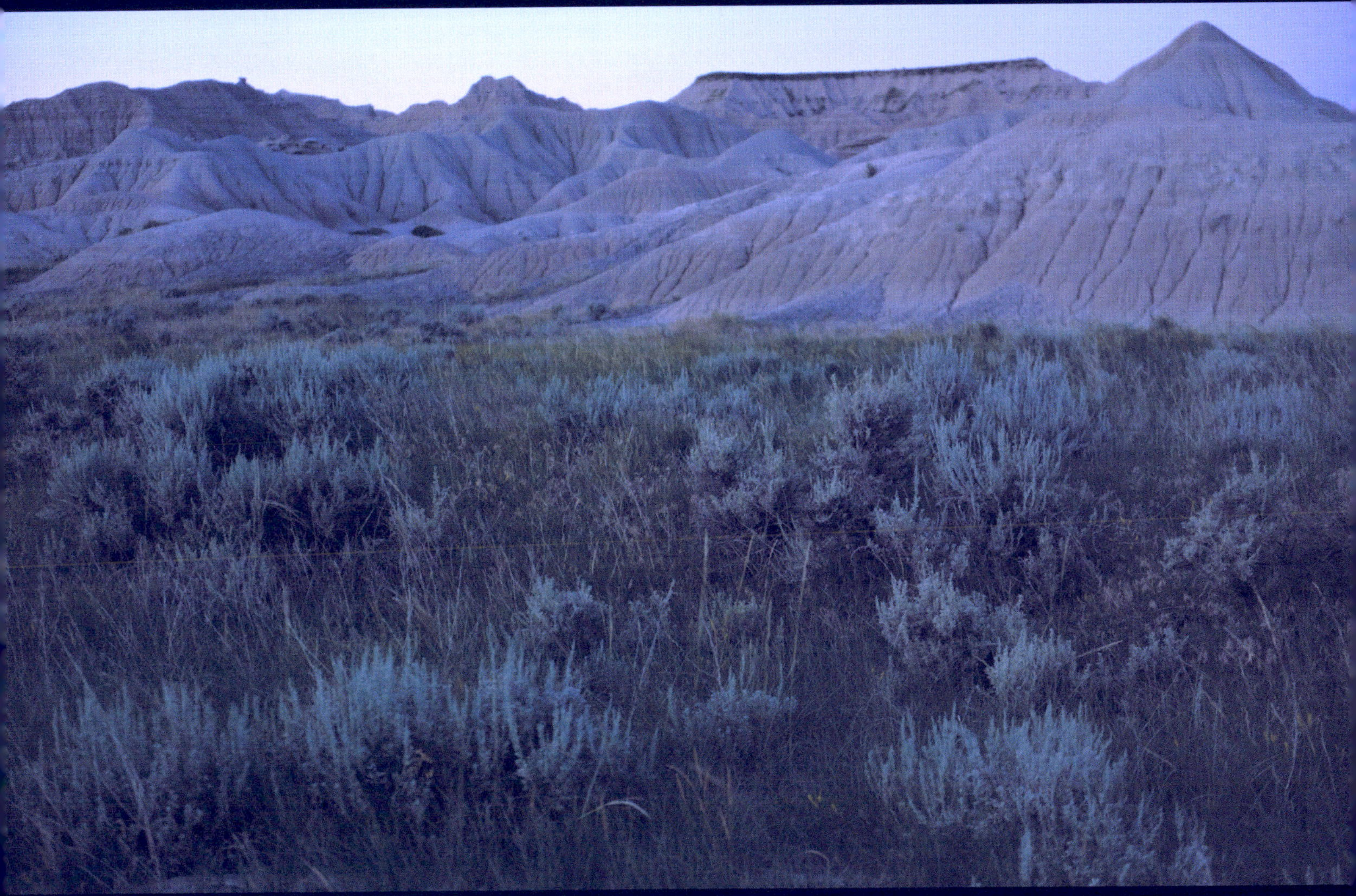

Grasses and Shrubs

Grass, shrubs gray and green
Grow densely intermingled
On soil washed down
From surrounding hills
By intermittent rain

The mat that they form
Is an offering of thanks
To the hills above
For soil in which they grow
For water which spurs them along.

The plants take these two,
The water and the soil
And make a perfume
Of dry grass and scented sage
To convey their offering.

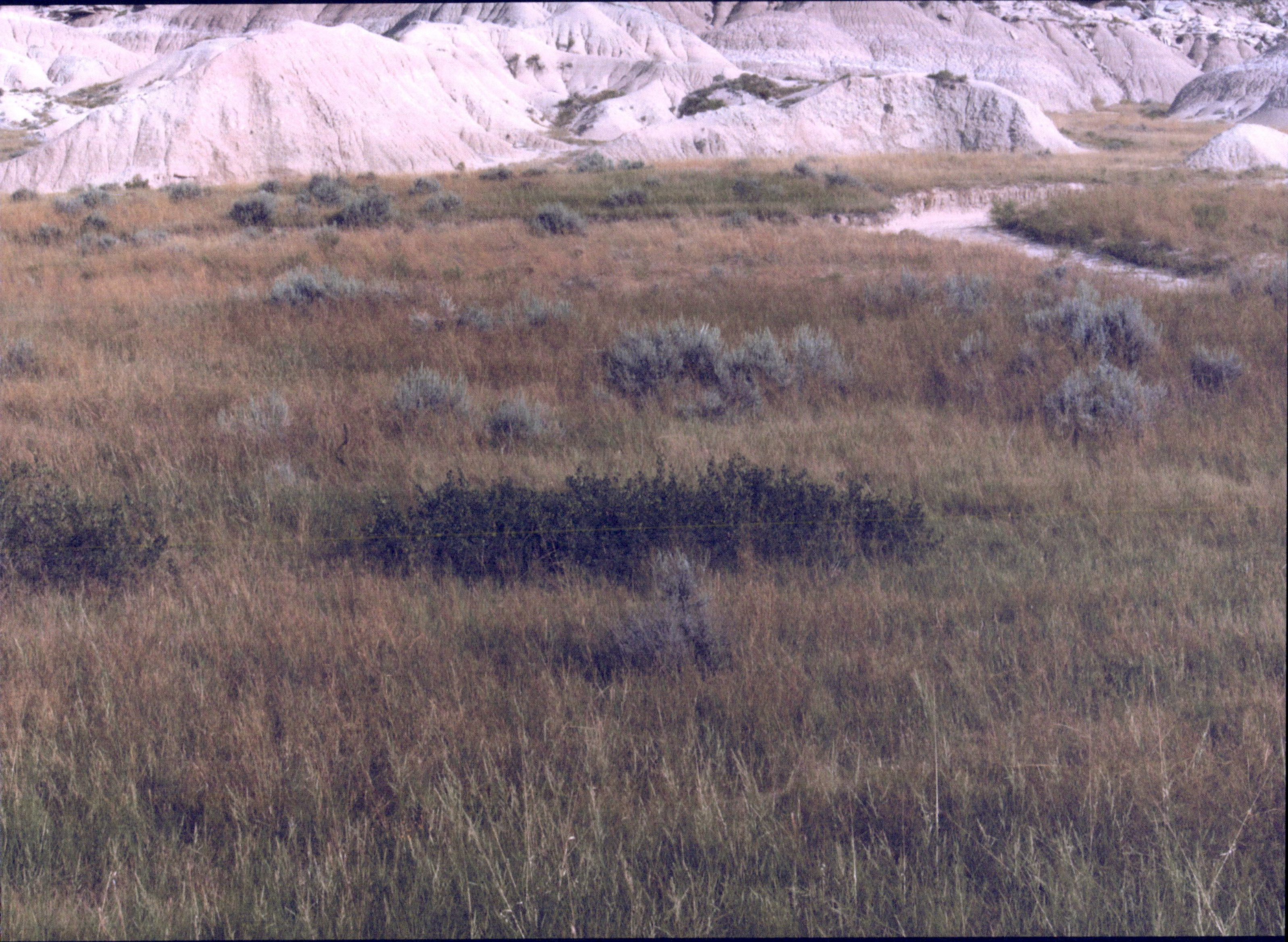

Day's End

As the daylight wanes
   sunlight lingers,
Trapped in lichens
   on rock surfaces.
And the earth and the heavens
Have an extended farewell.

The earth and the heavens
have an extended farewell.

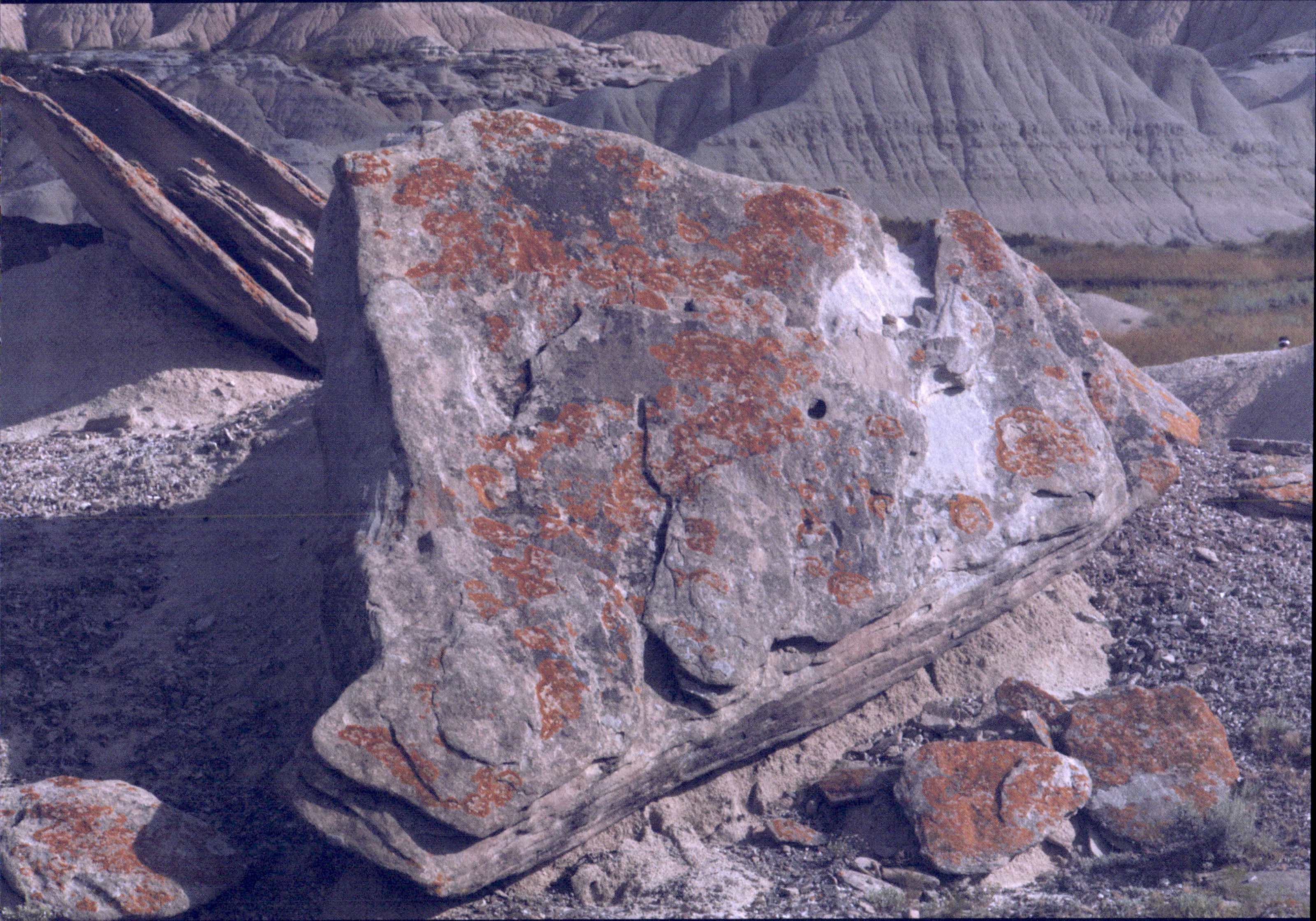

Sleeping Steppe

The steppe is sleeping
Waiting for the dawn, previewed
On the hills above.

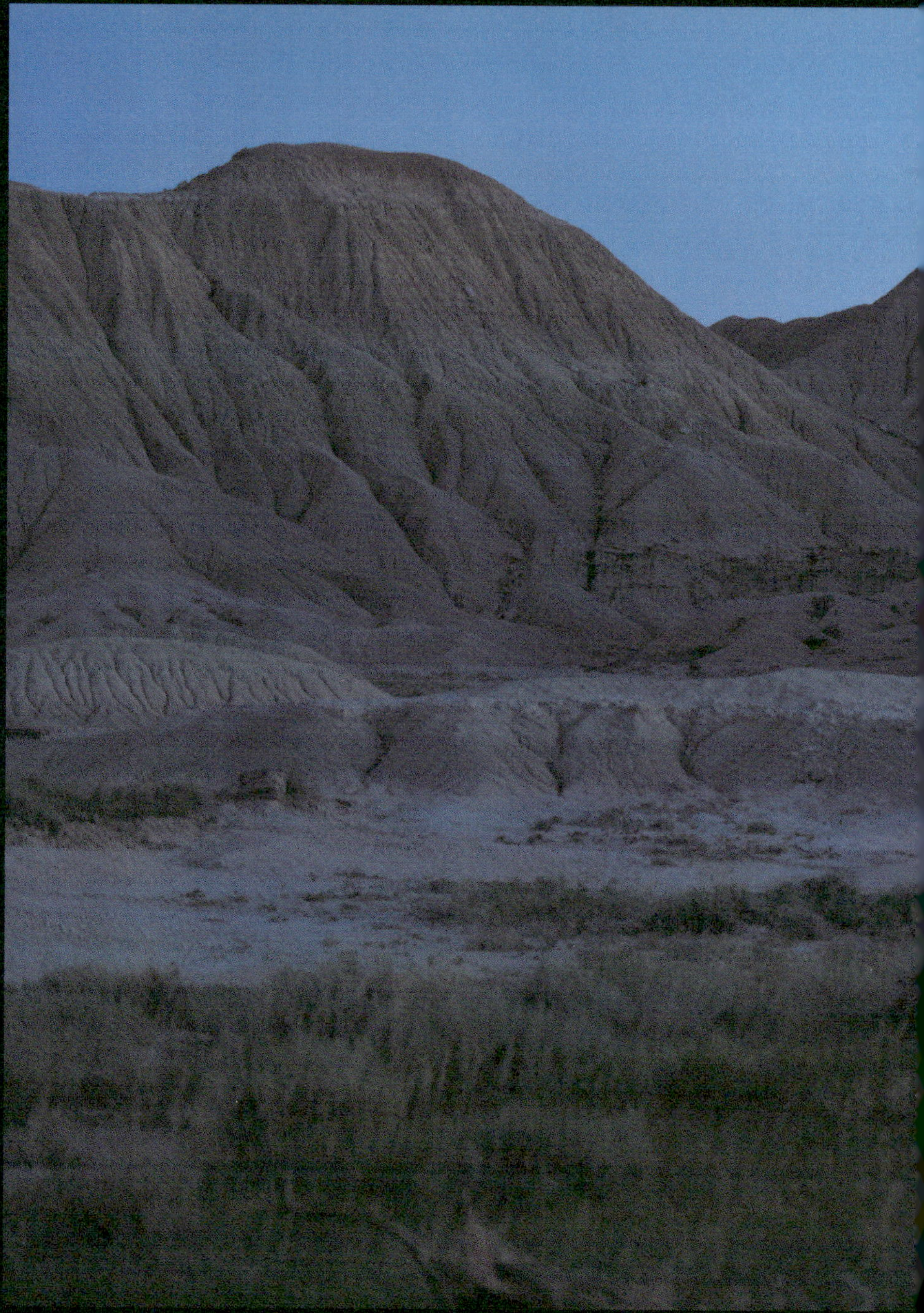

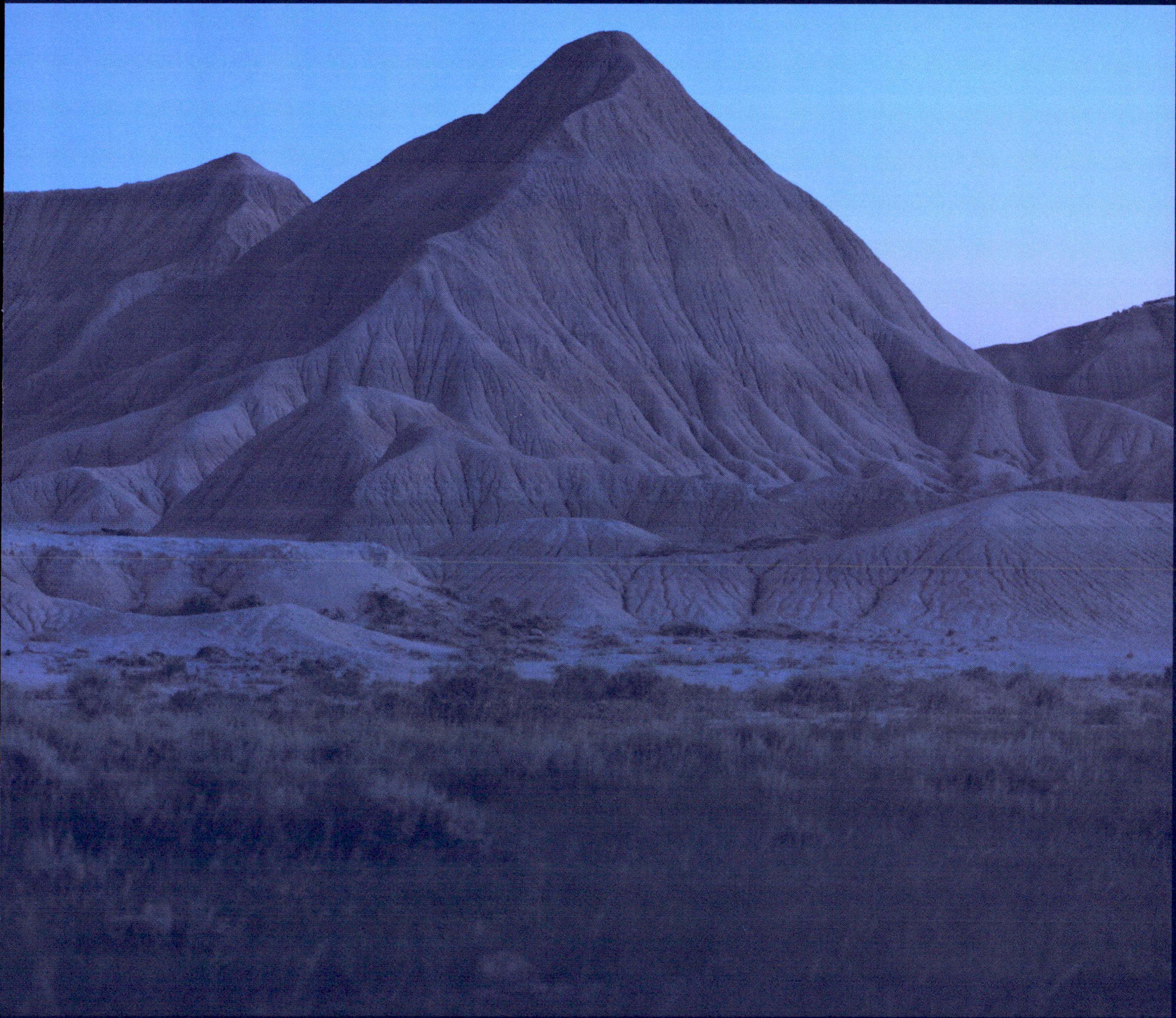

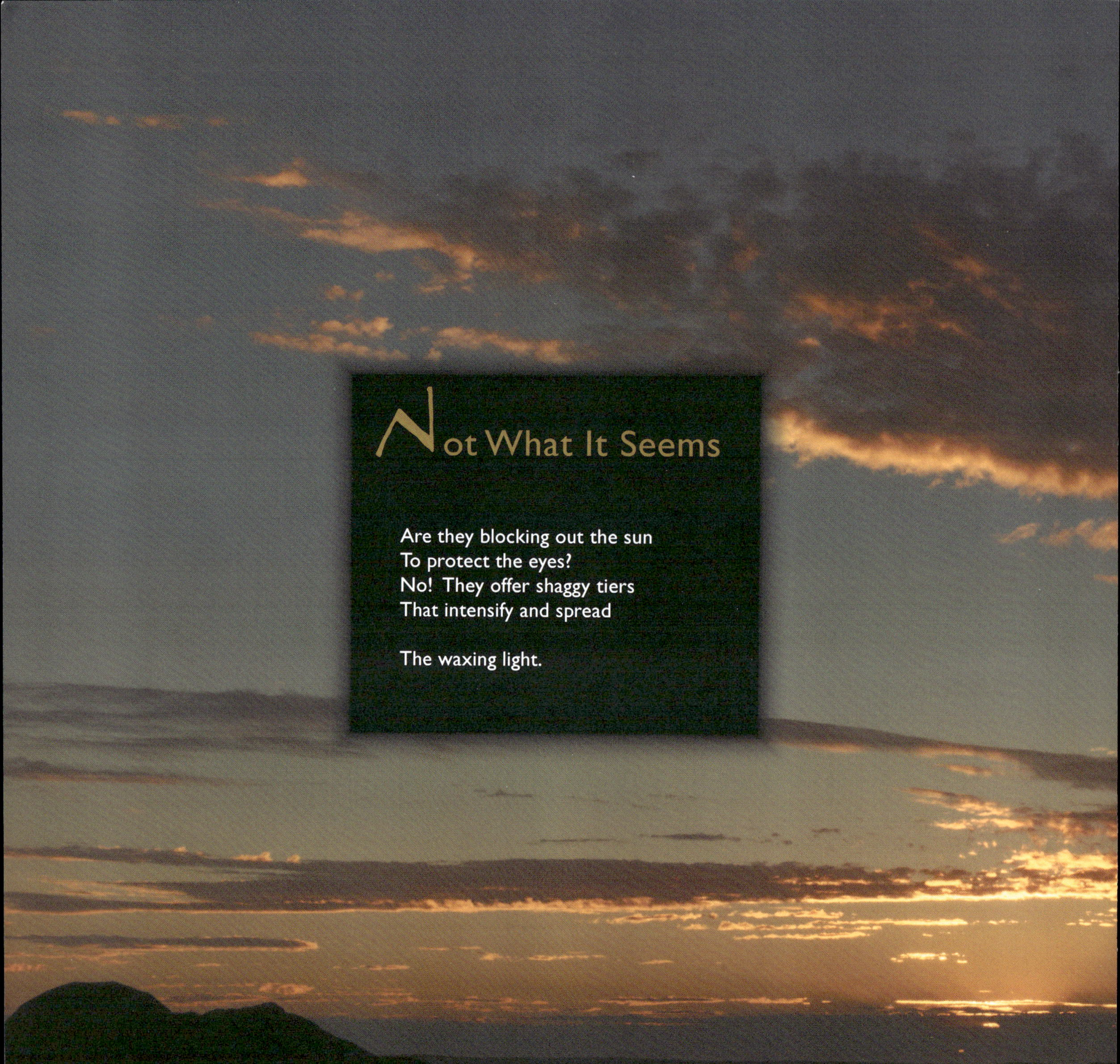

Not What It Seems

Are they blocking out the sun
To protect the eyes?
No! They offer shaggy tiers
That intensify and spread

The waxing light.

CPSIA information can be obtained
at www.ICGtesting.com
Printed in the USA
LVIW020705050313
322715LV00005B

* 9 7 8 0 9 8 4 8 0 7 3 2 1 *